THE LAST SECRETARY GENERAL

SEAN LESTER AND THE LEAGUE OF NATIONS

THE LAST
SECRETARY
GENERAL
SEAN LESTER
AND THE
LEAGUE OF
NATIONS

DOUGLAS GAGEBY

TOWN
HOUSE
DUBLIN

First published in 1999 by

Town House and Country House
Trinity House, Charleston Rd
Ranelagh, Dublin 6

ISBN: 1–86059–108–6

A CIP catalogue record for this book is available from the British Library.

Typeset by Typeform Repro

Printed in Ireland by ColourBooks Ltd

Cover design by Jason Ellams

Cover photograph:
The First Assembly of the League of Nations, 19 November 1920
(Reformation Hall, Geneva), from *The Palace of the League of Nations*
by Louis Cheronnet (L'Illustration, Paris, 1938)

To the memory of
Sean and Elsie Lester
and for their daughters,
Dorothy Mary, Ann and Patricia

Acknowledgements

Thanks are due to Pádraic MacKernan, Secretary-General of the Department of Foreign Affairs, for help with certain documents; also to Brian Cahalane and Bernadette Chambers of his staff; to Caitriona Crowe and Aideen Ireland of the National Archives; to Commandant Peter Young of Military Archives, Cathal Brugha Barracks; to John Bowman for sage advice and encouragement; to Amanda Gageby Bell; to Maria Gageby for almost daily help with her computer skills; to Ann Lester Gorski, for meticulously gathering, collating and indexing her father's papers and diaries; to Colonel ED Doyle, an old army comrade and military correspondent of *The Irish Times* for useful references to modern peace-keeping and peacemaking literature.

Then to Treasa Coady, the publisher, and Siobhán Parkinson for great patience and understanding with the text.

Contents

Foreword   viii

Chapter 1   The Making of an Internationalist   1

Chapter 2   From Journalism to Diplomacy   8

Chapter 3   Geneva and The League of Nations   20

Chapter 4   High Commissioner to Danzig   51

Chapter 5   Elections in Danzig   76

Chapter 6   Last Year in Danzig   93

Chapter 7   Back to Geneva   148

Chapter 8   Exit the League from Danzig   172

Chapter 9   War   177

Chapter 10   Wartime Intrigue at the Palais des Nations   188

Chapter 11   Interlude with James Joyce   222

Chapter 12   Ireland's Neutrality   231

Chapter 13   Towards the United Nations   240

Chapter 14   End of the League and Return to Ireland   250

Chapter 15   The Last Years   259

Index   265

Foreword

In the mid-1930s, Sean Lester's name was often headline news around the world as the Nazis raised the temperature in Danzig, a small city-state on the Baltic, under the protection of the League of Nations, of which he was then High Commissioner. After much persuasion and fair dealing all-round on Lester's part, the Danzig Nazis refused to co-operate with him in late 1936; the League withdrew him from Danzig and he became instead deputy Secretary-General of the League.

In 1940 he took over as acting Secretary-General in Geneva and, until the end of the war, kept together the structure of the League with its many ramifications in the economic and other spheres. He had sent his family back to Ireland. His greatest work for peace was surely in keeping going this now-depleted force of international civil servants which was able later to hand over to the United Nations a working structure on which to build for the future. Indeed, a United Nations publication of 1996 contains an essay by Alan James of Keele University in which he wrote: 'Much of what the United Nations has done has been clearly built on the foundations established by the League. The difference between them is thus more one of quantity than of quality.'

Roger Makins of the British Foreign Office wrote to Lester in 1942, urging him not to leave Switzerland for, while he might find it easy to get out (and, remember, it was then surrounded by German forces), 'whatever assurances you receive, you would in practice be prevented from returning to Switzerland.' And, he went on, 'there is nothing that would suit the enemies of the League better than to see the collapse of the organisation of the League at Geneva.'

Anthony Eden, British Foreign Secretary, had already written to Lester: 'The fact that you are keeping the flag flying at Geneva has, quite apart from the technical work which the Secretariat can still usefully do, a moral and political significance which could only perhaps be accurately measured if you were ever obliged to haul it down.' It was not hauled down. Lester, separated from his family, knew well that others around the world faced more immediate deprivation and danger than he did. He stuck to his post. He wrote, nearer the end of the war: 'I do not believe we are merely pumping a doomed ship. (If we are I'd still go on pumping till we get an order to abandon it.) All the glory and great activity may be going on elsewhere – which of us expects thanks in the end? ... Whatever the end may be, I, for one, shall not regret the personal effort and sacrifice in the years which have seemed stolen from my life.'

Lester, a lively but composed and resolute man, was born in Carrickfergus, Co Antrim, where his father was a grocer. The family later moved to Belfast and Lester received a startling and salutary illumination when he came into contact with the Gaelic League. A new history of Ireland opened up to him. He tells, movingly, of the impact. Then on to the IRB and the Irish Volunteers. He had become a journalist, first in provincial papers, and later was news editor or chief reporter of the *Freeman's Journal*, Dublin. In 1923 he was chosen by Desmond FitzGerald, Minister for External Affairs in the new Irish Free State, to help publicise the work of the new state. In 1929, now a fully established public servant, he was sent to Geneva where he became the Irish permanent delegate. He loved gardening and fishing. His wife Elsie, a Belfast woman, was a brilliant hostess and housekeeper. They were a perfect match. I was blessed with the good fortune to marry their eldest daughter, Dorothy Mary.

Lester's nationalism was summed up in a letter to a former colleague of his *Freeman* days, who asked for a brief biographical sketch. Lester wrote, in 1937: 'From the time I began to develop a mind and an individuality, I became an Irish Nationalist of the positive variety, looking for Irish freedom and happiness and development, while believing that only on the basis of Irish liberty could the two islands become friends.' He held these views for the rest of his life, though he came to learn that the gun was not the answer.

Lester took people as he met them; he had no airs. In the famous French politician Aristide Briand from Brittany (who claimed he had Irish ancestry, Brien or O'Brien) Lester admired 'an absence of what is called "dignity"'. This ties in with what a well-known medical consultant told me recently: as a boy he met Lester, then in his late sixties, as both were angling near Recess, Connemara. The man who had been that boy remarked how when they met on the banks of the river or lake, Lester spoke to him not as an elderly man to a young boy but simply as to a fellow angler. Now read on.

Douglas Gageby

CHAPTER 1

The Making of an
Internationalist

During the summer of 1909, two young men were to be
seen cycling over the rolling countryside of north
County Down, a lovely, fertile, well-farmed area, just a
few miles outside Belfast. One of the cyclists was a reporter; the
other, his friend, was out of a job and hoping to learn the
rudiments of journalism in his search for a career.

The reporter was Ernest Blythe, who was, not much more
than a decade later, to become a minister in the new Free State
government and, as Minister for Finance, deputy President of
the Executive Council, or cabinet. His friend, the aspirant
reporter, was Sean Lester, later to enter the newspaper life,
chiefly in Dublin; to step from that into officialdom in the newly
created Irish Free State; to become his country's permanent
representative at the League of Nations in Geneva and, from
there, to be invited to take the post of High Commissioner of
Danzig (now Gdansk), a Free City under the protection of the
League of Nations since the Versailles Treaty, which marked the
end of World War I; and eventually to become acting Secretary-
General of the League of Nations in Geneva, where he remained
throughout the war.

Few people can have experienced more intense, day-to-day
confrontations with Nazism than did Sean Lester in his three
years (1934–6) as High Commissioner in Danzig. He was
constantly facing the local Gauleiter and his deputies with their
bluffs, threats and blandishments, as he tried to protect the

1

constitution and the people of the Free City from insistent encroachment by the Nazis, with but erratic support from the great powers. When the Nazis finally refused to deal with Lester at all and his position as High Commissioner became untenable, the League saved face by offering him the post of deputy Secretary-General in Geneva. In 1940, he foiled an attempt by the Secretary-General at the time, a Frenchman called Joseph Avenol, to bring the League into Hitler's 'New Order Europe'.

After Avenol's resignation, Lester was appointed acting Secretary-General and held out in Geneva throughout the war, even though Switzerland was surrounded by the Germans and Lester's own fate as *persona non grata* with the Nazis, should Geneva be taken, can be guessed at. At any rate, he wisely kept his personal diaries buried in the garden, in case of invasion. The League continued to function in face of the German 'New Order' and many of its services were later merged into the United Nations.

Sean Lester was born John Ernest Lester in Carrickfergus, Co Antrim, on 27 September 1888 to a Methodist family. (Like many other young nationalist enthusiasts at the time, he later adopted the Irish version of his name.) His father, Robert, was a grocer and his mother had been a Mary Ritchie. The family later moved to Belfast, and Lester ended his formal education with two years at Methodist College, Belfast. He records no family history of scholarship or nationalism, but did recall a tradition that an ancestor had been 'out' in County Down with Betsy Gray and others in the Rising of 1798.

Lester's own political education was widened in that summer of 1909 when he accompanied Ernest Blythe, his lifelong friend, on many assignments in County Down. Blythe had to cover everything from Orange meetings and magistrates' courts to markets and meetings in parish halls.

Blythe and Lester had more in common than journalism. Both were members of the Gaelic League, the great cultural movement that swept much of the country in the early years of the century. Some time later Lester wrote that in the League he experienced 'the splendid hopes of an ancient nation's rebirth'. He recalled 'a strange feeling of intimate joy that [he] found in the Gaelic League, fighting for a new civilisation ... It was wonderful, this rising tide of youth and hope.' He goes on to say:

> When I first entered the rooms of the Gaelic League, I half hoped and half feared I would be the only Protestant in the ranks, but, of the first people I met, three were old school fellows. While I had been dreaming, they had been working, and I felt a due sense of shame! Soon however, the pride of initiation overcame other feelings.

Both Lester and Blythe were also members of a young revolutionary group known as the Dungannon Clubs, founded by another friend, Bulmer Hobson, and Denis McCullough. The Clubs had no finance behind them save the pence contributed by members. Not a single well-known name, and yet they set out to unite Protestant and Catholic Irish and to achieve the independence of Ireland – a group of young clerks and shop workers against the might of the British empire! They were, according to Hobson, the driving force at the centre of the more general Sinn Féin movement headed by Arthur Griffith, a ginger group in fact. Meetings were held further afield than Belfast: in Newry they spoke from a brake in the street. Mud, stones and decayed vegetables were thrown at them; in Castlewellan, Co Down, Hobson and his friends had to flee from an infuriated audience down a quarry, in the dark, with showers of stones following them. 'We had no hope and little desire to convert great crowds; we only wanted the men – a few in any district – who were capable of passionate sincerity and devotion,' wrote Hobson. This was of course the cell principle as employed by other larger organisations. They spoke at weekends when they were off work, in places as far away as London, Glasgow and Newcastle-on-Tyne, and were back in their offices on Monday morning.

The manifesto of the Dungannon Clubs (price one penny) called for strenuous effort and great sacrifice:

> We have but to let things drift, and continue in our old courses for another generation and the Irish Nation will have perished utterly; we have but to turn like men and take the helm into our own hands, and we can make it strong and great and independent.

The aims of the Dungannon Clubs were set out in eight small pages under headings which included 'The Building of Ireland Intellectually', 'The Building up of Ireland Physically', and 'The Organisation of Government'. Merely repealing the Act of Union with Britain was not their aim:

> Ireland her own, Ireland her own and all therein, from the sod to the sky ... the Ireland we seek to build is not an Ireland for the Catholic or the Protestant, but an Ireland for every Irishman, irrespective of his creed or class or rank or station.

The manifesto also strongly recommended abstinence from alcohol. They believed that in the past revolutionary movements had been ruined by tongues loosened in public houses. What they sought was 'Not to repeal the Union, but the Conquest: Not to resume or restore an old constitution, but to found a new nation and raise up a free people.'

Their nationalism also had roots in the world beyond Ireland. Their model was the Society of United Irishmen, which had sought help from revolutionary France. They knew of the Wild Geese, which had taken wing to every country in Europe in the eighteenth century to escape penal laws against Catholics. And of course they were conscious of the great fund of support that could – and would – come from emigrant Irish in America, many of them the embittered descendants of the million and more forced to emigrate after the Great Famine of the 1840s. Indeed in 1948, when Lester received an honorary doctorate from the National University of Ireland, his presenter, Dr JJ Hogan, reminded the audience of the many Irishmen of distinction who had gone out into the world 'as missionaries, soldiers, administrators to this nation or that. Mr Lester shows us perhaps the first example of a new sort of fruitful and honourable career for Irishmen in the services of all the Nations.'

Lester has described the evolution of his political thought in a letter to a friend:

> From the time when I began to develop a mind and an individuality, I became an Irish nationalist of the positive variety, looking for Irish Freedom and happiness and development, while believing that only on the basis of Irish liberty could the two islands become friends.

The third organisation in which Lester became involved was the Irish Republican Brotherhood. Like the Dungannon Clubs, membership was small, and in this case, secret. Lester was sworn in in Belfast by Ernest Blythe. In a questionnaire sent to him in 1947, Lester told the Irish Bureau of Military History (1919–23) that there were twelve members in the Belfast circle of which the head, or 'centre', was Denis McCullough. Another member, Cathal O'Shannon, later became a well-known trade unionist in Dublin and a member of the Labour Court, a novel type of tribunal for the post-1945 years. The meetings in Denis McCullough's shop in Belfast and in rented rooms were their Oxford and Cambridge Unions, their version of the College Historical Society of Trinity College, Dublin (where Wolfe Tone and later Thomas Davis and the Young Irelanders, on whom they also based their policies, had sharpened their political skills). They were a bookish crowd, looking beyond Irish history and Irish thinking – among Lester's books, as with many of his contemporaries, were volumes on Epictetus, Marcus Aurelius, Aristotle and others. In later life Lester wrote to one of his daughters, Patricia, from Geneva, recommending that she read *Sartor Resartus*. 'When I was twenty I used to moon about the shore of Bangor with a small edition in my pocket till the cover was worn off – and I read it too.'

There were senior figures in the IRB to give background to the young members: Francis Joseph Bigger, a solicitor, antiquary and enthusiast for local history, was a sponsor of writers and, above all, a social host in his house, 'Ardrigh', on the Antrim Road, Belfast, which had a fine prospect down to Belfast Lough. Over it towered the Cave Hill and Mac Art's Fort, on which, in 1795, Wolfe Tone and others had taken, as Tone writes in his autobiography, 'a most solemn obligation, which, I think I may say, I have on my part, endeavoured to fulfil – never to desist in our efforts, until we had subverted the authority of England over our Country, and asserted our independence.' In 'Ardrigh' there gathered poets and dramatists and nationalist believers of various degrees. Roger Casement stayed there often on visits home from his work in the British consular service. Like Bigger, Casement put money into nationalist cultural events such as the Gaelic language colleges and the Antrim Glens Feis – anything cultural that was to help the national movement.

Lester's first job in journalism was in Portadown, a notably Orange centre, with the *Portadown Express*, which he secured before the end of 1909. Excellent references accompanied his departure in April 1911: 'considerable literary ability ... steady, reliable, courteous and obliging...' And from the *Armagh Guardian* with which he spent two months: 'accurate reporting and avoids excessive verbiage ... his descriptive work which I have noticed in other papers has considerable merit' – the other papers might have been of a different political colour from the *Guardian*. After more than a year with the *County Down Spectator*, the proprietor, in his official recommendation, wrote that 'having been relieved of some public office' he could take over Lester's job of senior reporter. To the usual tributes to Lester's literary attainments he adds that he was a total abstainer.

His several moves, so early in his career, were perhaps signs of a young man trying to learn as much as he could of his calling. There could have been another reason: Lester's proprietors were all unionists. If his enthusiasm for the Gaelic League and his nationalist aspirations became known to them, then in spite of his professional abilities, they would have been glad to move him on. Lester's friend Bulmer Hobson had various clerical and office jobs in Belfast and used to tell how, as soon as his extra-office activities became known, his employers sacked him, sometimes with the words 'We want none of your kind here.' Hobson was a Quaker.

In the North of Ireland, the outlook of political opponents was often based less on policy than on racial and religious strains. His experiences in the North especially, and in the Irish national movement generally, gave the later High Commissioner for Danzig a certain foundation for approaching the intense racial contention between German and Pole.

CHAPTER 2

From Journalism to Diplomacy

In 1913 Lester moved to *The Connacht Tribune* newspaper in Galway. He fell in love with the west of Ireland, and while living there was a member of the local IRB circle. In later years he often shared a joke with a fellow member, Mickey Allen, that the entire membership of the IRB in that city in his day could have been seated on a jaunting car, 'and frequently was'. Later he was to buy a house near Clifden, Co Galway, and eventually retired to Recess, in the same county, where he died in 1959.

Next in his journalistic career he moved to Dublin. There he first worked for the group which included the *Dublin Evening Mail*, the *Daily Express* and the *Irish Weekly Mail*. The proprietors were the Tivy family who also had newspaper and other interests in Cork.

Lester was becoming known to the authorities in Dublin Castle as a member of revolutionary movements: Gerald Griffin in *The Wild Geese*, notes that because Lester had given help to Arthur Griffith, the leader of Sinn Féin, with some of his publications, Dublin Castle took 'an embarrassing interest in his movements, and on more than one occasion brought pressure to bear to have him dismissed by employers.'

This is clear in an irritable correspondence between Lester and Henry L Tivy.

Lester to Tivy, 28 July 1916:

Dear Mr Tivy,

As I was stepping onto the train for Belfast this evening, I was stopped by Mr Doig [editor of the *Express* and *Mail*] who gave me your instructions; consequently I returned to the office.

I presumed your action was owing to some important development in connection with my work. Will you kindly let me know if it would prevent me making other arrangements immediately either for myself or for some other members of the staff?

Tivy to Lester, 19 August 1916. From the *Constitution* office in Cork:

Dear Mr Lester,

I was intending several times to write to you about that unpleasant matter about the holidays. The fact is I might have been called on for explanation in case you, as you did about last Christmas, went without intending to do any wrong among these Blythes, Connollys and Becks and Hobsons. Some of these, I believe, are now in a sphere of high temperature and considering what was done to the office, I hope some of the rest will follow them. It is better for you not to go near Belfast or Lisburn for the rest of the year.

When Tivy wrote that 'he might be called for explanation', he presumably meant by the authorities in Dublin Castle.

Mr Tivy was essentially a merchant of Cork who also happened to own newspapers. Business was business. So, leaving aside his reference to the 'sphere of high temperature' (hell, presumably, though not all of those mentioned had been killed in 1916, if that is what he meant), he immediately switched to the problems of producing a daily newspaper – in this case the *Cork Constitution*:

Our Editor is away on holidays and will you write four suitable leaders of half a column for the *Constitution* of August 26th, 29th, 31st and Saturday, September 2nd. If you post them at night they will come here at midday next day and can appear on the days mentioned. The fee will be half a guinea each article and they could be addressed to me at this office.

And then the *envoi*:

If you like doing such work please take care and not to tell anybody in the office that you got the job. Keep it quite private.

Yours faithfully,
Henry L. Tivy

On the same day, a typed letter on paper headed 'Cork Constitution, 40, 41 and 42, Malboro Street, Cork, J. E. Lester Esq.,' expressing surprise on receiving the application of the reporting staff for increases of salary.

It is so much a matter of common knowledge proprietors are faced with most serious difficulties in carrying on newspapers at all. They did have all their pay without hesitation during that disastrous Easter Week and the work now cannot be very excessive.

Tivy would not treat with the staff as a whole.

One gentleman could well be done without, while others including yourself I regard as competent gentlemen, no doubt attached to the *Express* and *Mail* office.

Tivy to Lester, 22 August 1916:

Dear Mr Lester,
Yours received and as you were so anxious to visit the North, I will consult my son and turn over the matter for a few days and let you know. I am aware that your parents live at, I believe, Ormeau Road Belfast. If the same happens as some time ago when you went to the North, it would bring me as well as yourself into serious trouble. This I wish to avoid.

And then the frustration of the unionist proprietor who knew that things were changing around him:

> They [Dublin Castle] were inclined to class me as a Sinn Féiner whereas the fact is that I should be glad to do my bit in kicking the carcass of every Sinn Féiner and other rebel in Ireland into the Liffey.

On 26 August Tivy decides that he will make no objection to Lester going on holidays to the North:

> … but one condition I make, that is, that you will give me your word of honour that you will keep clear of persons (male or female) who are associated with disloyal conduct.

Lester's reply was, naturally, not pleasing to Tivy. But business was business. Tivy wrote back:

> I am going away for some weeks and I send a cheque for two guineas as to the four articles, two of which are to come. Your letter of to-day is not very definite and leads to the belief that you underestimate the position. If you again associate with those people and are reported for it, you will have no sympathy from me, but I hope you have a pleasant holiday.

In one sense all these young people in the Dungannon Clubs and in the IRB were romantics, but they knew something of the realities of political life in the North of Ireland. Hobson wrote in his memoirs: 'When one has learned to handle a hostile mob in Belfast, other audiences seem pretty easy.'

Henry Tivy, Lester's proprietor, was not alone in his bewilderment at what was happening in Ireland. Even the Nationalist MPs in Westminister did not know how the upheaval of Easter 1916 had come up without their being aware.

The cat-and-mouse game between proprietor and chief reporter went on when Lester told his editor that he had an offer of a job in the *Freeman's Journal*, a nationalist paper. Tivy wrote to Lester saying he had been informed that Lester had another position in view:

Sorry as I should be to part with you on my own account, it would now be a relief to me if you would avail of such an offer at the Freeman's offices you speak of. I never had a case of this kind before in all my long experience. I suggest that the occasion is a good time to announce your resignation at the Express office and thus end in a manner favourable to yourself, this most unpleasant matter.

Lester was later to refer reminiscently to the *Freeman's Journal* as the 'leading Nationalist newspaper in the world'. Desmond Ryan, a lively, humorous and honest chronicler of the times, worked as a reporter on the *Freeman* under Lester, who was then chief reporter or, in the modern idiom, news editor. He wrote in *Remembering Sion*:

> Before I joined the *Freeman* I had known another Ulster member of the staff very well, Mr Sean Lester, then News Editor of the *Freeman*, but afterwards the Free State representative at Geneva and subsequently High Commissioner for Danzig. I had first met him in a small lodge near Terenure, where Mr Bulmer Hobson lived, surrounded by shelves of books and smoked a genial pipe during many philosophical and political arguments with friends and critics.
>
> At that time Lester worked on a Unionist paper. He is a Protestant and Unionist by birth but he had joined the Sinn Féin Party and was regarded with a malevolent eye by Dublin Castle, which knew his journalistic ability shaped several Nationalist papers in forms not to its liking. Indeed, after 1916, in spite of Lester's strong MacNeill attitude during the crisis, some Castle busybody tried to get him sacked, until the staunch Tory editor, Henry Doig, told the Castle to go to hell and leave his staff alone!
>
> On the *Freeman*, Lester was a very pleasant and conscientious chief under which to work, and his younger lieutenants owed much to his sympathy and direction and unerring instinct for putting the right man on the right job. He is a dark-complexioned man, neither too tall nor

too short, with fine eyes which somehow sum up in one glance all his intellect, humour, reserve and capacity for untiring industry.

Lester did not take part in the Easter Rising of 1916. A planned mobilisation of the Irish Volunteers, which some members of the military council intended to use for an armed insurrection, was cancelled by Eoin MacNeill, the commander-in-chief. Lester and others were with MacNeill at his house on the slopes of the Dublin mountains above Rathfarnham when MacNeill made his declaration. The *Sunday Independent* of Easter morning 1916 contained this notice from MacNeill, commander-in-chief of the Irish Volunteers: 'Owing to the very critical position, all orders given to Irish volunteers for tomorrow Easter Sunday, are hereby rescinded and no parades, marches or other movements of Irish volunteers will take place. Each individual Volunteer will obey this order strictly in every particular.'

Roger Casement had landed on Banna Strand in County Kerry and been arrested. The German ship *Aud*, which was to bring arms, was blown up by its captain and crew. MacNeill placed Bulmer Hobson in charge of Dublin, and JJ O'Connell in charge of the southern forces. Hobson was abducted by the military council, which was determined on a rising. Leon O'Broin writes in *Protestant Nationalists in Revolutionary Ireland: The Stopford Connection* (Gill and MacMillan, 1985) that the military council could then blandly claim that they accepted MacNeill's orders 'as applying "to the manoeuvres" of Easter Sunday, so they decided to rise the next day.'

Military action had in any case been in the air for days. Lester used to tell how he and a few others, including Sean MacDermott, who was later executed, were passing the famous Jammet's restaurant on the Thursday before, when MacDermott said 'What about a last blow-out before it all happens?' They pooled their money and had one of the best meals of their lives.

The fact that he was not in the Rising did not prevent Lester being arrested and held until his editor Doig made a fuss and had him released.

Although he had gone through military training in the Irish Volunteers, Lester was never called out on active service. His journalistic and propagandist skills were known and valued in the movement. He was an observer of this, a participant in that, and the high regard for his work among the leaders was emphasised by Michael McDunphy, the director of the Bureau of Military History (1913–21), who wrote to him on 12 June 1952 about a meeting that he, McDunphy, had had with Mrs Tom Clarke, widow of the first signatory of the 1916 Proclamation of the Republic: 'She told me,' he wrote 'and has since confirmed in writing that some days before the Rising when she and her husband were talking about the possible results of that venture, he said he knew of no one better equipped to write the history of that time than you, and that you would write truthfully and sympathetically.' Lester's father was a shopkeeper. Tom Clarke's tobacconist shop was a regular meeting place for men in the various branches of the national movement. It is easy to picture Lester, after duty, calling down to 75A Parnell Street, to yarn with the old revolutionary and his customers, and to learn much of what was going on in various parts of the country.

Two standard questions from the bureau were 'To what extent and in what way were the IRB responsible for (a) the formation of the Irish Volunteers and (b) the direction of its policy. Lester wrote of (a) 'fully' and of (b) 'perhaps 80 per cent through officers and active members.' As to the question 'Were the plans [for 1916] specifically approved by the IRB?' he wrote: 'Never discussed at any general meeting of my circle.' As well as being a member of the IRB he was, of course, a member of the Irish Volunteers. To another question, 'Have you any information as to the circumstances in which the countermanding order was issued by Eoin MacNeill?' he answered 'Yes' – he had been there, but there is no record in the bureau of any details.

Although not an active service volunteer, Lester did attend

the third Coosan Camp near Athlone for training for officer rank in September 1915. In 1964, General Richard Mulcahy met Lester's eldest daughter (who is my wife) and me, at a reception, and as a result of the conversation sent the picture in this book which shows the Volunteers lining up for dinner in a variety of uniforms: leggings, puttees, high boots and headwear varying from soft hat to more military peaked cap. Mulcahy told my wife he had met her father before, 'but until I found him relaxing in his tent with the help of a book of Wordsworth's poems, I didn't quite realise what elegant company we were to have in our fortnight's camp.'

Lester had one memory of this camp, which he passed on to the family. On Sunday, all the others went to Mass, leaving him to cook the dinner. He filled out the stew by commandeering a few turnips from a neighbouring field, whether with the farmer's permission or not we don't know.

Lester was a sparky Ulsterman, with a self-confidence and self-discipline which enabled him to remain calm in difficult circumstances. As when, as one of his newspaper colleagues of Dublin wrote about Danzig: 'he was sitting on one of the powder barrels of Europe with the same *sang froid* with which he sat in his News-Editor's chair in the *Freeman's Journal* office and smiled as he read of the threats, now by the Black-and-Tans, now by the extremist IRA elements, to burn or blow up the building in which he was working.'

He has been described as a quiet man. He was not. In negotiations he did not speak unless he had something to say. He enjoyed the ironies of life, as when he told of his earnest conversation with a Polish diplomat about their two Catholic countries, finding, in the end, that they both were Protestants.

There were even some lighter moments in the Anglo-Irish war, as when, during the negotiations before the signing of the truce, the editor of the *Freeman* marked 'Proof to Archbishop' at the bottom of the typescript of a leading article – a direction to someone in the office to send the leading article on to His Grace before publication, either for comment or merely for information. In the very first edition, old *Freeman* hands swore, the leader duly appeared in the paper and, underneath still, now in print, the words 'Proof to Archbishop'. It must have been one of the quickest page changes in the history of the press.

In 1920 in Dublin, with Ernest Blythe as best man, Lester married Elizabeth Ruth (Elsie) Tyrrell, daughter of a well-off Belfast merchant, Alderman John Tyrrell, who lived in a big house on the Antrim Road, since demolished. Two of Elsie's brothers had been killed in the 1914–18 war. Another brother, a medical man, became Air Vice Marshal Sir William Tyrrell. Neighbours on the Antrim Road discussed the fact that a daughter of the alderman had married 'Jack Lester, the Protestant gunman'.

Elsie had a vigorous, original and determined mind of her own. She had no great respect for rank or title in itself, but had a high regard for sound and warm human qualities, no matter what the social or official position of the person. She had a perceptive eye for furniture, for comfort, for glass, silver and *objets d'art* in general, and the Lester house came to have a reputation for keeping a good table and cellar. She had learned the basics of household skills when she was deflected from her father's desire that she study medicine by a mother who wanted a housekeeper for her large, boisterous family. She was a dynamic element in Lester's subsequent rise on the international stage.

While Lester never wavered in his belief in the independence of Ireland, he became also a fervent apostle of the rule of law in international affairs, in the 'sublimely common-sense vision' of Woodrow Wilson, founder of the League. A good nationalist made a good internationalist, in his book.

The Civil War had petered out by 1923, but the threat of violence was felt for a long time. In the summer of 1923 Lester and his wife went on a tour into the Wicklow mountains with Ernest Blythe, the new Minister for Finance, and his wife Anne. They were travelling in the ministerial car, when the driver suddenly drew his revolver and fired into a field on the right. 'A hare,' he said calmly. 'I missed him.' What the minister said to him is not on record.

Lester once wrote that he was 'called into Government service' in early 1923. The call came from Desmond FitzGerald, Minister for External Affairs in the Irish Free State. FitzGerald himself had been a brilliant director of publicity during the War of Independence, believing always in delivering true information to the many foreign journalists who came to Dublin – and also to Irish journalists. Lester and he had been friends for some years. When overtures had begun early in 1923 Lester set out his views on the duties and limitations of the office of director of publicity in the Department of External Affairs:

> The work of the Publicity Office in my present view, would be roughly divided into two classes, the more urgent would be internal propaganda to meet the present situation; and the other more permanent and more normal work, external propaganda on the lines of the Departments run by Canada, Australia, etc. With the advent of more settled conditions, it would be highly desirable that foreign countries be kept informed of the political, industrial and culture progress of the young state, not as a matter of sentiment but for its reactions on trade and finance.
>
> Regarding the present situation, it seems to me that the question of propaganda for Ireland is simply the organisation of a good news service. This should include views occasionally, but 'leading articles' written by the publicity staff are, I consider, highly undesirable. Comment is occasionally needed and it should then take the form of brief statements of fact. To enter into discussions of 'principles', theories or indeed controversy in which our opponents cannot be smashed by brief statements of fact, would be both undignified and futile. This applies to articles from the Publicity Department. On the other hand, a pointed comment over the name of a Minister is frequently 'good news', acceptable to the Press and read by the public – if it is brief. Undisguised propaganda at this stage is useless.

I wish again to emphasise my view that given the conditions: 1. that the majority of the people support the Government and 2. that progress is being made towards peace and the development of the governmental machine, the best propaganda is simply a good news service.

Results would be slow. Anyone who expects the publicity staff to be more than a valuable auxiliary will be disappointed. Propaganda to be successful must be in accordance with the facts.' It is obvious that facts speak louder and more insistently than anything else. That is to say, there would be no use in trying to convince the Irish public of anything contrary to the actual situation of what they are fully cognisant. What is wanted is that they should see the situation clearly and see it all. Nothing short of extreme censorship (which is not warranted by the circumstances) will, for example, make the newspapers treat as negligible the violent activities of the Irregulars. Even if the newspapers suppress reports of these incidents it would not serve the government and would merely weaken the influence of the friendly press with the people. The most we can expect is that the news will be presented from the right angle with some degree of restraint and responsibility. The publicity staff should never be called upon to interfere in the direction of censorship, and should indeed be regarded by the newspapermen as advocate of the rights and privileges of the Press. If the Publicity Department can organise proper co-operation with the various ministerial departments, there should be plenty of incidents and news which the press would welcome and would have the desired object of impressing the public with the stability and advantages of the native administration and incidentally lessening the display given to reports of violence.

Another idea which he threw out, and which might surprise some people today, was that

Apart from the Press which is the principal and most important avenue of approach to the public, I think a weekly letter to the clergy would be valuable for a time at any rate. This would be partly informative and partly to suggest, delicately and indirectly, comments for use in sermons. Other minor centres of local opinion might be influenced by similar means.

In the same letter Lester set out his own qualifications as news editor of the *Freeman's Journal*, stating pointedly that almost half of his income was derived from connections with newspapers abroad, and that if he made any change he was not only breaking away from his own profession and giving up his position in the *Freeman* but breaking with other valuable connections: 'I have to mention this fact, as an appointment without some prospect of being permanent would, you will understand, hardly be a good proposition.' His conditions and pay were to be argued over for a long time and even at his retirement.

The Publicity Office was closed on 1 April 1925. Lester was appointed special correspondence officer of the Department of External Affairs, a post next to that of assistant secretary, in which he was responsible for correspondence between headquarters and offices abroad. In 1929 he became principal officer (equivalent to the later grade of counsellor), responsible mainly for the handling of correspondence with the British government on matters relating to the constitution and the international status of the Saorstát or Free State. In April 1929 he was appointed Irish representative to the League of Nations in Geneva, a post later described as permanent delegate to the League of Nations.

CHAPTER 3

Geneva and The League of Nations

G eneva in the late 1920s and early 1930s was, beyond doubt, the centre of world diplomatic activity, though whether it was the centre of world power is another matter. Each year there was a meeting of representatives of all member countries, known as the assembly; there was also a council made up of the 'great powers' and a number of non-permanent rotating members; this met quarterly; there was a permanent secretariat and a secretary-general, the first being an Englishman, Sir Eric Drummond, followed by the Frenchman Joseph Avenol.

The Irish Free State had been unanimously admitted to the League in September 1923 in the presence of a strong delegation led by William Cosgrave, President of the Executive Council (the equivalent of Prime Minister). The new state was thus a recognised international unit, status assured.

The League of Nation committees were in constant session. Foreign ministers of many states were regular visitors. Smaller states had permanent resident representatives. Contacts could be made at Geneva, not alone in the assembly and committees, but in the never-ending round of social functions. While Ireland was on the council – for three years, 1931, 1932 and 1933 – Ireland's prestige grew and its unremitting work and support for the League made an outstanding impression.

Lester arrived in April 1929 to succeed Michael MacWhite, who was transferred to Washington. Lester was to be there for many years and to make a considerable mark for himself, for his department and for his country. Speaking to the Irish International Society in the Mansion House, Dublin, in October 1948, he stressed the value to Ireland of the Geneva experience:

> It was one of the most important places for us, for there our new independence could be given its hall-mark. There we showed that, whatever problems remained outstanding between us and our great neighbour, we were not petty obstructionists, obsessed by the wounds and memories of past battles, and that while we might be rather conscious of our hard-won freedom and independence, we were also Europeans, representing an ancient nation and prepared to deal with every problem on its merits. Anything less than this would have been a betrayal of the character and will of the nation. What that meant for national prestige, in a world where sometimes less was expected of us, could not be estimated. Nor should it be forgotten that at that time the Department of External Affairs, including its representatives abroad, was a very small group of officials. Their work, often behind the scenes was as good as that of any other Foreign Office I know. Geneva was a place of work and it was also a University for the study of world affairs. I was still learning when I left it after eighteen years.

Comparatively new to diplomacy, Lester nevertheless brought with him a formidable array of talents, of experience in international and internal national strife – the Anglo-Irish War, the Civil War in Ireland, waged by Republicans against the government elected in 1922. He was, as a native of the North of Ireland, particularly aware of racial/religious tensions, and was sympathetic, as an Irishman, to the emerging countries in post-Versailles Europe.

Irish delegations to the League received much friendly unofficial help from Edward Phelan, who came from a maritime Waterford family. A member of the British delegation to the Paris Peace Conference after the 1914–18 war, Phelan was later a senior official of the International Labour Office in Geneva, and eventually its director general. He was accustomed to drop in on delegations of his compatriots to add liveliness and wisdom to their planning. The Lesters and Phelans became close friends, meeting weekly for bridge and, each time, trying out a new wine. Lester, who had never tasted spirits before the age of thirty, became a modest student of wine during his time abroad.

Not all diplomats and politicians were linguists – there were official interpreters and translators at the service of the League – but Lester picked up French quickly when he arrived, though he spoke it always with a Northern Irish tinge, and later he was to learn German.

One writer, an Englishman, wrote that Lester was a bulldog of a man – he was not, above all he was a man of sincerity and moral courage and, as the *Journal des Nations* wrote of him in 1933: 'In his three years at the Council, he has given the most brilliant proof (les preuves les plus éclatantes) of his independence of judgement, of his strength of character and of his attachment to the principles of the League of Nations.'

What makes a good diplomat? Harold Nicolson wrote in his book *Diplomacy* that the basis of good negotiation is moral influence, and that influence is founded on seven specific diplomatic virtues: Truthfulness, Precision, Calm, Good Temper, Patience, Modesty, Loyalty. In all of these, Lester would register well, as was to be seen most publicly in his period as High Commissioner for Danzig in the years of the rise of the National Socialist movement; nor would he have been offered the post had he not already, at the headquarters of the League of Nations, shown his qualities and distinguished himself in several disputes that came before the council, over which he regularly had to preside.

The Free State took its membership of the League seriously, but not uncritically. Thus the delegation to negotiate the admission of the state in 1923 had been led by WT Cosgrave, president of the executive council; the Minister for External Affairs, Desmond FitzGerald; Eoin MacNeill, Minister for Education who, as co-founder of the Gaelic League and founder of the Irish Volunteers in 1912, could be regarded as one of the great figures in the whole independence movement. There was also the Attorney General, Hugh Kennedy, three substitute delegates of wide and valued experience and Michael MacWhite, secretary to the delegation, who was to be the first permanent delegate of the state to the League of Nations. Later delegations included powerful speakers such as Patrick McGilligan, then Minister for External Affairs; Ernest Blythe, Minister for Finance; and when de Valera became head of government, he likewise brought a strong team. This dedication made it clear to the world that Ireland had not been engaged in a struggle with Britain merely to shake off her domination, but to reach out over the island that physically lay between her and Europe and to play her part in world politics. Cosgrave could claim that Ireland was a mother country: her people had been scattered throughout Europe as a result of laws against Catholics in the eighteenth century; she had negotiated with the French in the revolutionary wars after the 1789 revolution; her Wild Geese had made their way in Europe and into Russia; a million at least had gone to America after the Famine of the 1840s. Everyone who believed in the independence of Ireland carried in his or her head the famous peroration of Robert Emmet before he was condemned to death for his insurrection of 1803: 'When my country takes her place among the nations of the earth, then, and not till then, let my epitaph be written.' Not all of Ireland was represented at Geneva, but the independent part of Ireland was. Emmet's bones could have stirred.

It was a lively experience. A diplomat in another European capital would meet the Foreign Minister and possibly Prime Minister of that country from time to time. In Geneva, the representative eventually met them all. The men and women who were building the modern Irish state were conscious of the value of what they had done, and were conscious, too, of inheriting strength from their history; not unlike the Poles in many ways. They were not to be patronised. After the Imperial Conference of 1930 the Irish Free State emerged, as Donal O'Sullivan writes in *The Irish Free State and its Senate* (Faber 1940) 'as a completely autonomous nation, and the sole link between it and Great Britain was the King. But the King was to function entirely, so far as Irish Affairs were concerned, at the will of the Irish Government.' Winston Churchill was to complain in the House of Commons in 1931 that under the Statute of Westminster Bill the Irish parliament could at any time repudiate legally every provision of the Treaty of 1921, including the oath.

Lester was not a touchy person, but in his diary he tells this story about an encounter with Ramsay MacDonald, long-time Prime Minister of Britain:

> One St Patrick's day, I sat at a luncheon party of about forty diplomats in Geneva. I was wearing shamrock, and Ramsay was on the opposite side of the table. He spoke across to me, asking for a piece of shamrock. I pretended not to understand, and raised my glass to him. Then Benes, directly opposite, said to me in guttural English, that MacDonald wanted to share my shamrock. My hesitation had been to avoid either boorish manners or an anti-English demonstration before all the general members. So I smilingly passed a sprig. After luncheon R. [MacDonald] came up to me and hoped that I had not objected to his request. I hastened to assure him. He said he also was a Gael and our peoples had a common origin. This was charming; and I said that I myself had a Scottish Gaelic ancestor from Inverness. I still think it was as well that I should have let him see that the Irish shamrock needed no patronage...

An Englishman who was later to play a big part in his country's history was Alexander, later Sir Alexander, Cadogan. Cadogan was a member of the British delegation to the League of Nations in Geneva in the early years. In 1936 he returned to London, as deputy under-secretary at the Foreign Office and in 1938 became head of the Foreign Office. He held this post throughout the war and finally became Britain's permanent representative at the United Nations. Lester wrote: 'I knew him

continued on page 33

Good Friday 1916. From
left to right Padraig Ryan,
Eimar O'Duffy, David Boyd,
Sean Lester.

Portrait of three comrades in
the movement. From left to right:
Ernest Blythe, David Boyd,
Archie Heron.

Third Coosan Camp, near Athlone, in September 1915 for training officers. From left to right: William Mullins; Richard Mulcahy (later Chief of Staff of the IRA and eventually a minister in the Fine Gael government); Sean Lester; unidientified; Donal Barrett, Cork; Terence McSwiney, Cork; John Griffin, Castleisland, Kerry; possibly Liam Langley, Tuam; Pierse McCann, Tipperary; Austin Stack, Tralee.

Thomas Ashe, one of the
1916 insurrectionists.

Desmond FitzGerald, Minister for
External Affairs, who wanted Lester
to join the department as Director
of Publicity.

Bulmer Hobson was a great figure in the
Irish movement in Belfast in the early part
of the century where he set up Na Fianna
Éireann. He organised the Howth gun-
running, was secretary of the Irish
Volunteers, and implored the 1916 leaders
to adopt guerilla tactics throughout the
country rather than fight from buildings in
the capital. He was abducted by the leaders
of the Rising, and kept incommunicado.

Arthur Griffith

Believed to be an outing of the
editorial staff of the *Freeman's Journal*.
Lester is the third from the right in the
front row.

Tom Clarke, who hoped that Lester
would write the history of the period.

Kevin O'Higgins, Minister
for Justice in the Free State
government, murdered in 1928.

Sean Lester, 1920

Denis McCullough, who, as a young man had been head or centre, as they deemed it, of the Belfast circle of the Irish Republican Brotherhood (IRB).

Constitution committee, from left to right: Ron Mortished; John O'Byrne; Elim France; Daryll Figgis; EM Stephens; OP O'Toole; James MacNeill; Hugh Kennedy; James Murnaghan; James Douglas. Absent were Kevin O'Sheil, Professor Alfred O'Rahilly and Michael Collins, chairman. Mortished, Stephens and O'Toole were secretaries.

Irish representatives at Geneva (and wives), 1932/3. Back row, from left to right: Frank Cremins, unidentified, Sean Murphy, John Marcus O'Sullivan, Patrick McGilligan, John Costello, Sean Lester. Front row, from left to right: Elsie Lester, Ann McGilligan. (The rest are unidentified.)

Sean, third from left, with Patrick McGilligan, Minister for External Affairs (writing) and from left to right, John Costello, John Marcus O'Sullivan and Thomas Coyne.

The Irish delegation entering the Salle
de Reformation at Geneva for the tenth
assembly of the League of Nations.
Lester and Cremins (secretary to the
delegation).

Delegates at the League of Nations
council table. Delegate from Guatemala
on left and delegate from Spain on right.

Sean and Elsie Lester mountaineering with
friends, the Petersons, on Alp Matze, 1932.

Sean and Elsie Lester, with their eldest
daughter, Dorothy, centre, accompanied
by Ned Phelan (of the International
Labour Organisation) on the left, with
his wife, Fernande, on the right, 1932/3.

The family on holiday at Forte dei
Marmi, Italy, August 1932.

well as head of the British Foreign Office League Section. In Ireland and Europe he would be described as a typical Englishman, very reserved, an air of indifference, if not superiority, those characteristics which are not, I think, a national asset.' Lester was later to write of the great respect he had for Cadogan.

The small nations were, in many ways, the workhorses of the League. And the principles of the League of Nations and the practices were difficult to reconcile.

Major General AC Temperley, long-time chief military advisor to the British delegation, wrote, in regard to the Sino-Japanese dispute: 'In no spirit of sarcasm it must be said in the case of the small powers, that their moral fervour and determination to carry out the Covenant to the letter, varied noticeably in proportion to their geographical proximity to the scene of action.' It was only natural, he said, that all the great powers, with a considerable stake in the outcome of the discussions, should have a much more sober outlook. He concluded, pessimistically, that the members of the League had completely failed to protect a fellow member and that collective security had proved a sham.

The Irish Free State had ample opportunities to show that it would act as an independent unit in foreign affairs, subservient to no other power. As Lester wrote, the permanent delegate of a small country at Geneva 'may be called on to attend all kinds of international conferences, from purely technical ones dealing with conditions of labour, control of drug traffic, to those relating to disarmament and high politics – experts not being available from the small countries to advise.'

Eighteen months after his arrival, Ireland was elected to the council of the League. From time to time Patrick McGilligan, Foreign Minister, and later, after a change of government, President de Valera, were available to represent the country, but on many occasions the duty fell to Lester. The Sino-Japanese dispute relating to the invasion of Chinese territory by Japan, both members of the League, and the Disarmament Conference, were only two of the major problems he soon had to face. Further, he was appointed by the council as president of two conciliation committees, firstly on a dispute between Peru and Colombia and also that between Bolivia and Paraguay. Later he was to be rapporteur on minority problems.

As to Temperley's remark about the moral fervour of small nations, Lester, lecturing to the Geneva Institute of International Affairs in the summer of 1933 on the viewpoint of small states, said:

> That point of view is perfectly simple; it is that the Covenant must be applied as completely and as firmly against a powerful aggressor as against any small state which tries to take the law into its own hands. The organisation of peace is not a question of sentimentality nor even of an abstract justice, but of vital concern, perhaps of life or death, to the states which are not militarily strong.

Japanese action in invading Manchuria, he went on, was:

> ... except in one respect, no more amoral than the action of other Powers in the past. They may, therefore, feel themselves unfortunate in being treated on a different basis because their action took place in 1931 and not in 1901... The outstanding differences in the Japanese case were, of course, the existence of the Covenant, a solemn contract between Japan and fifty-six other nations.

The confidence that Desmond FitzGerald, Minister for External Affairs, had in Lester's shrewd mind and knowledge when he called him into government service early in 1923 was not misplaced. He had seen peace and war. He had gone through the growing pains of a new young country. Geneva was a world to which he adapted quickly and to which he brought useful gifts. As he wrote to a friend:

> In September 1933, four and a half years after my arrival ... I had learned that modern diplomatic life can only mean hard work. Certainly a diplomatic picture in popular

34

imagination some years ago, would nowhere look so ridiculous and out of place as amongst the leaders in the international field at Geneva, which was, and remains the greatest centre of international life in the world.

He now and then simulated – or genuinely felt – amazement at the fate which had cast him on the international scene: 'What am I doing here?' he would ask himself in Geneva or Danzig or New York or San Francisco. He referred nostalgically to his own small department in Dublin and to a house full of family, friends and books, not too far from a trout stream, which he did much later achieve, to his great satisfaction.

One of the greatest of all figures in Geneva was Aristide Briand, a far-seeing man who proposed in 1929 a form of federal Europe, primarily economic in aim. Briand was ten times Prime Minister of France but made his mark internationally as Foreign Secretary, particularly at Geneva. Lester remembered Arthur Henderson, British Foreign Secretary, 'smacking Briand on the shoulder a little heartily and declaiming: "Cabinets come and cabinets go, but Briand goes on for ever".' Adds Lester: 'Neither of them understood the other, of course, so perhaps it was all right.'

Lester found that he had two things in common with Aristide Briand, apart from zeal for the League – both were anglers, and Briand, a Breton, claimed to have Irish ancestry, O'Brien or Brien. Lester had raised a voice against procedure in regard to the Sino-Japanese dispute where the great powers had formed a kind of informal committee, leaving other members of the council without full knowledge of what was going on. Briand, then president of the council, accepted the claim of equality at once. He was 'more than gracious (as only a Frenchman can be)' wrote Lester in his diary.

Briand had a heavy moustache. In photographs of the time, he looked somewhat dishevelled. His delegation swore that he never read the papers they brought him. He always refused invitations to evening parties and it was rumoured that he had really read all his documents before 8.30 each morning. His fishing was, as Lester describes it, *à la française* – sitting for hours on a stool by the river back in Brittany or in Switzerland, waiting for the cork to bob. A story told to Lester was that Briand once went fishing in Switzerland in particularly old and disreputable clothes ('though, Lord knows, he never was a dude') and was met by two gendarmes, who thought him to be a doubtful-looking tramp. They asked for his papers and he said he never carried identity papers. Asked who he was, he said he was 'Président du Conseil'. For this impudence they brought him to the village gendarmerie:

> It is so easy to picture old Briand, with his humanity and sense of humour and absence of what is called 'dignity' trudging along between his captors. Of course he made them go with him to the café afterwards to solace them with a glass of wine.

Briand was a serious politician: 'The greatest Frenchman I have ever met.' He died in 1932. Some years later Lester, writing in Danzig of the days of Briand's presence in Geneva, reflected that France would be feeling more comfortable then, if she had given Briand's policy of conciliation with Germany a trial.

Lester met Anthony Eden many times, particularly over the case of Danzig:

> He is such a likeable fellow, with the gift of making friends, and without the drawback of so many Englishmen abroad – what is called, perhaps rightly, their superiority complex, in evidence. His honesty and sincerity count for much in League affairs and [this was written in December 1935] Geneva is still Europe's diplomatic centre.

On 26 September 1932 Eamon de Valera, president of the League council, made a speech at the assembly which shocked his audiences so much that, neither during it nor at the end, was a handclap, or a murmur of appreciation or assent heard in the chamber. In the opinion of more than one of the serious journalists present, it was the best speech ever heard from a president of the council: De Valera went through the year's events as presented to him, in the routine fashion, by the League secretariat, but he had much more to say. He told the delegates that they should not think that the League could live on the commendations, however merited, and expressions of satisfaction which it received from its friends or from the assembly itself. With the Sino-Japanese conflict and the Disarmament Conference in mind, de Valera said:

> Friends and enemies of the League alike feel that the testing time has come; and they are watching to see if that test will reveal a weakness presaging ultimate dissolution, or a strength that will be of the assurance of a renewal of vigour and growth ... We are defendants at the bar of public opinion with a burden of justification upon us which is almost overwhelming ... the one effective way ... is to show unmistakably that the Covenant of the League is a solemn pact, the obligations of which no State, great or small, will find it possible to ignore.

He spoke of the Economic Conference:

> Twenty five millions of unemployed are crying out for the recognition of the right of themselves and their families to work and live; a hundred million people are faced with starvation in the midst of a world of plenty ... no state should be permitted to jeopardise the common interest by selfish action contrary to the Covenant, and no State is powerful enough to stand for long against the League if the Governments in the League and their peoples are determined that the Covenant shall be upheld.

Of the Disarmament Conference, on the success or failure of which he calculated the League would be judged, he said: 'Without progressive disarmament, it is impossible that the League should survive.'

The year 1933 brought serious blows to the League – perhaps a fatal blow, with the withdrawal of Japan, formerly a model member, and with the failure in the second year of the

Disarmament Conference. But it was not without its hopes and victories, illusory as they may seem from this distance.

On 4 March 1933 Lester wrote optimistically to his department in Dublin:

> We have been making history in Geneva this week. On the one hand a committee of which I have been President has proposed, and the Council have accepted the formation of an international army[1] to take over temporarily a disputed territory [Peru-Colombia]. For the first time also, arrangements are in progress for the declaration of a League embargo on arms for two countries, Bolivia and Paraguay, and I think also for the first time, three States will exercise their friendly rights in invoking Article 11[2] in a dispute between two countries.

Lester's activity was all patient step-by-step reasoning and listening and coaxing and now and then putting his foot down. Maître MW Suès, a Genevese lawyer and journalist, spoke on 22 March of Lester's handling of the Colombia–Peru affair, referring to 'Monsieur Lester qui a beaucoup de tenacité, jointe à une droiture au dessus de toute éloge.' ('Mr Lester who has plenty of tenacity, together with an adroitness above praise.') The delegation of the United States of America wrote to him: 'This happy occurrence is a definite contribution towards world peace and an event for which you, as President of the Advisory Committee, deserve so large a measure of credit.' This was

---

1. When Lester wrote of Geneva making history in setting up an international army in South America, he was verbally correct. But Frank Walters, author of *A History of the League of Nations* (OUP), wrote: 'The Commission of Leticia had under its orders a small detachment which was considered as international, and wore armlets with the Letters SDN (League of Nations).' But it was composed only of Colombian soldiers and was not, therefore, an international force in the full sense. The first truly international force was called together in 1935 to supervise the plebiscite in the Saar. The force was 3300 strong, the largest contingent – and the Commander – being British. Also included in the forces were Italians, Swedes and Netherlanders.

2. This Article states 'Any war between two countries or threat of war, whether immediately affecting any members of the League or not, is hereby declared a matter of concern to the whole League, and the League shall take any action that may be deemed wise and effectual to safeguard the peace of Nations...'

signed Hugh R Wilson, who was a delegate to the Disarmament Conference, and not to the League of Nations itself.

Lester was to need all his qualities for the next problem on his agenda, which concerned the fate of the Jews in German Upper Silesia. Here German discriminatory measures against Jews were clearly and legally visible as being counter to a treaty to which it was party.

When the industrial region of Upper Silesia was divided between Germany and Poland after a plebiscite in 1921, minorities were left on both sides, and each government signed the Geneva Convention on Upper Silesia in 1922. The German government assured absolute equality to all residents there, without distinction as to race, language or religion: the rights of Jews as a minority were expressly guaranteed. These were declared 'Obligations of International Concern' and were placed under the guarantee of the League of Nations. So when, in May 1933, Franz Bernheim, a Jew, submitted a petition against Nazi discrimination, it was declared urgent and went before the League council.

The Germany of 1933 was very different from that of 1922. Germany first tried to stop Bernheim's petition coming before the council on technical grounds. Was Bernheim a member of a minority at all? And no *de facto* situation had arisen in Upper Silesia from the Aryan decrees of Germany. The French member of the council, Paul-Boncour, reminded Germany that it was she who had desired the minority treaties after the war, and had insisted very strongly that, in her own territory, she would see to the rights of minorities.

Lester, as rapporteur for minorities, stressed the gravity of the case in a memo of 30 May to his department in Dublin: 'Apart from other political motives, there are about three million Jews in Poland and, in other countries, Jews have considerable political influence.' He instanced Léon Blum in France, then Prime Minister. Lester had invaluable help from John Hearne, legal advisor to the Dublin Department of External Affairs, and

Lester's own number two, Thomas Coyne, who was also a barrister.

During the discussions Hearne or Lester or Lester and Hearne together saw representatives of France, Italy, Poland, Britain, Norway, Spain and Czechoslovakia and to some extent the other four members of the council. All the time Lester and his Irish colleagues aimed at an 'objective impartiality', also showing 'every possible courtesy and consideration of the views expressed on behalf of Germany', which views were often delivered in a heated manner. On the Saturday Lester insisted on working through the night to 2am in order to achieve an agreed draft report merely as a basis for discussion. He wrote later that he was not going to be drawn into a showdown, but patiently, and in the face of unpleasantness, had insisted on going through 'our own text' paragraph by paragraph to find out what was acceptable and if not acceptable, the reasons for the German attitude.

The leader of the German delegation, von Keller, was consistently courteous, but that could not be said of his colleagues. When the text was looked at there was a great divergence of standpoint. At 11am on Sunday they met again and at 6.30pm there was no advance except in the 'final clarification on our respective attitudes'.

The committee offered the Germans two versions: one which they could submit to the council and defend, if they agreed to accept it; the other which they could put forward if they refused. On Monday evening the Germans informed the committee that they would not vote for either.

A final report went to the council, going to the limit of concessions to the Germans, but maintaining all that was necessary to give complete protection to the minorities. Lester notes that 'the absence of extraneous denunciation in the Report which the Germans were to refuse to accept would, in fact, add to its strength'.

The German delegation, of course, was bound by the strictest instructions from Berlin. The new National Socialist government was, writes Lester, extremely stupid about the whole affair. The Germans themselves had taken a leading part in insisting on the carrying out of minority treaties. They had, for example, 250,000 of their own people in Poland, protected by the same treaties, and they were anxious that 'the treatment of Jews in Germany should not be exploited further than the minimum in this case'.

The reputation of the Irish Free State for independence and courage, which had been a source of approval before, was more firmly established than ever by these negotiations. Suès, who broadcast a regular daily review of the proceedings of the League, referred to Lester's work on the council and committee in these terms: 'Monsieur Lester qui n'est pas irlandais pour rien.' ('Mr Lester who isn't an Irishman for nothing.')

The Italian representative of the council later told Lester that his government had sent a dispatch to Berlin, urging them to give in and give in quickly, because of the bad impression all around. The committee's report was adopted by the council and, wrote Lester some time later, was 'the first League protest against a policy which subsequently led to a series of unparalleled horrors.'

It was a precursor to Lester's later experiences in Danzig and his appointment as High Commissioner, of which he had then no inkling. Lester noted that while the Poles had every reason to be pleased in this special case, the 'firmness of the Council in the German case is a fore-runner of, if anything, increased firmness with the Poles themselves.'

The German delegation seemed, in the end, to concede the logic of the Bernheim petition without a genuine admission, and agreed that such errors as might have been committed could be corrected. Von Keller asked, however, that the provision 'that the people concerned should be reinstated in their position' could be omitted. He was told it could not. In a note to his department in Dublin on 6 June 1933, Lester said that he thought this particular petition would not be heard of again except indirectly. He was wrong. The League was now dealing with a country under the new regime of National Socialism, which played only by its own rules – and often on the whim of one man, the Chancellor, Adolf Hitler, and his immediate associates, notably Joseph Goebbels, Minister for Political Enlightenment and Propaganda.

On 20 September 1933 Neville Laski, president of the Board of Deputies of British Jews, wrote to Lester that no substantial improvement had been produced in Upper Silesia: 'even where a formal rectification had taken place, it has been nullified in practice by the German Government and the National Socialist party'. He enclosed three damning articles by a special correspondent of the *Manchester Guardian* of 18, 19 and 20 September 1933 and asked if the League would not send out a 'competent authoritative Commission to establish the true position'. The *Guardian* articles showed how a minimum of face-saving had taken place. The Polish Jews in the territory, who had gone to their counsel and had achieved intervention by him, were all driven out of the country. Forged lists of Communists were drawn up, and employers told to sack them. Sacked they were, and were refused unemployment pay. Up and down the professional, business and workers scale, the story was the same. Lawyers were affected too. No German was allowed to employ Jewish counsel in court. Overdrafts and mortgages taken out by Jews were called in. Some were sent to a concentration camp, and thousands – small traders or those in modest jobs – were destitute. Wrote the *Guardian* correspondent:

> About 150 Jewish professionals – doctors, lawyers, judges, dentists and civil servants – lost their positions under the Nazi Government's anti-Jewish legislation. A good many of them have been reinstated since June, but they are working under conditions that make the practice of their professions almost impossible. Some two thirds of the Jewish professional classes have, at all events, partly regained their rights of earning a livelihood. There still remains, however, the whole mass of the Jewish minority, over 10,000 artisans, shopkeepers, shop assistants, and working men and women who are wholly deprived of the

means of getting a living. Their lot is as unenviable as that of the Jews in any part of Germany ... Unlawful arrests, detention, maltreatment and expulsion of Jews are of frequent occurrence.

Further damning reporting by the same correspondent told of the boycott of Jewish firms and shops. Large posters with swastikas were prominently displayed: 'Every purchase in a Jewish shop strengthens international Jewry: buy only in German shops.'

In September 1933 Lester was already going through the process of appointment to his new job as League of Nations High Commissioner in Danzig, where he was to run into the full force of the anti-Jewish policy of Nazi Germany.

It had often been said that, during the thirties, the peoples of Europe were more enthusiastic for the League of Nations than were their governments. Early in 1935, in Britain, a 'peace ballot' was held in favour of the League. Over eleven million ballot papers – equal to half the total number of votes cast in the previous general elections of 1929 and 1931, were handed in. Over ten million of these favoured non-military sanctions against an aggressor, and seven million accepted the principles of collective military measures. Stanley Baldwin, the Prime Minister, received a delegation from the League of Nations Union for formal presentation of the figures, and assured them that the League remained 'the sheet anchor of British Policy', though he had earlier tried to make a connection between collective security and armed strength as a substitution for the League disarmament formula.

RAC Parker, in his book *Chamberlain and Appeasement*, writes that most ministers, while more sceptical than devoted League supporters, would, of course, have liked the League to be in some way able to prevent aggression. They thought of the League as admirable and desirable but unattainable in an imperfect world, though in 1935 'they had to try to make it work or make a convincing pretence of trying to make it work'. Reason and persuasion and ultimately self-interest should prevent war, which many serious people thought might bring an end of civilisation: in the 1920s and 1930s the war graves were still fresh; so, in the case of the dispossessed in Versailles, were the resentments and the desire for revenge. Even moderate Germans like Stresemann, the German Prime Minister, strove throughout the 1920s to be given some concessions to bring back to his people from Geneva. France made sure they did not get the concessions.

In April 1929 Stresemann spoke with Robert Bruce Lockhart, author of *Memoirs of a British Agent*. The Germans, said he, had not been given one single court card by France and Britain. Nothing remained but brute force: 'Now the youth of Germany, which we might have won for the peace and the new Europe, we both have lost. That is my tragedy and your crime.' Six months later Stresemann was dead and a few short years later Hitler was Chancellor.

Brooding on the interview, Lockhart recalls Churchill's dictum: 'In war resolution, in defeat defiance, in victory magnanimity.' 'In the post-war policy towards Germany,' wrote Lockhart, 'there had been neither magnanimity nor good will' (*Retreat from Glory*, Putnam, 1934).

Much had happened in 1933. On 30 January Hitler became Chancellor; on 27 February the Reichstag was burned; in elections on 5 March the Nazis gained a clear majority; on 23 March the Enabling Act was passed in the Reichstag, effectively making of that body a mere rubber stamping agency for a dictatorship. On 1 April the organised boycotting of Jewish businesses and of Jewish doctors, lawyers and other professions began, to be followed, on 7 April, by a law governing the expulsion of Jews from the civil service. On 2 May, just before Bernheim's petition was considered in Geneva, the trade unions were disbanded and then all political parties except the National Socialist party were disbanded too. Germany quit the League on 14 October.

Goebbels was then the driving force behind the anti-Jewish momentum in Germany. Already on 26 March he and other leading Nazis, including Julius Streicher, editor of the pornographic anti-Jewish rag, *Der Stürmer*, discussed the campaign against the Jews. Then on 1 April Goebbels, in a speech broadcast on all German radio stations, described the boycott and smashing of Jewish business windows and raiding of synagogues as 'our proud mission'.

At a dinner early in 1933, when the Disarmament Conference was going on, Lester sat beside Edouard Benes. Benes was for fifteen years Foreign Minister of Czechoslovakia, and played a big part in League affairs until he was chosen as President of his country to succeed Masaryk. Small, unimpressive in appearance, friendly and intelligent, a university professor of humble origin, he joined Masaryk's Revolutionary Committee in Paris when the 1914 war broke out:

> I said to him that a country like Germany could not be kept down and that no peace could be built in Europe with Germany kept in a condition of inequality. To my surprise he agreed. But he said that any geographical changes or proposals would mean war. I said it often seemed to me that the geographical frontiers had been drawn not so much to help the new States as to weaken Germany.

Benes then told Lester that he had been in Paris during the Peace Conference after the war, and that when had he learned the details for his country's frontiers, he went to the great powers to ask them to take away a million Germans who were to be included in Czechoslovakia. They refused, he said, and now the frontiers must remain.

In 1938 Sudeten Germans, after the Munich agreement, were returned to the Reich, and next spring Germans marched into Prague and took over the rest of the country. But the conversation with Benes took place before Hitler came to power, before Germany left the League and before she rearmed.

Complaints about lack of backing from the home government may be common in diplomacy world-wide, but the new Irish

Free State was having serious economic troubles, and the Department of Finance in Dublin ruled much of Lester's life.

He and his wife and three daughters had a 'good address' at 43, Quai Wilson, in a flat overlooking the lake; but for long it had to act as home and office. One small room was given over to the typists, filing and archives for the entire service of Ireland's delegation to the League. Lester used a small sitting room as an office by day, and in the evening it reverted to being the family sitting room. Another room was the office reception room. Mrs Lester used the bedroom as her sitting room. Three children who in Dublin had a night and day nursery shared a small combined room for day and night. They did have, though, a splendid view over the lake to Mont Blanc. One of Lester's daughters remembers sitting on the knee of Eamon de Valera, and wondering if she dare ask him if he could provide the family with a house that had a garden, as they had enjoyed back in Dublin. She didn't ask.

Other Irish diplomatic representatives had more salary and allowances than the man in Geneva, and while Lester never applied for an increase in his salary, he did protest about the inadequate expense allowances for entertainment. And in spite of all his responsibilities on the council and as a rapporteur and a chairman of committees, he was not given the title of 'minister plenipotentiary', as were so many from other countries.

His predecessor, Michael MacWhite, wrote (in 1928) of his embarrassment at not being able to return acts of courtesy of which he was the subject. It would be better, he suggested, to close the Geneva office until funds adequate to the position could be raised. He himself had survived through making use of private means, he said, but 'family reasons' had not allowed him to continue doing so.

Lester, calm and equable though he normally was, would now and then become testy with the department back home, chiefly through their lack of response. Thus in a letter of 11 May 1932: 'I cannot even get an acknowledgement from the Department when I ask on what grounds my salary was reduced last October.' He asked the secretary of the department, Joseph

Walshe, 'would you like me to go over for a few days? … I would pay my own expenses if necessary.' And 'I cannot help taking my job seriously even if nobody else does.'

A note from the head of the Department of Finance to the Department of External Affairs informed Lester that the Minister for Finance had decided that the outlay for international and other external organisations and conferences should be cut by 20% in 1933/34, and by 50% in 1934/35. Indeed, 'amongst other things, the possibility of effecting economy by closing down the permanent office of your Department in Geneva was mentioned'.

But there were happy days rowing on the lake and swimming in it; excursions into the mountains of both Switzerland and France. It was an expansive life for the Lester family in so many senses, though a very hard-working one for Lester himself.

If the spirit of Calvin still permeated the city of Geneva it was not evident to the huge international population that surged and ebbed through conference after conference; dinners, luncheons and cocktail parties as well as solemn deliberations and wranglings.

The *Daily Telegraph* man in Geneva wrote an article entitled 'The Most Fascinating Lobby in the World'. This was about the *salle de conversation* of the huge building, the Bâtiment des Commissions, which the city of Geneva built for the Disarmament Conference. The *salle* was a vast expanse where delegates could pace up and down after escaping from the offices and conferences rooms. And everyone, says the *Telegraph* man, was to be seen there eventually. There was a bar too, and 'the best-equipped press room ever conceived by man', a post office, a shop where newspapers could be bought – '…all in all, it is the most perfect thing in Geneva.' He lists some of the greats and the not-so-greats that passed through: Herriot, Paul-Boncour, Lord Lytton, Ramsey MacDonald, Captain Anthony Eden, Baron von Neurath, Eamon de Valera and Sean Lester 'with the shrewdest face in all Geneva'. And the great ones pass in and pass out 'never tiring in their never-ending pilgrimage towards a better and more stable world'. The date was 4

February 1933, when hopes had already begun to ebb at a fast rate.

Cartoonists had a busy time, and the new informal Leica camera, easy to conceal, gave a vitality to the recording of the life of the conference-goers that had not been possible with heavier photographic gear. Dr Eric Salomon has left a huge collection of visual images of the life of conference-goers in the 1930s, including in Geneva, which is unequalled. Briand called him 'Le roi des indiscrets', not without foundation, for while he often worked openly, many of his pictures were shot secretly. The dust cover of his book shows Briand pointing straight into the lens, smiling.

The Minister of State at the British Foreign Office, Philip Noel-Baker, at the last session of the League in April 1946, said:

> Those who have come to know Geneva have learned to love it. During twenty years the Secretariat members lived here, their children were born on Geneva's hospitable soil. These children have been scattered like the chosen people by the tides of war. Wherever I travel, in whatever continent, I find them now; and always I find them longing almost with a nostalgic passion to go back. They are longing for the beauty of Geneva; they are longing for the order and tranquillity of its life; they are longing to renew their memory of their happiness in the International School; above all, they are longing to touch again the inspiration of the work on which their parents were engaged – the Secretariat of the League.

Of that secretariat he said:

> I worked in it as a humble member in its earliest days. I also worked in four Government Departments in London between the wars. I am as proud of our British Civil Service as any man could be, but I can say with truth that in none of our Departments did I find a higher standard of technical efficiency, a higher level of personal and official probity, a greater industry.

The achievements of the League are often minimised, but today in Geneva and elsewhere organs of the United Nations build on the groundwork laid by the League in health, in the care of refugees and in economic and social matters.

If Lester did have communications difficulties with the department in Dublin, one topic galvanised it: the spectre of birth control had raised its head, they thought, in a League document. It was a foretaste of the infamous squabble two decades later on the Mother and Child Scheme of Dr Noel Browne which was abandoned by the coalition government in the face of furious attack by the Catholic Archbishop of Dublin, Dr John Charles McQuaid, leading the hierarchy.

Lester explains in a letter of 25 July 1932, in answer to a letter of 10 July from the department:

> Regarding certain matters appearing in the League document CH 1060, the report in question was prepared by a sub-committee consisting of professional men at the request of the Health Committee. They were asked to study and prepare a memorandum on maternal affairs and the hygiene of infants.

The Irish Free State was not represented on the health committee, he noted, but it contained a number of Catholics and representatives of Catholic countries. Among them was Velghe, president of the Ministry of Health in Belgium. 'He is not only a Catholic,' writes Lester, 'but what is described as a militant Catholic, and I understand, is President of the Belgian Catholic Doctors' Association.' Moreover the 'paragraph in question' was considered most carefully by the committee in view of the concern felt by the various churches, especially by the Catholic church, in the matter it refers to. He was assured that it was referred to a Catholic priest in Paris 'Monseigneur Beaupin [or Bopain] who seems to have reassured them that the wording was not contrary to Catholic views.... The Committee was concerned with medical reasons only,' wrote Lester, 'and the words "It is necessary to explain what steps she and her husband should take to prevent this [pregnancy] from happening" were purposely made general in order that no recommendation might be given which would cause offence to any Government or religious body ... These steps might well include total or temporary abstinence from conjugal relationship, which are the only contraceptive measures permitted to Catholics ... The Committee emphatically disclaims any intention to take any position with regard to birth control or the use of contraceptive measures for other than medical reasons.' But 'in spite of the views of Monseigneur Beaupin, the *Osservatore Romano* is said to have had some reference objecting to the document.'

Lester went on leave shortly after this and Thomas Coyne, his deputy, carried on. He pointed out in a letter to the department: 'I foresee some difficulty in securing the suppression of a technical document with the express authorisation of the League, through the assembly of the council, and, in this connection, the possibility (and the desirability) of a public discussion will have to be borne in mind.'

CHAPTER 4

High Commissioner to Danzig

DANZIG GOVERNOR'S FAMILY IN PERIL?

TENSION INCREASES IN DANZIG WITH MASS
ARRESTS

HIGH COMMISSIONER DASHES TO GENEVA

NAZI COUP FEARED TO CAPTURE DANZIG: CRISIS
AT ANY MINUTE NOW

DAS RINGEN UM DANZIG
(THE STRUGGLE FOR DANZIG)

THE NEW PUSH BY THE NATIONAL SOCIALISTS

Such headlines were commonplace in the summer of 1936, while Sean Lester was High Commissioner to Danzig, and had erupted, from time to time, as Berlin decided to heighten or release the pressure on this most sensitive spot in Europe. Many times it seemed that war would break out over this small city in the Baltic, but it was not until 1 September 1939 that the first bombs of World War II did land on the Free City.

The Free City of Danzig was in fact a small state of about 750 square miles – for purposes of comparison, Ireland's smallest county, Louth, is almost 318 square miles – including, as well as the beautiful, dignified and historic city itself, several towns, a favourite holiday resort, Zoppot, and Oliva, seat of the Catholic bishop, many farms and estates and much woodland. Altogether it had over 85,000 households and almost 400,000 inhabitants, of which Danzig city's administrative district had just over 200,000.

When the Council of the League of Nations invited Lester to become High Commissioner of Danzig (now Gdansk) he at first declined; but when the invitation was repeated he felt bound by his sense of duty and accepted in late 1933, the year of Hitler's accession to power in Germany. The duties of the High Commissioner, from early 1934 when he arrived in the lovely old Hanseatic city, were to take a threatening turn, as the National Socialists, with a small majority, began a serious campaign to undermine the constitution of the city, a constitution voted into place by the citizens themselves and confirmed by the League. The setting up of Danzig as a Free City following World War I had been a compromise between Polish demands for annexation and the British and American desire to avoid placing purely German territories, as they saw it, under alien rule. In the end, it was separated from Germany as an autonomous city under the protection of the League of Nations. 'The most distasteful and unsuitable of the tasks imposed by the Peace Conference upon the League... a task which could never be brought to a safe and satisfactory conclusion.' So wrote Frank Walters, official historian of the League, in his *History of the League of Nations* (Oxford, 1952).

While Danzig spoke mostly German, it had for long been associated with Poland without being a part of it. A Polish writer, Casimir Smogorzewski, put it thus in *Poland's Access to the Sea*, a book published by George Allen and Unwin in 1934:

> Danzig has had a strongly Teutonic character since the
> fourteenth century, but the townsmen have always been

on their guard against separation from the Polish hinterland by a political frontier. Placed at the mouth of the Vistula, the Polish national waterway, Danzig was and always will be the principal port of Poland. Poland has always respected the internal self-government of the town; she will also respect, therefore, its present status [under the League of Nations]. But Poland will never renounce Danzig.

The Versailles Treaty set up the Free City as a customs union with Poland. Poland was to be responsible for the city's foreign affairs and defence, and also ran its railways and post office. There was a harbour board with a non-Polish and non-German chairman.

The corridor which gave Poland direct, unrestricted access to the sea was over 1600 square kilometres in area, 230 kilometres long and 240 kilometres wide at its base. It narrowed to 30 kilometres to the west of Danzig, and to the north had a sea coast of 76 kilometres.

The High Commissioner was to arbitrate between Danzig and Poland. Germany was not in his brief. His duties can be summarised as follows: he arbitrated on all matters in dispute between Poland and the Free City of Danzig; when a decision had been taken by the High Commissioner, Poland and Danzig had the right to appeal against this to the council of the League, whose decision was final; he supervised the manufacture, storing and transport of all war material in Danzig; he approved the external loans of Danzig; he exercised the right of a veto on international treaties applying to Danzig; he sent to the council reports on all questions which fell under his jurisdiction, and followed the instruction of the council on these matters.

Danzig in the 1930s was commercially only a shadow of the Danzig that had dominated the Baltic and loomed so large in the Hanseatic League centuries before. But it was a busy place, small and intimate, and above all outstanding for its wonderful architecture. The Marienkirche was claimed to be the largest brick-built church in the world; its tall, narrow houses in the more fashionable streets a rich mixture of styles, mostly bearing Dutch influence. The Free City still had its busy manufacturing bases: the international shipyard, the railway wagon factory, sugar refineries, distilleries including the famous Lachs, makers of the liqueur Danziger Goldwasser. It had a busy amber trade. It had huge and architecturally satisfying warehouses or *Speicher*. It had long been the outlet from which the grain of Eastern Europe went out to the world; and from the east, through Danzig, came spices for the tables of Europe. The main physical impression to the newly arrived was the smallness of the city, its beauty and above all its dignity.

The High Commissioner's residence, a former military command post, was well in the city, a few hundred yards from the railway station. Three minutes away, on foot, were the rich private houses of the merchants and the expensive shops. The size allowed easy access to any official in any office. Lester had no bodyguard or ceremonial cover. His office staff was small, the domestic staff large and the German butler, of course, a spy.

Early in 1934 Germany and Poland were concluding a treaty of friendship and non-aggression. A move which, in effect, shifted Poland from her longstanding attachment to France, and which, for that reason, gave great satisfaction to Berlin. Poland was to be lulled into a false sense of security vis-à-vis Germany. Danzig was useful for anti-Versailles arguments and airing of German grievances, but German long-term plans for a land empire stretching eastwards, which would save her from ever suffering a sea blockade again, and which would enrich and make her the supreme land power, required comparative peace with Poland until war broke out.

The German–Polish pact of January 1934 had repercussions on the running of Danzig as well as accomplishing Hitler's strategic aim of moving Poland from French influence. Ulrich Sahm, in a book on Rudolf von Scheliha, a German diplomat against Hitler, executed in 1942, writes:

> For the free city of Danzig, the Treaty brought, after many years of tension, a relatively long period of lasting calm.

Both Governments were, as was the Danzig Senate, interested from differing motives, in the weakening of the control of the Free State by the League of Nations through limiting the scope of activity of the High Commissioner of the League of Nations (1934–1937 the Irishman Sean Lester, after that the Swiss, Carl J. Burckhardt).

Lester in Danzig

When he took up the post of High Commissioner, Lester was going from the civilised argument at the League of Nations and the open society of Geneva to a place where, as time went by, he could not be contacted safely in the High Commissioner's office by supplicants and others regarded by the Nazi government of the Free City as traitors (often elected members of the opposition in the parliament of the Free City). It became not unusual as he went on walks through the woods for the family to be told to go ahead slowly, while Lester was stopped by a man who would not risk being seen to make contact officially. Another regular feature of Lester's Danzig experience was to receive a visit from the future head of the government, Arthur Greiser, to explain that a vituperative speech he had made against Lester was not, of course, personal, but solely an attack on the office. And the same Greiser would complain that he had been forced into speaking so strongly by the Gauleiter of the Free City, Albert Forster, a favourite of Hitler, and to plead with Lester to do everything he could to have Forster removed: an Orwellian world.

Nothing was to be done about Forster and, as the German Foreign Minister Baron von Neurath explained on one occasion to Lester, who had called on his way through to Geneva: 'You know our policy on Danzig. It is to keep turning the knife in the wound.' And regularly during the three years that Lester spent in the Free City, the world's headlines reported threat after threat, imminent disorder, provoking unease throughout

Europe: 'Sean Lester: Man with the most dangerous job in the world', 'Spy ring around Danzig's Irishman', 'Danzig to be made military base: Secret Berlin arms plan reported'.

The High Commissioner had 'a multitude of responsibilities but no power of enforcement,' wrote Tom Johnson, former Lord Privy Seal in a Labour government in 1936. And at a period when police surveillance of all visitors was intense, another British MP, Arthur Jenkins, after a visit to the city, wrote of Lester as 'a man of great courage ... with a fine and moving dignity ... and if our Consul there were treated in this disgraceful manner, the British Government would see that Herr Greiser was put in his place at once.'

It would have been difficult, if not impossible, for the League of Nations to find a candidate more suited to represent it at that time in the Free City of Danzig than Sean Lester. In temperament and in experience he was the man to meet the challenge of the new, aggressive National Socialist government there. Lester's experiences back home from 1916 to 1923 gave him a natural inclination to sympathise with Poland, newly arisen; at the same time he could feel for the German people, heavily defeated in the war of 1914–18. He was used to the fact that newly arisen patriotism was often expressed in truculence, and could make allowances for strident sloganising.

His task, more than any of his five predecessors, was, above all, to strive to maintain intact the constitution, which was constantly under attack and openly flouted by the National Socialists, not long come to power with a slim majority, but already acting as if the elected opposition had barely a right to exist. In other words, he had to be a guarantor of the constitution and the constitutional rights of the population.

Lester's arrival in Danzig on 24 January 1934 was reported all over Germany – and the world – but the German news agency's formal report was followed the next day by a most friendly and expectant dispatch from the *Völkischer Beobachter*'s own correspondent on the spot. The *Völkischer Beobachter* was the official organ of the National Socialist party and therefore of the German government. This was a glowing welcome to 'the new man' whom Danzig came forward to meet with eager confidence:

> It is only natural that the manly Irish freedom-fighter appears as a sympathetic figure to the thoroughly National Socialised Danzig ... It is a coincidence which we at any rate see as a good omen for co-operation, that both Lester and the Danzig Senate President, Dr Rauschning, in their earlier public careers, were chiefly writers and journalists. That seems to guarantee a broader outlook than the stifling air of bureaucratic office. Lester, still in his prime, his early forties, is seen as straightforward, unaffected and open-minded.

The line about open air, man-to-man diplomacy being superior to talk between walls was a favourite with some of the individuals with whom Lester was to have dealings. 'Danzig believes,' continued the dispatch 'that when necessary he will be a good and honourable mediator between the Free City and Poland.'

Later in the same article Lester is quoted as expressing 'in a friendly gesture' the hope that he and his wife would spend in the beautiful, historic city of Danzig 'three of the happiest years of our lives'. Diplomats express such sentiments in similar circumstances. It need not be seen as cynical or thoughtless. Lester took people as he found them, and was prepared, in the new circumstances, to make generous allowances. He had seen, in the affair of Bernheim, how Germany was dealing with Jews. This was Danzig, not Germany. But already he had been made aware of the authoritarian, heavy-handedness of the government, even under the relatively moderate president, Hermann Rauschning: the council of the League had summoned Rauschning to Geneva to explain how not only had two newspapers been suspended, but their editors had been arrested because they had appealed to the then High Commissioner, Count Gravina. Rauschning, in Geneva, claimed they were arrested because they had neglected to exhaust all legal measures open to them before seeking to petition the League. The League would not accept this explanation. Lester, who had not yet departed to take up office in Danzig, sat in at the meetings with the Council but preferred not to offer any remarks. He was to see in Danzig, again and again, the suppression of newspapers without any valid cause.

Government of Danzig

The senate or government of Danzig consisted of a president and a vice-president along with ten others, elected from its members by the Volkstag (popular assembly). This body, seventy-two in number, was elected by all Danzig citizens over twenty years of age by proportional representation for four years. Danzig had no state president as such. The president of the senate was *primus inter pares* within the government.

The campaign for reunion with the Reich was a never-ending source of trouble for Lester, but there were lesser Polish–Danzig quarrels about trade and the harbour. Sometimes he got settlement on the spot, but when he had to bring matters to the council of the League, he got promises which, he said, were not always kept.

The High Commissioner's influence was linked with the prestige of the League. He had no forces at his disposal. As time went on, the Danzig Nazis were encouraged both by the failure of the League members to stand by the covenant, and by Hitler's onward march. The Italian victory over the League in the case of Abyssinia encouraged the Danzig Nazis to more audacious moves. Mussolini's Abyssinian triumph led de Valera to say that the world was facing a choice between the covenant and the law of the jungle.

There were three main *dramatis personae* on the German side in Danzig: Rauschning, president of the senate or government, who was typical of the old Nationalist party from which background he came; Albert Forster, the Gauleiter; and Arthur Greiser, deputy president and later president. Of the three,

Albert Forster, a Bavarian, not a citizen of Danzig, but a favourite of Hitler, was the supreme boss as head of the Nazi party; all elected politicians and the rest of the Nazi organisation came under his sway. Forster arrived in the city with all his belongings in a cardboard box. There was nothing unusual about that in the Irish experience, but a year later he owned a town house and a country residence and travelled in a fine Mercedes car as befitted a Gauleiter. 'But,' said Lester in a speech to a Dublin audience in 1948:

> ... more corruptible than easily-acquired wealth was unbridled power and the absence of any control on the growth of a vast vanity. Provided he showed sufficient adulation to the Dictator, he could do as he pleased. A Nietzsche-esque lord of the lives of the people. Forster was a great mob orator and a fanatic, very impatient of legal obstacles to the institution of a Nazi dictatorship.

Von Neurath, German Foreign Minister, confirmed to Lester on one occasion that even he could not influence Forster. Only Hitler could.

The second player in the drama was Arthur Greiser, who was hanged after the war by the Poles in the market square of Poznan (Posen in German), before a crowd of ten thousand. He had been made Gauleiter of the province of Poznan, or the Warthegau as it was renamed by the Germans, on the outbreak of the war. But in Lester's time and until the war, he was second to Forster and a successor to Rauschning as president of the senate (the government of Danzig). Greiser was a crude, simple man, always running to Lester to assure him that no offence was meant by some outrageous speech of his – he was attacking not the man but the office. He often complained to Lester that Forster was ruining his life. He was simply a batman or valet to Forster, but according to Lester, he had no moral scruples about carrying out orders. Nevertheless he often used Lester as a father confessor. It seemed at times like the classic operation of the hard interrogator and the sympathetic one, Forster and Greiser. Forster, too, was tried after the war by the Poles and executed.

Colonel Beck, the Polish Foreign Minister, was an enigmatic character. From the time when a German–Polish rapprochement in the form of a 'treaty of friendship and non-aggression' was signed in the month that brought Lester to Danzig, he gave the impression of detaching himself somewhat from the League view of what was going on in Danzig even though he sat on the council. Nevertheless, in the cat-and-mouse game that went on in Lester's time, the Nazis knew that, in extreme circumstances, the League could have called on Poland for armed protection for the city and its High Commissioner; it was the greatest and most dangerous sanction of all, for it could have led instantly to war. When the League accepted the function of guarantor of the Free City, no special difficulties had been anticipated that could not be settled in a democratic way. There did not seem to be any need to give the council of the League, or its servant, the High Commissioner, any special power of enforcement. The League was tempted at times, after the excesses of the Nazis and the sometimes ambivalent tactics of Colonel Beck, to abandon not only its function as guarantor of the constitution, but its whole connection with the Free City.

The first man with whom Lester had to deal was Hermann Rauschning, one of the very few there, in Lester's mind, who had any conception of Europe and the world outside the Nazi movement.

How a moderate Nationalist like Rauschning – moderate by German standards though no western democrat – came into the National Socialist movement is explained in a book he wrote in England in 1941. The youth had to be won, he urged, by speaking a language that articulated great emotions, movement, passion, sacrifice and ideals. 'In spite of all that could be said against the Nazis, there is an energy at the back of it, a rhythm and new life. This was political capital which must not be squandered, it must be got into the right hands.' So he had joined the party in 1931. It would mellow. 'We are attracted,' he wrote, meaning people like himself, 'by an element that existed in Nazism and in no other German party: faith in Germany, and vitality.' Above all, he was attracted by the energy of the party

60

and its holding out to the youth of hope for the future. He was discarded after a short period as president of the senate once his usefulness as a respectable front had come to an end. He was to write several books which exposed to the world the Nazi mentality and intentions, notably *Hitler Speaks*, accounts of many talks face to face with the Führer. He describes how Field Marshal von Brauchitsch, who later became commander of the German army, 'advised me to carry on the struggle with the party in such a way as to provide evidence that a workable democratic order was quite possible after Nazism'. The idea behind these cryptic words was that an anti-Nazi coalition of all parties in Danzig from the German Nationalists to the Social Democrats should be formed, organising the trade unions for the preservation of civil order. Forster, the party leader, was to be deported as an undesirable alien, the SS and SA formations to be dissolved and the chief leaders to be arrested. 'We could rely on the Danzig Police which, at that time, were overwhelmingly anti-Nazi. ... It would have been a sort of *coup d'état*. I rejected the idea, for the good reason that I could not protect the Constitution of the Free State against Nazi demands, and at the same time myself break it.' Not that Rauschning was unaware of the expressed boundless imperial, racist and destructive ambitions of Adolf Hitler. He had put up with them, or perhaps he had not believed them fully.

The Free City

Danzig was not a problem in isolation. The temperature rose and fell according to the general state of Europe, and major issues in Europe reacted on Danzig, especially after the blow which the Abyssinian affair dealt to the prestige of the League of Nations.

Poles were not numerous in the city itself, but were everywhere around the territory: Cashubians to the west, Masurians to the east. No wonder that Günter Grass, born a Danziger, could, decade after decade, mine rich literature from the city, as James Joyce did with Dublin. The Poles and other minorities amounted to no more than ten per cent of the voters. But much more than the fate of the city itself was at stake, great though that was. There was the fear among Western powers that, if concessions were made on Danzig to Germany, all the frontiers deriving from the Treaty of Versailles would come up for revision.

Rauschning aimed to give an intellectual basis to the new rapprochement evolving between Germany and Poland and between Danzig and Poland. He set up a Danzig Society for the Study of Poland, and delivered the inaugural speech in March of 1934. The recent German/Polish pact, he stressed, was not to be seen as a temporary truce and could lead to a really effective way of working together. Poland had just emerged as a new state. 'National Socialists,' he said, 'had also fought for a new state, where class war had been eliminated. Poland, from a democratic constitution, had gone on to develop into an authoritarian state with a character of its own, through the work of a great personality [Pilsudski], surrounded by enlightened associates.'

But even with Rauschning as head of the senate, Lester was almost immediately into the routine of press suppressions, quarrels over uniformed organisations, 'protective custody' and all the time guarding the constitution against new decrees and laws. It was like trying to square a circle, to arbitrate in an entity where a totalitarian government incessantly strove against the constraints of a democratic constitution.

Early in 1934, Lester's first year, Danzig had a visit from Himmler, head of the SS. A parade took place of twelve thousand uniformed men, infantry, cavalry and motor cyclists. 'Like a parade of a military division without arms,' as Lester reported back to Geneva. He went on to say:

> The situation as I find it on my arrival in Danzig is, therefore, that a minimum of twelve thousand (some estimate twenty thousand) men in the territory of the Free City are organised on what is no doubt a semi-military basis, and drilled and uniformed. They carry the same flag

as in Germany; their officers have made the same declaration of loyalty to the Führer; they are occasionally inspected by superior officers from Germany itself.

Typical of Lester's struggles to keep Danzig newspapers in being was an early incident, when on 1 March 1934 he interviewed Rauschning on, among other topics, the seizure of the *Volkszeitung*, organ of the Centre party. The disputed article was on the constitutional position of the Free City. Lester told Rauschning that the article appeared to him to be very innocuous, and not in any way threatening to the state. It was a conservative newspaper, anything but extreme in its policy. Rauschning said he had been urged to suppress the newspaper altogether, but agreed only to the seizure of that issue. The government, he said, was suffering from press attacks. Articles hostile or embarrassing to the government were then being picked up by other opposition papers in such a way as to misrepresent the government and hinder it in its work. The article concerned, Rauschning argued, picked up a few sentences from a report of Sir John Simon to the council of the League and gave a false impression of the whole report. The *Volkszeitung* gave the extreme socialist an opportunity to quote and comment in an undesirable way on the matter, he said. The paper also questioned the sincerity of Rauschning's recent declaration to the League about his respect for the constitution.

Lester asked for an *aide-mémoire* on the subject. It arrived the next day, stressing that it was a question only of the seizure of one issue and backing up the decision by quoting a law of 7 May 1874 and a decree of 30 June 1933 and going over the ground covered the day before. Rauschning ended: 'I hope I have succeeded, dear Mr Lester, in convincing you that the not very severe measures taken against the *Volkszeitung* were absolutely necessary for the Government.'

Lester might have asked 'Why not just demand a public apology, or issue a forceful government denial?' That wasn't the National Socialist way. And worse could have happened in Germany itself.

Rauschning's wife Anna was less sanguine than her husband about the prospect of turning Nazi ambitions into more conservative channels. When he was elected president of the Danzig senate in May 1933, she had to move into the presidential residence in the city from the farm they ran some miles away, and entered into the constant round of public engagements with less than enthusiasm. In a book published (in French) in exile in 1942, *Au Pied du Mur* (Eyre and Spottiswoode, London, 1944), she found it laughable that Nazi women went around the small town of Danzig, raising their arms in greeting to their friends and shouting 'Heil Hitler'. Even when they went into a shop, it was: 'Heil Hitler, two litres of milk,' or 'Heil Hitler, can you sole my shoes?' She had no kind word for her husband's colleagues. They were corrupt men who had just graduated from street fighting, and were soon property owners on a large scale. She mentioned the Gauleiter, Forster, in particular. They tried to corrupt the young, including her own children, by immoral teachings on sex in the various youth movements. Girls were told, she asserts in her book, that from the age of seventeen the greatest good for the Reich was that they should give the Führer young soldiers, in or out of marriage. Young boys were taught that nature was cruel and they too must be cruel.

The Rauschnings stopped going to church. Their old pastor left for Switzerland in despair, and what a new generation gave out from the pulpit was hardly distinguishable, she says, from speeches from Nazi platforms. Rauschning tried again and again to persuade her that all this was a temporary phase. They both were, after all, members of the party. But as time went on, as the family came to realise that every servant in their home and farm at Warnau and in the presidential residence at Danzig was, and on party orders had to be, a spy, even Rauschning's enthusiasm was dampened.

Lunch at Rauschning's farm in May 1934 introduced the young Lester girls, aged twelve, ten and eight, in an unforgettable way, to the realities of livestock rearing. Lester was in Geneva and Rauschning himself was not present. Around the luncheon table were, in addition to Elsie Lester and her girls, Mrs Rauschning and her four children, the eldest a girl of some eighteen years, and a few other young visitors. During the meal there was a flurry outside – a calf had run amok and was to be slaughtered at once. A senior Rauschning girl led the procession in a rush out to the yard, picking up on the way a large knife that hung conveniently. And there, before the eyes of all the children, the calf was slaughtered in a shed, blood flowing profusely. Then they all went back to their meal. Writing to her husband later that night, Elsie worried that their sudden introduction to the slaughtering carried out before their eyes might prove a traumatic shock for the girls. When she tucked them up in bed, she was reassured that none mentioned the incident, one even worrying that she had failed to pick a pansy that had attracted her. But the fact that they did not say anything to their mother meant nothing more than that they had stored away in their minds something they would never forget. Sixty years afterwards, they remember the occasion – the interrupted luncheon, the shed, and all the blood flowing. And the fact that they all went back to the table afterwards.

Rauschning had long felt a strong personal commitment to easing relations between Germany and Poland. When the Polish–German borders were redrawn after World War I, Rauschning, an ex-officer, had found himself in Poland. He worked for years to improve relations between the two peoples and saw the culmination of his efforts in the non-aggression treaty of early 1934. He later realised that on Germany's part, this was merely a holding operation, effectively leaving Poland to the mercy of Germany. Once that was signed, it may be, Rauschning's value to the National Socialists had diminished to vanishing point. Rauschning had told the party he would not resign as president unless they forced him out. Eventually a vote of the senate was taken and he was brought down. On 17 October the Danzig press carried a statement by the president of the senate categorically denying the rumours about a clash between himself and Mr Forster. A month later on 23 November Rauschning sent his letter of resignation to the president of the popular assembly. He announced, in a letter published in the press on the same day, that he had 'for special reasons' decided to lay down his office. He appealed to the citizens to realise their joint responsibility for the greater interest of the community as a whole, and to thrust all petty and personal consideration into the background: 'To yourselves be true – such is the foundation of loyalty to and faith in the State and the National community.' The national community, presumably, being all Germany. And he finished on an impeccably national note expressing 'steadfast confidence in Divine guidance to this land and this people, and to the German cause in the East with the heavy task by which it is confronted.' A sentiment with which the government in Berlin would heartily agree.

From then on began a campaign to isolate and destroy him and his family. His stud farm, where horses and cattle were bred and where general agriculture was extensively practised, was boycotted. Notices were put up outside the property calling him traitor. Local people would come only at night to buy – at miserable prices – their produce. They lost their famous and favourite stallions.

Eventually Rauschning felt that his life was in danger. He fled for a time to Switzerland. His wife and family held out until 1938. Just ahead of the Gestapo, she believes, Anna Rauschning, having sold the farm, escaped through the Polish Corridor with her family to the port of Gdynia bound by steamer for France.

Years later, writing in England, Rauschning wondered if he had taken the right decision in emigrating. Many conservative nationalists clung on to their posts, hoping, like Rauschning, for a turn in the tide. His associates, and people of a like mind, were simply engulfed in the tide of war, and, as far as the Allies were concerned, seemed to be culpable by association or omission, and thus no better than their masters. Lester maintained contact with Rauschning on a social basis afterwards and this was the alleged reason for a later diplomatic incident.

The departure of Rauschning and his replacement by Greiser meant a change of tempo. Lester had not been long in his office as High Commissioner before the National Socialist majority realised that they were going to be confronted every time they exceeded the limits laid down in the constitution. Their rush towards what, in the Reich, was called *Gleichschaltung* – forcing into line all opposition – had to be tempered.

Mere confrontation was not Lester's purpose. He spoke with reason, tried to move events with persuasion and moderate pressure, as he had been able to do when Rauschning was president, not always with success, but without heightening the temperature too much. Forster and Greiser, however, worked on the principle of strong language in public, followed, where this raised protest, by protestations of fidelity to the constitution.

Political upheavals aside, 1934 was a difficult year economically, too, for Danzig. The senate noted that it succeeded in bringing about a further permanent reduction in unemployment by such measures as the transferring of four thousand unemployed women to domestic service and work in agricultural practices, or labour service camps, and training on the land. Vigorous efforts were made to put an end to double earning. The senate complained that the Poles, by so-called customs control over trade with Danzig, frustrated the Free City's efforts to stimulate shipping and inland waterway traffic.

There was another major factor. The Poles had been given access to the sea by their rights over Danzig, but they also set up a large port of their own, transforming a small fishing village on the new Polish Corridor, Gdynia, with incredible energy and speed, into a harbour with full facilities, which in a few years outstripped the volume of trade of Danzig itself. From exports of 9186 tonnes in 1924, Gdynia went to 4,761,400 in 1932, very close to Danzig's 5,047,949.

Lester notes in his diary that Count O'Rourke, Bishop of Danzig, called to see him on 14 June 1934. The O'Rourkes had emigrated from Ireland during the eighteenth century and had finally settled down in Russia. His Lordship did not speak much English but was able to converse in French with Lester: 'His Lordship came in, ostentatiously carrying a copy of *Ireland's Own*, and insisted on smoking Irish cigarettes, on patriotic grounds, as he said, although I know that His Lordship's taste is very much in the direction of Russian cigarettes.' This was an official visit but Count O'Rourke was regularly in the Lester household as a very welcome guest. The three young Lester daughters thought of him as a smiling Father Christmas.

The bishop was concerned this time about two matters. One was a decree recently issued by the senate dealing with collections of money for the poor. This, said Count O'Rourke, was directed against Caritas, which included the St Vincent de Paul organisation for men and the St Elizabeth organisation for women. Collections were not allowed to be made at the houses of the parishioners who had promised a monthly contribution, but contributions must now be sent by post or delivered at the offices. This obviously would mean a very considerable reduction in the income and activity of the Caritas organisation and the bishop lodged a strong protest with the senate, of which he was to send Lester a copy. He hoped for help, and indicated that if he didn't get satisfaction from the senate he would come to Lester officially with a petition.

The other point which the bishop mentioned was parades of the Hitler Youth boys outside Catholic churches. These boys were assembled in line, and when the congregation left the church, they shouted anti-Catholic and insulting verses. At one of the churches the police were present, but the only result was apparently that a young member of the congregation named Bergmann was arrested and charged with resisting the police. The bishop said fifty witnesses could be produced to refute this charge. Fortunately he had some satisfaction. On 11 July Lester records that Count O'Rourke called to see him and to thank him again for his intervention with regard to the collections for the Catholic charitable societies and other matters.

He said that following Lester's conversation with the then president, Rauschning had gone to see him and had agreed that permission would be given to Caritas to collect from its members. There had also been, for some time, a question of a state contribution to the organ fund for the cathedral and Rauschning had presented him with 17,000 Danziger gulden for the purpose. He had been informed that, as part of land reform, the land belonging to the churches would have to be distributed as in other cases, but had since received from Rauschning an assurance that this would not be done.

Some years later, Lester was discussing Bishop O'Rourke with the Bishop of Galway, the formidable Michael Browne, known to everyone in the west of Ireland, and farther afield, simply as Michael of Galway. Michael had met Count O'Rourke on several occasions. Lester told him how welcome Bishop O'Rourke had always been in their house in Danzig, how much the family appreciated him. 'He's so good-natured,' said Lester, 'so easy to talk to. He's so good, er ... so Christian.' He stopped and looked at Michael, realising what he had said, then asked: 'Is that an awful thing to say about a Catholic bishop?' Michael shook his head: 'Not at all. That's quite all right.'

The fact that Lester had been a successful negotiator and facilitator in Geneva did not mean that he sought the easy way out of difficulties, or strove for a conclusion on any terms. He sought justice. Nor was he the entirely pacific, smooth dealer. He did not often raise his voice, but when he had to, he did, as was the case frequently in Danzig, even in the relatively (for Danzig) quiet first year of 1934. While his annual reports to the League of Nations are cast in diplomatic terms, his personal letters to Avenol, the Secretary-General, and his own diary show the frostier side. The disputed points concerned, early on, the persistent banning of newspapers in the Free City; the violent provocative language of the Nazi senior figures against the opposition, often including the word 'traitors', as if everyone who was not a Nazi was an enemy of the constitution; the constraints put on the churches and their youth organisations; the over-reaction of the police to non-Nazis; the anti-Jewish restrictions; the use of 'protective custody'; in fact, all the paraphernalia of the German Reich except for concentration camps, and this gap was filled on the outbreak of war in September 1939, with the building of Stutthof a few miles from the city. To this day, the remains can be seen, with its crematorium, its piles of old shoes, its crop of human hair and the usual photographs of emaciated corpses.

It was a heavy programme for Lester, to be for ever watching, cautioning, protesting, pacifying and laying down the law. As he wrote to de Valera, in June 1947, when his secondment from the Irish foreign service to the service of the League was coming to an end:

> I could have had an easy time by accepting various hints and proposals or by yielding to the threats which followed, and abandoning to the fate – which did ultimately overtake them – the non-National Socialist majority of the population, including the Catholic Party, the Conservative Party, the Labour Party and the Jews. Feeling, sometimes, what with the confused European situation, the absence of any real power behind me, and the intense activity of the anti-Constitution Party, rather like a fly on the wheel, I endeavoured, with a sense of proportion, with much patience and, when necessary with firmness, to maintain in Danzig the elementary human rights. Looking back on this period, I can honestly say that I did my duty, tolerating a personal situation which, especially during the later part of my term, at times might have been thought intolerable, not too much impressed by threats and ignoring conditions which, to say the least, were novel in international life.

Already in the spring of 1934, the depths of anti-Jewish feeling in Danzig could be seen. A Jewish student in the school of St Patri wrote an essay on the famous equestrian statue at the cathedral of Bamberg in Germany. The teachers thought the essay well-balanced and mature, but the new state commissioner for education, Herr Schramm, a friend and disciple of Albert Forster, the Gauleiter, declared that

> a Jewish pupil was not in a position to write an essay on the Bamberg Horseman, who was a symbol of Germanness, and in any case, such an essay could not obtain the best

marks. (*Nazi Conquest of Danzig*, Hans L Leonhardt, p 29)

As time went on, especially after Rauschning's resignation, it became strikingly obvious to visiting foreigners, writes Leonhardt, that showcases for the prurient anti-Jewish rag, *Der Stürmer*, multiplied on street walls. Leonhardt describes the paper as 'a unique example of cultural degeneracy, often read by the growing generation.' I came across the unease this paper caused among some older Germans myself, when I was in Heidelberg before the war. My kindly and cultivated landlady noted that I had bought *Der Stürmer* and protested: 'Oh, Douglas, why do you bring that awful publication into the house?' I pointed out to her that her son was an officer in the SS and that the paper was obviously approved by the régime or it wouldn't have been allowed to appear. 'The trouble is,' she explained, 'that Hitler is so attached to his old comrades of street-fighting days. He cannot let them down now.' Julius Streicher, editor of the paper (and governor of Franconia) was one of these old comrades.

I have seen a copy of a standard news agency photograph of Lester, published in *Der Stürmer*, but with artificially lengthened nose and the caption, 'Lester the Jew'. (It was customary with many Nazis to label anyone they didn't like as a Jew, for example renaming President Roosevelt as Rosenfeld.)

Leni Riefenstahl, who made the film *Triumph of the Will*, which recorded the Nuremberg Nazi rally, met Streicher and asked him how he oculd publish such a nasty newspaper. She relates in her memoirs, *The Sieve of Time*, how he laughed, in no way ashamed and said, 'My newspaper isn't written for intelligent people like yourself. It's for the country populace, so that the peasant girls can tell the difference between Aryans and Jews.' Riefenstahl's reply was: 'I find you loathsome,' but, still laughing, Streicher took his leave.

The disease of anti-Semitism was not confined to Germany, but nowhere did it reach such depths of criminality. In Danzig, not part of the Reich, the constraints were many and heavy, but at this stage they did not have a concentration camp, in spite of Forster's regular threats that enemies of the state (in other words, anti-Nazis, even publicly elected ones) would find themselves in just such a camp.

In July 1934, President Ruschning had issued a declaration reminding the citizens that the constitution of the Free City made it impossible to injure the rights of inhabitants on account of their race or religion, but four days before this, Forster, the Gauleiter, not a Danziger and not an official of the state but the dominant Nazi there, issued a manifesto to leading Nazis:

> To a National Sociaist, there are no decent Jews. The race is, and must remain our mortal enemy. Our hospitality must not go so far as to make us support the Jews in small Business. The Jew must be eliminated wherever possible.

Among the problems presented to Lester in 1934 was a formal petition lodged by two Catholic priests against the banning of uniforms of young people's organisations out of doors: National Socialist associations and Polish young people's organisations were exempt from this. The High Commissioner passed the complaint on to the president of the senate. The senate considered that the complaints were not justified, and so the petition was sent on to the Secretary-General of the League of Nations with the request that it be put before the Council.

Local elections were to be held on 18 November 1934 in two districts of the city. Lester went to the president on 30 October and formally handed over an *aide-mémoire* setting out his observations, which included his confidence that the government would see to it that all parties could exercise their rights in regard to propaganda within the limits of the constitution: the vice-president gave the usual assurances of the government's consciousness of its responsibilities and so on. In spite of this, and naturally enough in the circumstances, the newspaper of the Social Democratic party was suspended on 8 November for three days for accusing the police of partiality in reporting some election incidents.

There were incidents, too, in which the Polish government's

actions were questioned by Lester. He noted in a conversation with Papée, the Polish representative in Danzig, and others, that Poland was placing restrictions on Danzig's exports to Poland. One firm, which had a licence to export to Poland, was suspended because a bottle of ink found in its office had been bought from another Danzig firm – not one of those approved by the Polish authorities. Lester told them that this was economic war.

Interlude in Geneva

On 18 January 1935 the League council in Geneva considered the High Commissioner's report on the year 1934. While noting an appreciable improvement in relations with Poland, it was damning enough in detail. Internal politics had on occasion, Lester said, given rise to 'serious apprehensions in the most varied spheres, such as the creation of new institutions, measures regarding the press, speeches delivered by official personages and, in general, the struggle between the various political parties.'

He related the circumstances of Rauschning's withdrawal and quoted at some length from the statement of the new president of the senate, Arthur Greiser. This began by inviting all classes of the people of Danzig to co-operate in the great work that lay ahead of them. The conditions, were, of course, that there should be no 'unpatriotic activities' such as the picking of holes in every government achievement by the opposition, 'which represents a fast vanishing minority'. Internal peace and order were of course said to be fundamental.

Lester did record some alleviation of restrictions agreed by former President Rauschning. He also quoted from President Greiser's New Year address to the population of Danzig, professing the 'peaceful disposition of the National Socialist Government'. Here Greiser said that if in the coming year, 'certain small opposition parties, protected by the Constitution of the Free City, but otherwise of little account, imagine that they would be able to disturb Danzig's great work of peace for

Europe, we will not tolerate such sabotage…' and spoke of 'perpetual recriminations of diehards who refuse to realise that their political role is over, even under the Constitutional laws of democracy'. He was referring, again, to the lawfully elected opposition.

On the same occasion, Lester reported, von Wnuk, senator and president of the Volkstag, had said that those who voted for the National Socialists at the last elections were proof that 'the people had seen through the traitors' machinations' – traitors, again, being constitutional political opponents. Lester's report also recorded the fact that goods traffic at the port of Danzig had quickly gone from being the leader among Baltic ports, to being superseded by Copenhagen and Gdynia.

The council meeting on 18 January was also the occasion of Greiser's first appearance. The rapporteur, Anthony Eden, referred to the petition from two Catholic priests in Danzig, Fathers Emil Moske and Walther Winke, forwarded via the High Commissioner. After receiving this petition Lester had also had a petition from the Centre party with similar complaints. The Danzig government had expressed its willingness to open discussions with the latter. Lester informed the council of this later communication in case it wished to take the two petitions together at a future date. The council agreed to defer. It was a not uncharacteristic attitude, and explains why Lester tried always to have disputes settled in Danzig. He knew the sidelines in Geneva into which submissions could be diverted, the delays and, often, the fudging that might follow.

Eden gave a lecture to Greiser, on the basis of Lester's 'impartial and dispassionate' review. 'Understated' might have been a better word; understated in the interests of his continuing efforts to come to grips with the government of the Free City. He emphasised that the League's guarantee of the constitution implied the right of the council to be the sole judge of its own action in any case that might arise, and noted the assurances given by President Greiser of the loyalty of the senate to the same constitution.

Greiser said he was well pleased at the deferring of the two petitions, as the interval would give the senate an opportunity of seeking a settlement. He then went on to refer to the 'sacred principle of democracy whereby the majority of the population determined the general direction of the government's activity, which that majority guided'. They would be led by the principles of National Socialism to govern the city within the limits laid down by the constitution. The satisfactory relations between Danzig and Poland were due to National Socialism's desire for peace. And more references to the usual bogey, 'persons and associations who were unwilling to bow to the principle of the will of the majority on which the Constitution was based' – once again, the elected opposition. Eden concluded the proceedings by emphasising the word 'Free' in Free City with respect to the constitution of the Free City of Danzig, 'which was, of course, the name by which the City was called at the Council table'.

Eden would have been popular in National Socialist circles for his kid-glove handling of the question of the two petitions. No wonder that he was referred to not long after in the Nazi *Danziger Vorposten* as 'a respected and distinguished Englishman'.

CHAPTER 5

Elections in Danzig

T he Saar, a coal-rich basin between France and Germany, near Luxembourg, had been placed under a League of Nations commission after World War I to compensate the French for mines destroyed by the Germans in northern France. Under the terms of the peace treaty, a plebiscite was to be held whereby the Saarlanders could decide whether to remain with France, to return to Germany or to stay under League jurisdiction. In 1935 they voted overwhelmingly to return to Germany. This landslide encouraged the Danzig party members to try for another German victory, so, two years before the due time, Danzig Nazis decided to hold elections for the Volkstag and thus the senate or government. Their aim was to reach two-thirds of the votes, which would allow them to petition the League of Nations to change the constitution of Danzig to what they wanted. They felt confident that they would reach a much higher figure, maybe even eighty per cent.

1935 elections

Elections were to be on 7 April 1935 and, as the date approached, some of the most important figures in Germany came to speak and to be seen in this small Hanseatic city. Newspaper headlines told of Danzig ringing with the tramp of marching men, of 'forty miles of cheers' for General Göring, Air Minister and President of Prussia, whose motor car was escorted by two air squadrons.

Rudolf Hess, the Führer's deputy, came too, and Goebbels,

Propaganda Minister. Even Julius Streicher, publisher of *Der Stürmer* appeared.

Danzig was not German territory, as the *Manchester Guardian* pointed out, and for these notabilities to electioneer in the Free City would be the equivalent of Marshal Pilsudski, the leader of Poland, addressing meetings on behalf of the Polish minority. Or for that matter, Eden of Britain, or Laval of France. To the *Guardian* all this was a small but significant step towards the creation of the greater Germany which was the supreme object, they claimed, of German foreign policy. (In fact two Poles did address meetings during the campaign, but they were not of the seniority of the Germans.)

The election campaign saw one of the many passages between Lester and Greiser – Lester patiently pointing out what he saw as irregularities, if not breaches of law; Greiser arguing back and then, lumpishly, giving in.

Lester wrote to Greiser on 25 March, informing him that attacks on people and property had been reported to him and that, whether National Socialists or opposition, he wished to point out that it was incumbent on the senate to protect citizens exercising their constitutional rights. Further, and this was presumably the main point, he had been informed that the police had taken into protective custody, or *Schutzhaft*, several candidates for the Volkstag belonging to the opposition parties. Greiser replied that liberty for the citizen did not reach so far as to allow citizens during an election to break the laws and regulations at will. Sometimes, he replied, the police are forced to detain even those culpable of acts which outrage the natural sense of justice of the population, for their protection. Often it is not possible for them to recognise that the person concerned is a candidate for the popular assembly. Four candidates, he admitted, had been taken into protective custody in recent days in the interest of their safety: 'In the hope that, in spite of their attitude, they will not be molested by the population, I have ordered, notwithstanding the grave drawbacks which this measure involves, that these persons be set at liberty.'

For three years Lester lived with this regular pressure of

distortion and unreason often followed by honeyed tributes to his straight dealings. He was not impressed. He was not flattered. He went on carrying out the duties of his office, one man without any power behind him, and often let down by his employers, the League of Nations.

Lester tried always to leave a door open for the Nazis to come back. He did not, in spite of the strain on his own mental resources, ever try to put them into a corner out of which they could not, with any shred of dignity, emerge. He knew fighters and guerrilla types from home. Allowances had to be made for leaders to do some strutting.

In the case of the 1935 elections, Greiser blandly and mendaciously declared from the start that this was not to be seen as aiming at the constitution of the city, but was an election of the normal kind, prescribed in the constitution and wanted by the majority of the population. Again and again during the campaign, National Socialist leaders stressed that they aimed to reduce the minority parties to an insignificant number, and thereby to make it clear to the League of Nations that no importance should be attached to complaints about the constitution from these people.

Goebbels told the voters that the architects of the Treaty of Versailles had separated Danzig from Germany not to maintain peace but to create a lasting centre of discord among the peoples. Those who wanted to maintain what they called the independence of Danzig, he said, were only the mercenaries of the Treaty of Versailles. Germany did not want to alter boundaries by force, but to show to the world what the sentiments of this city were. Germany had got rid of different political parties; it was time for Danzig to follow that example. Rudolf Hess, Hitler's deputy, had told a meeting of nine thousand Hitler Youth of both sexes that he bore a special message from the Führer for them. 'He always has you in mind,' he told them, 'for all his efforts are devoted to you, who are the future of Germany. Abolish all class distinction among yourselves, and be worthy of the new nation of which you are the forerunners.'

The Saar had had an international force to keep the peace during the plebiscite there. In Danzig there was no such force. Violence from all the Nazi organisations was widespread and insistent throughout the election campaign.

Among the voices raised against the National Socialist list of candidates was that of Hermann Rauschning, former president of the senate. He did so in the form of an open letter to Gauleiter Albert Forster. Rauschning's letter was backed up by a similar message from Dr Ernst Ziehm, his predecessor as head of the Danzig senate and a venerated Nationalist leader, who denounced the Nazis for stigmatising all opponents as 'separatists'.

In spite of the best efforts of the National Socialists, many of the brave Danzigers followed the advice of the two former presidents of the senate and so the Nazis failed to achieve their two-thirds majority.

The headlines of newspapers throughout Europe were large: 'Shock for Nazis in Danzig Elections; 40% against,' said the London *Daily Express*. The New York *Herald Tribune* headed its report 'Nazis Fail to Gain Control of Danzig, Polling Only 60%'. The *Echo de Paris* said the results of the vote in Danzig 'bring consternation to Hitlerites'. Second headline to that was 'In Spite of Unheard of Pressure, the Nazis have not achieved 60% of the Vote'.

It was a remarkable tribute to the fearlessness of so many Danzigers and a remarkable setback for the Nazis, who had even brought into the circus the famous Marshal von Mackensen, one of the great heroes of World War I. During the campaign Greiser, president of the senate, had made a particularly violent attack, even for him, on the High Commissioner. The High Commissioner, he said, was in Danzig to act as an arbitrator on the relations between the Free City and Poland. He accused him of seeing less of the Germans in Danzig (meaning the Nazis) than the representatives of bankrupt parties, 'who, if they put into practice the democratic principles they are constantly advocating, would have bowed to the will of the majority'. This again supported the frequent claim that because the Nazis had a majority in the city, no other voice should be heard. Lester replied, in a letter, that there could be no question about the right of citizens of Danzig to appeal to the League of Nations in matters affecting the constitution of the Free City, and he expressed his surprise at frequent references by members of the senate to the opposition as traitors and separatists, principally on the ground that they exercised their right of appeal to the League, and refused to admit a discussion in the senate regarding the way in which the High Commissioner carried out his duties. Greiser's response was that the more the opposition appealed to the League in regard to even the most trivial matters, and misrepresented incidents, the more the government's work was damaged and its authority was undermined.

> If, for example, newspapers or parties can send petitions to the League regarding any trivial prohibition or regarding the seizure of a newspaper (as indeed they do) they regard it as an opportunity – which they utilise to the utmost – to write in the most provocative and insulting way about the government and the government parties ... every small incident is magnified into a sensation and every slight scuffle into an act of terrorism.

In short, the seizure of a newspaper was a trivial event: it was so held by the Nazi party throughout Lester's stay in Danzig, and of course in Germany itself the newspapers were, from the outset, completely controlled. At the time of the 1935 election, the *Danziger Volksstimme*, the socialist organ, was seized on 4, 6, 8 and 9 April. Months earlier, on 8 June 1934, the newspaper had published the following undertaking:

> Should reports published in the *Danziger Volksstimme* give rise to objection or misunderstanding, we will at all times place ourselves at the disposal of the competent organs of Government ... in order to discuss such questions, since we do not close our eyes to State necessities and are desirous of serving State interests.

Hans Leonhardt, who quotes this in *Nazi Conquest of Danzig*, adds: 'At no time did the chief of police make use of this gentlemanly undertaking.' And while Danzig's constitution laid down, in Article 79, 'There shall be no censorship,' Lester sent to Geneva a new decree of 8 May which included the following:

> A copy of every printed publication of a political nature shall be submitted by the printer to the local police authority before the issue for the purpose of circulation. The issue of printed publications may not take place earlier than one hour after a copy has been submitted to the local police authority.

The result of the election of April 1935 was that the National Socialist party gained an increase of one seat with about 57.3% of the votes cast (128,619 out of 224,442 votes). The council of the League subsequently affirmed that laws affecting conditions under which the election had been held were unconstitutional. But, wrote Lester, the manifest existence in Danzig of a very large minority opposed to the National Socialist party did not check the efforts to apply, to a still greater extent, the principles of National Socialism. This was evident from the Danzig government's attitude to the press, with constant bannings and seizures. Lester wrote:

> The Senate idea of what constituted reasonable criticism by the Press, seems to have been based upon National Socialist principles rather than upon those laid down in the Constitution. My representations to the Government on this subject, I regret to say, ceased to be effective.

Already in November 1934, musing over his *modus operandi* in a letter to Frank Walters, assistant Secretary-General of the League of Nations in Geneva, Lester wrote:

> I do not like the prospect of the Constitution being left an empty framework, and the League guarantees in consequence being a thing for laughter. As you know, I have a great deal of sympathy for Danzig, and have taken

a general guiding principle that there should be as little interference as possible with their internal affairs, and where there has been reasonable doubt, I have taken the responsibility of giving the benefit of that doubt to the Government elected by the people here. It has been possible to go far enough in this direction mainly because of the confidence which I had in Rauschning.

But now Rauschning was gone.

Danzig and the League council

Lester sometimes had difficulty getting Danzig questions put on the agenda of the League council. In the same letter, he says,

> ... in spite of the agreements between Germany and Poland and now between Danzig and Poland, Danzig is still one of the test points in Europe and my anxiety is that no situation should be allowed to develop which might later be found to have reached a point where more serious possibilities would arise and it would then be impossible, or very much more difficult to retrace one's steps.

He was a man on his own.

On 24 May 1935 the council of the League in Geneva had Danzig on its agenda once again. Anthony Eden, as rapporteur, took issue with a speech by Greiser in which he said that the work of his government was disturbed by the opposition's sending continual complaints to the League; and that the High Commissioner did not confine himself to his task, which was only to act as arbitrator between Poland and Danzig. Eden again corrected the notion: the High Commissioner stood as guarantor of the constitution of the Free City. Greiser excused himself somewhat by remarking that as the Danzig constitution ensured the right of free speech, it was sometimes the duty of the government to express popular opinions. He regretted that the High Commissioner should have interpreted 'in the way that he did' the speech which he, Greiser, 'had been obliged to make in the course of the electoral campaign'. He assured them as regards the High Commissioner's competence.

The jurists reporting to the council on the April elections in Danzig were from countries which had not taken part in the 1914–18 war: Baron Marks von Württemberg, former president of the Stockholm Court of Appeal (Chairman); Dr Jan Kosters, vice-president of the Supreme Court of the Netherlands; and Dr Fritz Fleiner, Professor of Public Law in the University of Zürich. They met at Geneva from 22 to 26 July, and submitted their report, which Eden presented on 23 September.

Eden said that the League of Nations, while according to the judgements of the courts of Danzig the respect and authority which must be due to them, could not be prevented by a decision of any organ of the Free City, whether judicial, legislative or executive, from intervening in cases where it considered such intervention to be necessitated by a breach of the constitution – in other words, the council of the League had the last say in everything.

The jurists found that the constitution had unquestionably been infringed at several points: they found the five-month banning of *Volksstimme* on 5 April to be an administrative action incompatible with the freedom of the press, which was guaranteed by Article 79 of the constitution. It was pointed out, in fairness, that the order was rescinded and the paper reappeared on 1 July, but, said Eden, 'A few days ago the same paper was again seized.'

The petitioners strove to show that, in the widest spheres of the political administrative life of the Free City, equality of treatment was violated in favour of the National Socialist party. According to the petitioners, although certain measures taken by the government ostensibly applied equally to all the citizens of the Free City, they were in fact interpreted exclusively with the object of protecting the organisations of the National Socialist party.

But the senate had argued that the criterion taken by it had always been and would continue to be 'just and equal treatment for all Danzig Nationals'. Said Eden:

> In view of the fundamental divergence of views in the interpretation of the Constitution, which is revealed by the documents now before the Council, your rapporteur has reached the conclusion that, in order to facilitate the Council's task, the best method of procedure would be to appoint a committee of jurists composed of three members whose duty would be to examine these petitions as well as the observations thereon of the Danzig Senate and to report to the Council whether this examination reveals the existence of violations of the Constitution either in the form of legislation, decrees or regulations or in the form of administrative acts or omissions.

Greiser said that if the council, in the light of the opinion of the committee of jurists, should reach the conclusion that the constitution had been infringed on certain points, the senate of the Free City of Danzig would modify its opinion on the basis of the council's interpretation and would take appropriate measures – his usual style of answer.

With regard to complaints in the petition of the Jewish organisations, the jurists said that they could not form any opinion on the failure of the government to regard the equality of a further law without holding an inquiry into certain facts on the spot – which was outside their province, but when the senate claimed that 'The public ... is no longer willing to submit to strictures from a Jewish judge' and spoke of an official as being 'acceptable to the people', the impression might be given that the whole Danzig population was National Socialist, whereas there were large groups in the population who undoubtedly preferred an able official to a less able official, whatever the former's political position might be.

The government, in short, could not be allowed to apply a party programme which was contrary to the constitution, even if adopted by a majority of the people.

The jurists asked was it not 'disturbance of public security when a whole section of the population is subject to constant and serious defamation on the sole ground of its race or religion?' The High Commissioner had pointed out, in a letter following the Jewish petition, that the National Socialist party had been displaying great activity *inter alia* by promoting the wide circulation of a publication intended to incite its readers against Jewish citizens – *Der Stürmer*.

The jurists were damning about a petition of the Deutschnational, Social Democrat and Centre parties concerning a decree of August 1929 and in 1935 amending the penal code: the old maxim of *nulla poena sine lege* had been superseded by a sentiment which rendered punishable any person who committed an act which was deserving of penalty according to the fundamental conceptions of law and healthy national consciousness, i.e. subjective Nazi party feelings.

Lester pointed out that he had done all he could to save the council from having to deal so much with the affairs of Danzig. He tried to settle all he could on the spot. And while there had been many declarations of loyalty to the constitution, there had also been many declarations showing unfriendliness to constitutional principles. He spoke of 'the malaise of Danzig and [of] the discontent which had led the representatives of 40% of the people to appeal to the Council' and noted that the rights for which protection had to be asked were thus the rights of thousands of men and women of German culture.

He therefore appealed to Greiser and his colleagues that, having failed to reach sufficient votes at the April elections to enable them to be in a position to change the constitution, they should now agree to accept it not only in letter, but also in spirit.

He hoped the council would, in the near future, take note of a happier situation in Danzig.

Mission to London

The opposition parties had challenged the result of the 1935 general election, only the Polish group failing to join the rest. The Supreme Court of Danzig gave judgement on 14 November 1935: while the judgement criticised such excesses as Forster's declaration that officials who did not vote Nazi should forfeit their jobs, the decision was that the elections were, overall, valid. Then the opposition thought of sending a delegation to Geneva, but doubted if the council would or could receive an anti-governmental delegation. One other proposal, however, was that two representatives of the opposition should go to the British capital. There were fears that secrecy could not be kept and that the whole venture would give the senate a pretext to clamp down completely on the opposition. And there was anxiety that either the High Commissioner or Anthony Eden, or both, might be offended by such extra-legal steps on the part of the opposition. In the end, these hesitations were overcome, probably because the opposition had little to lose. Leonhardt, a Volkstag deputy, informed the High Commissioner of the contemplated journey and the latter, he says, 'expressed neither approval nor disapproval'. It was to be a depressing experience for the travellers, for they were bluntly told in the Foreign Office that the great British public had no enthusiasm about, and maybe not much knowledge of, their remote little city on the Baltic. The full story of the expedition is told by Leonhardt in *Nazi Conquest of Danzig*.

On the day after Christmas 1935, two Danzigers left by sea, carrying certain letters with them as evidence that they were acting in agreement with leading circles of the opposition. It was an unfortunate time for them to arrive in London. They were not familiar, as Leonhardt says, 'with the spacious nature of English holidays'. Moreover, public attention was absorbed by the Italo-Abyssinian conflict, with the resulting problem of oil sanctions. Additionally, public opinion was distracted by the first bulletins of the king's serious illness. The Danzigers, says Leonhardt, almost envied the Abyssinians, who stood in the limelight of public attention. They themselves had the Herculean task of convincing indifferent London that Danzig, in its way, was as much a challenge to the League's authority as the Italian attack on Abyssinia. In actual fact in their minds the Free City situation was perhaps even more menacing, since the Nazification of Danzig, although advancing less noticeably, represented the first active steps towards 'revision' in Europe. If the council of the League were not to act now, it could mean the surrender of Danzig to Germany, in fact if not in name.

The Danzigers' first calls were to journalists who already were well acquainted with the conditions: Elizabeth Wiskemann, FA Voigt, and the London diplomatic correspondent of the *Manchester Guardian*. Later they paid a visit to a Mr Craven of *The Times*, a Mr Ewer of the *Daily Herald*, who had written well on Danzig and others. Major Vyvyan Adams, a Conservative MP, interviewed them and wrote afterwards a vivid article on Danzig in the *Sunday Chronicle*. The British League of Nations Union received them with special marks of friendliness and also the New Commonwealth organisation. Lord Robert Cecil, president of the League of Nations Union, gave them a long audience at his country seat and showed a keen interest in the affairs of the Free City. He had at one time been rapporteur to the League council on Danzig. A statement was prepared by the League of Nations Union which was read to the Danzig representatives before being sent to some three hundred newspapers throughout the country. In it, attention was drawn to the seriousness of the situation in Danzig, and the British government was reminded of the League's special obligation in regard to the constitution of the Free City. The point they kept making to all their British listeners was that the League council should, in its next session, restore constitutional conditions in the Free City, which end could only be achieved if the council should decide upon a radical remedy – a repetition of the elections to the Volkstag.

Fair elections, it was suggested, could be guaranteed only by the presence of an international police force. German and Polish troops would obviously have to be excluded, but British, French or Scandinavian and Dutch forces would be welcomed by the parties of the opposition, as had been the case in the Saar. The delegates made the point that events in Danzig were watched with particular interest from Berlin, where they were regarded as yet another test of the reality of the League of Nations.

The most important call was to Number 10 Downing Street. There they met Maurice (later Lord) Hankey, assistant private secretary to the incoming Secretary of State for Foreign Affairs, Anthony Eden. They asked for a personal interview with Eden, particularly since he continued to officiate as a rapporteur for Danzig affairs in Geneva. A few days later the delegates were invited to call on RCS Stevenson, assistant advisor on League of Nations affairs to the Foreign Office. Stevenson expressed the Foreign Secretary's regret that formal reasons hindered him from himself receiving any representatives of the Danzig opposition, but added that Eden took a special interest in the fate of the Free City and had instructed him to give a very detailed report of the conversation. 'Every word said to me,' he emphasised, 'will be conveyed to Mr Eden.'

Stevenson was 'to an astonishing degree' conversant with the many intricacies of the position in Danzig. He was in fact the official of the Foreign Office permanently charged with the duty of drafting for Eden the resolutions proposed to the council of the League of Nations. And soon the conversation drifted away from the strictly local aspect of the question and turned to discussion of a more general nature. From the Danzig side it was stressed that the League ought to act soon if it intended to accomplish anything at all. The Danzigers declared that they could vouch for an impressive defeat of the National Socialist party in Danzig if elections were to take place under a minimum of constitutional conditions. This Stevenson did not seem to doubt, but he did not conceal his manifold hesitations. The British empire, he said, had many obligations in her far-flung possessions, and he doubted, speaking candidly, whether British public opinion was prepared for an adventure in a city whose very location was unknown to the overwhelming majority of his countrymen. The Danzigers replied that they had received a very friendly reception in various journalistic quarters in London and had gathered a very definite impression that the press seemed eager to take up the matter; at any rate they could not quite see why British public opinion could not be brought around to a more realistic attitude and, the Danzigers added bluntly, no organisation in the world would be able to preserve the status of Danzig if the terror were once allowed to gain definite hold of the people – German rearmament, they said, had not yet advanced so far that Hitler would dare to risk complications over the Free City. The opposition once eliminated, the Führer could produce at any moment the unanimous plebiscite on the issue of 'zurück zum Reich' (back to the Reich). The National Socialist menace was, they said, precisely the same in Danzig as in Austria and elsewhere, and a defeat of National Socialism in Danzig was bound to have wholesome effects beyond the territory of the Free City.

Leonhardt writes that the discussion took place in an atmosphere of perfect frankness. Stevenson 'seemed sometimes a trifle amused,' he thought, 'at the seriousness and intensity of his foreign guests, but he listened with respect and attention to all they had to say.' One of the obstacles to which he called attention was that of a legal character. He admitted the *de facto* existence of the League's guarantee of the constitution of Danzig but he said it was nowhere specified how this guarantee should be practically enforced. Without entering into a legal discussion, the Danzigers replied merely that the guarantee was not worth the paper it was written on if the powers did not find ways and means to implement that guarantee. Leonhardt puts it bluntly: 'In a general sense the atmosphere in London was one of sympathy – and of sympathy only.'

To some extent the supporters of the idea of collective security, such as the League of Nations Union, were ready to demand more vigorous action in Danzig. But the Foreign Office seemed reluctant to add new problems to the existing ones and the omens for the coming session of the council were scarcely encouraging, even though, before the Danzigers had left London, the Polish embassy had let it be known that the Poles were not unfriendly to the course proposed by the Danzig opposition.

Leonhardt points out that Count Edward Raczynski, the Polish ambassador in London, was following a policy which did not strictly conform to that of Foreign Minister Beck: he was in favour of a more active policy. The British Foreign Office, however, was reluctant to antagonise Berlin by the ordering of new elections in Danzig, and Leonhardt refers to a *New York Times* report of 13 January 1936 which notes that Danzig was alive with rumours including the news that vigorous action had been promised on the part of Great Britain. It had not, of course. The Danzig mission had been told that no action could be expected from the British or, indeed, the League.

Admiral Scheer *incident*

Social life in Danzig was generously convivial, even in the midst of political wrangles and worse.

The first of two diplomatic incidents concerning visits to the city by German naval personnel came about at the end of August 1935: the visit of the German pocket battleship *Admiral Scheer* to the Free City caused something of a storm in a teacup. Writing to Avenol, Lester told of a dinner he gave to thirty people, strictly official, which passed off smoothly. After dinner, one hundred and fifty guests arrived for the reception, among whom a few, 'probably less than 5 per cent,' were politically objectionable to the National Socialists. Lester had invited President Greiser's two predecessors, Ziehm and Rauschning. Ziehm was unable to come.

In addition to the representatives of the National Socialist newspapers he had included a Social Democrat deputy in the Volkstag, who represented the *Volksstimme*. And among the honorary consuls were one or two Danzig citizens who were supporters of opposition parties: Deutschnational and Centre.

> When President Greiser saw some members of the Opposition, he left my house abruptly, bringing with him a few of the senators who were present and was followed by some other National Socialists. He said good night without making any remark and subsequently an SS man, the adjutant of Mr Forster, was sent to order some others to leave. [Forster had not replied to the invitation and was taken off the invitation list from then on.]

When these had left, the party went on. But the Danzig radio station and the newspapers the next day made a stir. The *Vorposten* wrote that the captain of the warship, Marshall, and the other German officers left 'very soon afterwards'. Lester was sure that the German officers had not allowed themselves to be a part of this demonstration and, for the first time, issued a statement to the press, setting the record straight: 'No holder of the office of High Commissioner,' he wrote, 'could show partisanship by confining his list, on the occasion of a large reception, to either Polish or Danzig people or to members of any one party in Danzig.' He deplored the attempt to drag visiting officers into local political controversies and stated emphatically that during their visit the commander and officers 'have, of course, shown complete courtesy and correctness towards the representative of the League of Nations in Danzig'.

Lester saw Greiser the next day ('mild and apologetic') and first pointed out that at a dinner given by the senate on the day before his own dinner, the League had been slighted by the table placing which gave precedence to the visiting captain. It was a breach of all standing arrangements, and a public affront. Greiser said he thought it right to give the guest of the city pride of place. He was apologetic as to the incident in Lester's own house: Greiser pointed out that he was subject to party discipline and it was a rule of his party that they should hold no communication with a member who had been expelled, in this case Rauschning.

Lester replied that President Greiser, having undertaken the responsibility of the Head of the Government could not expect any behaviour contrary to international good manners to be excused on the ground of the discipline of a political party.

The local Nazi papers had indeed made a minor sensation out of it. In big headlines the *Vorposten* had 'Embarrassing incident at the High Commissioner's house'. And then 'The Senate and the officers of the German warship along with Marxists and other Opposition representatives and Dr Rauschning invited to the reception – the Danzig guests and the officers of the *Admiral Scheer* thereupon leave the house.'

The story was also widely reported in Europe: 'Incident at

Danzig: High Commissioner's rebuke,' in the London *Times*, which gave Lester's statement: 'Nazis provoke an incident at a reception given by Mr Lester,' wrote the *Journal des Nations*, Geneva.

Lester's patience was sorely tried. He wrote after this to Avenol:

> I must have a show-down, have the intention to say at the Council table that if the Council's decisions are not applied so as to bring public life in Danzig into accordance with the Constitution, I shall very shortly ask the Council to appoint (or authorise me to appoint), a Special Commission with power to investigate the administration from top to bottom – to expose the things I know to exist but which need personal investigation in detail.

CHAPTER 6

Last Year in Danzig

T he year 1936 opened on a rare, genial, bucolic note, with a long account in the Nazi *Vorposten* of a hunt, presided over by Jägermeister (chief hunter) Greiser, photographed rifle over shoulder against a woodland background, while two smaller pictures show Lester and Papée, the Polish minister, rifle at shoulder. They were taking part in the second of two shoots, the profits of which were to go to the Winter Relief Work (the Winterhilfswerk). Lester had missed a hare that came straight at him – he couldn't swing around to follow it, because of people in the background. There were jokes about that at the evening's celebration. At the end of the day's activity two huge bonfires threw flames high in the air, outside the police praesidium torches blazed while, on fresh green foliage was laid out 'the bag': 121 hares, one rabbit, 4 foxes. Presumably it was the proceeds of the sale of these that went to the needy. Police bands blared away, male voices were raised in songs of the chase, hunting horns were blown, and Greiser, in his dual capacity as master of the hunt and president of the senate, led the revelry. Earlier he had made a hearty speech, suitable to the outdoor setting. He thanked the High Commissioner, in particular, and the Polish minister and other distinguished guests for taking part. Such occasions, he said, gave an opportunity for people to get closer together than they could between four walls, where they normally met.

The *Vorposten*'s report ended with an assertion by the writer that the participation of Lester refuted the conjectures of the opposition about strained relations between the president of the senate and the High Commissioner.

In Danzig Lester managed to get an occasional outing for his trout-angling. On one river he was surprised to find that, though it had a good reputation, he landed no trout. The water- and game-keeper assured him that ten thousand young trout had been put in for the season. He added with pride that a stock of no less than thirty thousand pike had gone in at the same time!

Lester's occasional expeditions fully dressed in thigh boots and other accoutrements of the angler once started a scare. Seeing him making off purposefully, it was rumoured that the High Commissioner was fleeing the city by plane – the gear not being so very different to inexpert eyes. This canard even got into print.

Another social occasion took place before the serious business of the League council meeting in Geneva early in 1936. Lester notes in his diary that on 11 January they had Greiser and twenty other principal Danzig officials to dinner. It was the first time Greiser had been in the High Commissioner's house since the walkout over the *Admiral Scheer* incident. 'Nothing for G. to walk out about this time.' All went well, 'lashings of good drink' and 'many thanks to Elsie as usual'. Greiser had asked for champagne at 11pm. 'It is always nice to see guests enjoying their drink.'

On 14 January Greiser hosted a dinner in the Rathaus (town hall). For the first time in the history of Danzig, women were allowed to dine in the Red Room, decorated with fine panelling, the pictures on the wall above the panelling being directly illuminated, and the dinner tables lit with candles. In his speech Greiser gave a special welcome to the High Commissioner as the representative of the League, guarantor of the statute and constitution of Danzig, and made cordial references to the collaboration between the two of them. 'Anyone listening to this complimentary speech would have thought that there was not a cloud on the horizon.' Greiser was making this speech before the Polish representative, the president of the harbour board (from Holland), the German consul general and other prominent people. Forster was not present. Lester noted to himself that such soft talk was often preliminary to other meetings of the League council.

He had, of course, already written his report for the year 1935, to be presented shortly. Next morning he was off to the ninetieth meeting of the League council in Geneva. He presented his report for 1935 on 17 January 1936. A degree of satisfaction was expressed with Polish/Danzig relations. Not so with other aspects of public affairs. 'The year,' he wrote 'has seen an intense development of the policy to create a National Socialist community *de facto*.' And neither the exhortations of the council at each of its three sessions in the year nor his own unceasing efforts had prevented the steadily increasing application of anti-constitutional policy.

He detailed the seizures and suppressions of newspapers which to him appeared 'to a very grave extent to infringe the principle of free expression of opinion'. This is diplomatic language for wholesale blotting out of opinion, for outrageous reaction to criticism. 'My representations to the Government on this subject have, I regret to say, ceased to be effective.' He listed some of the suppressions and concluded that section of his report with the observation that 'The authorities would appear to have been guided more by what is legally possible in the National Socialist State than by what is legally right in a community governed by a Constitution like that of Danzig.'

As to the parliament, he noted that the Volkstag had met on seven occasions during the year. The meetings usually lasted an hour and 'did not give much evidence of a desire to use the Parliament as a means of ascertaining public opinion'.

He pointed out that the opposition parties, representing not very much less than half the population, had time allocated to them in such a way that the Social Democratic party got five minutes, the Centre party four minutes and the Deutschnational and Polish Communist groups each one minute. And they made a new rule that a deputy who received no authorisation to absent himself, or who abstained from taking part in a nominal vote, was excluded from the assembly for a period of ten meetings. In practice, thus, for a year.

Lester then dealt with the activities of Albert Forster, not a citizen of Danzig, to whom, nevertheless, in the code of Nazism, public representatives belonging to the Nazi party from Greiser, president of the senate, down, were all subordinate, and bound to give loyalty and obedience as he, Forster, was bound to give to his superiors in the Reich. Lester quoted from some of Forster's speeches, in case the point was not yet driven home, including his assertion that 'Our purpose remains unchanged; to work for a great and powerful Germany. A day will come my friends – we shall take good care of that – when all these fellows who dare to oppose us will be flung into a concentration camp, which is where they belong.'

These were only the political highlights of a long report covering finance, trade and other matters.

Lester's diary tells us much of the political state of mind at Geneva. He notes for 17 January 1936:

> Avenol [the Secretary-General] greeted me with the remark, 'This is literature!' – waving my Annual Report. I interrupted his rhapsody by saying that I was more concerned to know that he thought it good politics. He seemed to be 100% satisfied. I said I had done my best, while fulfilling my duty, to leave the Council plenty of latitude – not to present inelastic proposals. I had tried methods of persuasion in Danzig for two years and when the question of the League guarantee was now brought to an issue, it was not by me, but by the Senate refusing to carry out Council recommendations, and accompanying that refusal with an impossible speech about the League.
>
> I had, furthermore, personally interviewed the members of the Council most concerned, six weeks ago, to warn them of the situation and had endeavoured by diplomatic means to find an issue from the situation. But he [Avenol] had not the slightest doubt that I had done excellently in my report. Walters [English under-Secretary-General] just

back from London and suffering from a chill, did not seem quite so happy. But the Polish/British conversations in London on the subject seemed to have been on the whole satisfactory. If the Danzigers insist on their defiance, Poland is prepared to accept a mandate from the Council. Of course I imagine the case makes special difficulties for Britain as rapporteur and Danzig, one must remember, involves all kinds of questions relating to Eastern Europe in which Britain is wary of interfering, or becoming committed. Nothing one may suppose will or can prevent Danzig becoming again a focus of international trouble and danger. But if League prestige can be maintained in this case, it may help – even if only postponing or lessening the crisis a little. Senatorial Adviser Böttcher, looking rather grim, shook hands with me as he walked into Krabbe's office today. [Krabbe was the League of Nations official who looked after Danzig affairs in Geneva.]

To Krabbe, Böttcher said the High Commissioner's report had shocked them; he added that the High Commissioner was the only source of trouble in Danzig, that he [Böttcher] was German and that Germany would not allow this to continue. So the cat comes out of the bag again. This confidence is the real explanation of Danzig's defiance of the League.

Böttcher has all the fervour of a convert. He is now more Nazi than Mr Hitler. But that would not matter if he had an intelligence and gave wise advice to his President. It looks as though Danzig was going to fight. Böttcher was twice in Berlin. Has he any mandate from Berlin, and if so, from whom? For, of course, Berlin is divided too.

Well, I have spent two years persuading, advising, coaxing and warning; it was not enough. It was answered in November, with defiance and a high and mighty 'this closes a chapter'. I am worried and anxious, as is my nature. Perhaps they were right when they said, in effect, that the realists in Geneva will understand that now that

Germany is strong, the League has ceased to count in Danzig.

Next day, Sunday 19 January 1936, Lester spent four hours with Stevenson, Eden's speech-writer and right-hand man in his function as rapporteur.

I have read a large number of minutes relating to discussions in the Foreign Office and the conversation with Raczinski, Polish Ambassador in London. All show that the problems are being faced, but the way out is not clear. Even the abrogation of the Articles in the Versailles Treaty were considered and the withdrawal of the High Commissioner. Malkin, Legal Advisor to the Foreign Office, raises legal difficulties from the first. It seems to be recognised that a situation might arise in which I should feel compelled to resign. There is no sign of any tendency not to give me 100% support.

But is the problem insoluble? Military occupation is to be ruled out. Economic pressure by the League would require an Assembly decision; and even if it were possible, it would look somewhat peculiar to have the entire Assembly machinery brought into motion against a recalcitrant provincial town!

The alternative would be economic pressure by Poland acting under a mandate from the Council. I don't like it really – unless it can be effective merely as a threat leading to complications, as it would, between Germany and Poland. Poland seems inclined to say 'Yes'. I still have some hope that the more reasonable elements in Berlin may win the day before the crisis develops.

The German press has opened a broadside rather concentrating on the question of the elections. This is not conclusive, as the question of new elections is not, really, the key to the Council's difficulties which are concerned, in the first place, with the refusal to carry out recommendations and the general attack on the Constitution and the League guarantee.

King George is dying. Even here telephones are busy and the latest bulletins sought for. The succession question is smooth, but the formalities will involve Eden's return to London should death occur while he [Eden] is here. This would mean an upset, perhaps ultimately serious in effect, on my own problems. The full authority of the Secretary of State himself is required in the discussions.

And when publicity at last could be of value, Danzig, at its worst, would be smothered out of the press, as it was in September by the Italian war.

Monday 20 January 1936, Lester's diary continues:

First day of the Council and news of George V somewhat better in as much as the appointment of a Regency Council suggests there is no danger for some days at any rate. I never before felt such a personal interest in H.M.'s health!

Count Lubienski [Beck's adviser] called this morning early and received from me confirmation that my talk with Stevenson yesterday had not resulted in any specific proposals. 'You know,' he said, 'we admire you very much. That might be nothing from me, but I know that it is Mr Beck's opinion. Then he told me that the Polish Press this morning was unanimously in support of me, as a contrast, I suppose, to the German campaign with its veiled threat under references to Knox and the Saar. But I mustn't exaggerate that: I see a note of restraint so far in the press of Germany. They have published a bowdlerised summary of my report. Only this afternoon has it been officially released here.

Short talks with Walters, Krabbe and Stevenson. In the middle of a conference Eden came in, looking much older and lacking the boyish verve of formerly. I hope his high office won't age him too quickly. He said it was Avenol's suggestion that there should be a preliminary Council discussion before the Report was drafted. I fully approved: it should help the rapporteur's task if a few Council members expressed suitable opinions. Secondly, and perhaps most important, a preliminary expression of views may help the reasonable elements in Germany and give time for Greiser to reconsider his position before we come to positive proposals. Eden asked if Greiser was here and expressed his astonishment and annoyance on hearing that he would not arrive before tomorrow night. He sent Stevenson to tell Böttcher to telephone at once and Böttcher promised he would suggest an aeroplane from Berlin. It is exactly what I warned them about before leaving Danzig.

Beck saw Eden today. The situation is becoming a little more clarified.

Beck will act on a *mandat diplomatique* from the Council, as the State most interested, and in conjunction with the High Commissioner in ensuring the execution of the Council's recommendations and the maintenance of the Constitution. They don't want a military mandate.

What will the other mean? Empowered by the Council to talk to Danzig – and to Germany, I suppose. One reflects also, that it helps the League to shed some of its responsibilities and one must remember that other alternatives are more dangerous than that. After all, the Free City was created to meet a Polish need. One can well guess that the Wilhelmstrasse people won't like it. It will increase Polish standing in relation to Danzig. But it may well be followed by more complications. ... the hint is dropped by Beck that the next High Commissioner should be a Pole!

Well! The sardonic Gods would laugh if this were the outcome of the stupid policy pursued by Danzig Nazis. Wilful, blind, unintelligent partisans, without a glimpse of an intelligent policy. I find it hard to envisage. But there would be a certain logicality, superficially at any rate. Germany and Poland on good terms; Danzig boasting the same, while attacking the League and its High Commissioner. Poland asked to take the major responsibility on behalf of the Council in the present conflict. Logically, it might be asked 'why not?' People like Böttcher and Forster may tell the League to carry out its duty about the Constitution. What sort of a 'bust up' would follow the appointment of a Polish High Commissioner! To hint at it is, perhaps, a new indication that Poland is in earnest about her own rights and, as someone said, she might not make any difficulty about a few German (opposition) heads being broken in Danzig by the Nazis, and everyone be more comfortable! I think the Polish idea too fantastic – a nominee, perhaps, but not a Pole.

I reflect with some satisfaction that I have done my best. Smug? No, too anxious. I have advised – in vain; I have taken risks to avert the crises – and failed; I have then bluntly put the cards on the Council table.

Later, I heard that the idea was regarded by the French as impossible. I suppose a Polish nominee might be different. The Poles are subtle enough to have put up the greater with a view to getting the less.

Lester's diary for 22 January 1936:

George V died at midnight.

A day of great anxiety, and nervous over the Danzig situation. Watching points in the rapporteur's draft with an effort to judge effect in the future. German press campaign turns out to have been more virulent than I had thought from reading one or two extracts.

Much congratulation, of course, from circles here. Borberg, Danish delegate, a reserved fellow, said, 'A courageous report and as political judgement excellent.' Starkey, a wise old veteran of the American press, and many other delegates, probably sincere, echo this. As I warned people here six weeks ago, Danzig is again hectically in the front line.

I am prepared to resign of course, but that, said Walters, would be a disaster. I am equally prepared to hold on, especially in view of the attacks. I left Danzig with a somewhat irresolute intention of hinting at another year of office – although I have previously and consistently declared my sincere intention to go at the end of my term. Certain personal considerations arose. I am, however, more afraid of my health than anything else. I am so constantly under nervous strain and frequently have, for the first time in my life, bouts of sleeplessness. And I get no holidays, so that I long for a quiet corner and simple work for a period. And, of course, it will be thankless whatever I do in Danzig. (George V was a model King of England. But why did he pass away just in time to smother Danzig?)

Laval, French Premier, recalled suddenly to Paris where his Cabinet, in the accustomed French way, had crumbled under him. A new Cabinet formed by Sarraut with Flandin as Foreign Minister and Paul-Boncour coming back to Geneva as permanent delegate. Cabinet rather more pro-League and pro-British.

Irreverent wits said Laval's hasty departure was because his black tie had been left in Paris. Perhaps it sounds more of a joke in French.

The question of Lester's extension of office, due to expire early in 1937, was to come up at the League council meeting in January 1936. At his request, consideration of it was postponed.

Eden, on 24 January, dealt with the 'important suggestion of the High Commissioner relative to the appointment of a Commission of Investigation'. While understated, this proposal by Lester was in fact a call for help, a call for more back-up. Eden proposed that the council should reserve the matter for consideration on a later occasion.

Leonhardt reasoned, early in 1936, that as the League had offered so little backing to Lester, he had two courses open to him: to resign immediately or to start labouring again with Greiser. He chose the latter. 'Possibly because Danzig and its Opposition had become endeared to him,' wrote Leonhardt, 'in spite of the unpleasant conditions under which he had to perform his duties.' The main reason, those who knew Lester would be sure, was that he was not a quitter. His Northern blood was up. He didn't have to like Greiser and the others. He still had something to contribute, if even only to hold back the tide just a bit longer. Even without much help from the League. And, like many of his generation, he was conscious of service to his country. He was, of course, now seconded to the League of Nations, but still felt he was contributing to the standing and prestige of the Irish Free State. Lester's diary for 23 January 1936:

> In spite of the King's illness and death, I find Danzig has been figuring in the English press. Good. Saw Avenol for a few minutes and found him very sound and rather firm. He is against letting the idea of a Commission of Investigation drop. He wants it to be reserved as a potential weapon; and the election petition, too. At a vague hint that I would be ready at any time to give up my mandate, he emphatically said that would be a defeat for the League of Nations.
>
> Met Greiser and a delegation of eight advisors in the Council room. Cordial handshakes. Göring provided him with an aeroplane to answer Eden's summons. Eden opened the Council debate with a good declaration (including a compliment – 'A High Commissioner in whose impartiality and good judgement the Council has complete confidence'). The French, Spanish, Turkish, Danish, Portuguese and Polish representatives followed. I made a short supplementary statement – including a declaration as to absence of any political bias or prejudice. Then Greiser made an oration – declaring his attachment to the Statute of Danzig including the High Commissioner – lightly passing over the failure to carry out recommendations; only a difference of opinion between jurists, and 'we politicians' care more for peace than such trifles. Anthony Eden deflated him a little and we adjourned.

Lester spoke 'briefly': the situation in Danzig had become acute because the government there had found itself unable to comply with certain recommendations of the council, and because of the spirit evinced in the declaration made to the Volkstag by the head of the government. And though the government consistently maintained that the guarantee of the League was limited to certain matters, which the council refused to accept, the senate of the Free City had also maintained that it did, in fact, keep within the letter of the constitution. Lester did not say it, but it reminded any who knew *Through the Looking Glass* of the words of Humpty Dumpty – 'When I use a word, it means just what I choose it to mean – neither more nor less.'

Lester had striven to be just and fair. In any case where there was a reasonable element of doubt, the benefit was given, and properly given, to the views of those responsible for government. If conflict arose at the present time it was due to the attitude of the government even towards formal decisions of the council itself. Still, he could not believe it was impossible for a clear understanding to be reached between the council and the Danzig government, and while he remained in his post he would continue to work in that spirit.

Then Greiser spoke in what was, for him, the normal double talk of his régime: He could state, as president of the senate, on behalf of his government, that the government of the Free City of Danzig had never had, and had not, the least intention of attacking the Free City's statute as conceived by the League of Nations, and established by treaty. Moreover the senate's attitude to the High Commissioner's position was the same as its attitude to the statute. He thought that this statement would remove any fears which members of the council might have entertained regarding an aggravation of the international position in so far as the Free City of Danzig was concerned. As to not carrying out the recommendations of the council, he pointed out that four of the six had been duly carried out. In the case of the other two, it was not lack of goodwill, but a difference of opinion by jurists. That is, the Supreme Court of Danzig decided that the laws and decrees to which the two recommendations were not yet carried out were absolutely consonant with the constitution. For twelve years Danzig had been the powder barrel of Europe. The present government had emptied the powder barrel and he was grateful to Beck for having so frequently borne witness that the Danzig government really was actuated by the League spirit. He was able to say that for the people of Danzig, the League was the embodiment of peace and justice and he had no hesitation in saying that the whole world, and not least the Free City of Danzig, and the people of Danzig, regarded it with every confidence.

Eden, speaking as rapporteur, would not accept Greiser's interpretation that the main differences were differences between jurists. It was wholly untenable in face of the evidence before the council. Lester noted other reactions:

> 'Such an impudent speech I never heard,' said Ferguson, the calm and shrewd representative of Reuters. Others seemed also to be badly impressed, but others not. I am so accustomed to it, and worse, that I was almost amused.

Anthony Eden once said to Lester, 'I wouldn't have your job for all the money in the world': the frustrations were great. Lester was tough enough and had seen, in a revolution at home, how the heart becomes a stone. There were times when he could listen to Greiser and the other members of the senate, point out where they were infringing the constitution, and try to convince them that it would be more sensible to settle the matter there and then with him rather than refer it to Geneva, where it would possibly receive a watery answer or a half-yes, half-no, after a long interlude.

On the ground Lester himself did not give them any reason to believe that he was soft. He fought them all the way, and to refer a matter to Geneva was not a victory.

Looking back on the events in Danzig and Germany in general, today, the reader must ask how could it be that the dictators, Hitler and Mussolini, could get away with so many acts of aggression, often with hardly a protest from the League.

One of the answers is that no one quite realised to what excesses Hitler could lead not just his own Nazis but also the vast majority of the German people, including its disciplined army. But the major powers in the League of Nations were divided and irresolute. France and Britain were strongly for the League when it suited their own national policy. Eden said it quite bluntly to Lester in January 1936 in Geneva when the council was meeting. From Lester's diary, 25 January 1936:

> I had talked with Eden alone in the forenoon, thanked him for all his work and hoped it would not involve political trouble at home. I appreciated that England did not want to get much involved in East Europe. 'That is so,' he said, 'and people don't distinguish between a Council rapporteur and one's representative duties. My Cabinet colleagues may well ask me what I have been doing.' He also referred to a *Daily Mail* leader, 'Keep out of Danzig,' which described him as 'Dangerous Mr Eden'.
>
> I told him that only the gravest circumstances would bring me back to the Council with Danzig. I was not at all convinced as to the future, but had some hope and would work it to the last degree. Eden said to me he could not risk it being made the subject of a big attack on him in Germany. I bowed to that – he had already done so much.
>
> On the Forster paragraph [in which Lester in his report had pointed out that the main force behind the Nazi movement in Danzig was not from the elected senate, Greiser and other people, but from the Gauleiter, a non-Danziger, Forster] he said he could not afford to aggravate Germany, and had the Italian business already on his hands. I inclined before high policy.

As to the *Daily Mail* and its 'Dangerous Mr Eden' line, its stable companion the *Evening News* wrote strong leaders too:

> Membership of the League of Nations is, short of actual war, the most dangerous luxury that this country has ever indulged in. Its activities, of which our statesmen have an

unhappy knack of appearing to be the prime inspiration, have earned it the ill-will of our former allies, Japan and Italy, have caused a large section of the French people to regard us as a source of danger to themselves, and are now threatening to earn us the ill-will of Germany, a great country that really desires our friendship and respect. Danzig means nothing at all to this country. Its internal affairs solely concern the German and Polish peoples. Even the High Commissioner belongs to a Dominion that regards its Empire membership as an oppressive necessity. Why was dangerous Mr Eden appointed rapporteur of the Danzig dispute? The logical man for the job was Mr de Valera. Even if it were desirable that a British Statesman be appointed, Mr Eden, already identified with the disastrous policy of sanctions *à l'outrance* was the worst possible choice. Surely there is too much danger in the international situation for us to be throwing this dangerous firebrand about.

Soothing talk was often to be heard from German sources. On 26 January 1936 Lester, still in Geneva, had a talk with Krauel, the German consul general, meeting him for tea in the flat of Frank Cremins, Lester's successor as Irish representative in Geneva.

Krauel said that the Forster difficulty was only due to Hitler's affection for his old comrade 'ein alter Kämpfer'. Forster had now done Germany and National Socialism a great deal of harm. Lester said that his principal difficulty, 'apart from Forster's dictatorship,' was general stupidity. The German consul general appeared to be slightly alarmed at the hint in Lester's report that Poland might be brought more into the affair, to which Lester replied that he had expended every diplomatic resource open to him and got no results. It was very nice of Hitler to stick by old comrades – but it was sometimes a difficult principle to apply when the interests of a great empire were involved. Krauel said that he knew of Lester's visit to German Foreign Minister von Neurath 'and that the latter had appreciated the openness with which I spoke. Perhaps the Geneva events would now strengthen the influence of the Wilhelmstrasse.'

Before leaving Geneva on 26 January, a sentimental entry in his diary, which he does not often allow himself:

> From the windows of the Hotel de la Paix, this morning Geneva does not look its best, with mist and rain. The lake steamers tied up for the winter, their mooring chains closely festooned with seagulls; the drifting patches of wild duck and bald coot, also winter refugees, passing slowly towards the outfall of the Rhine. On the other side of the lake rise the bluff towers of St Pierre and beyond, the crest of Mont Salève above Geneva's blanket of fog. The tramcars rumble over the Pont du Mont Blanc and I am only longing to be back at home with Elsie – for home is where Elsie is.

On 3 February Lester wrote in his diary:

> I have been waiting for the situation to develop a little. Last week the 30 January celebrations [of Hitler's first reaching power in Germany] in Danzig led to several public speeches. Greiser and Forster on the same platform. Greiser also gave a carefully prepared interview. He studiously avoided any very harsh remarks either about the League or myself – although making the best of the situation from the National Socialist point of view. Forster, on the other hand, impertinent and irresponsible, made me the object of a tirade. 'How could we expect a foreigner to understand us or our movement? The High Commissioner lends too willing an ear to the Opposition.' There were also remarks about my emoluments that were not printed in his newspaper. He again declared he was Hitler's agent etc.
>
> So I rang up Greiser, and he and his wife lunched with us *en famille* today. He afterwards told me he was most willing to co-operate. 'Have you the power?' I asked. He said that Hitler was leaving Polish and Danzig matters to

Göring; that he had seen Göring in Berlin and had now the backing which he had not had before. There would be a clearer division now between Party and Government and he did not want any question from Danzig on the May agenda [in Geneva], I hardly needed to guess Göring's orders. I said I hoped it would work out like that, but that things could not go on as they had been during the last six months.

My poor German got me through the conversation sufficiently well. Then when we were talking of a short holiday I was thinking of taking in the Harz Mountains, he offered to have us sent from Berlin in an S.S. car!!

After all the Press outburst, it's a little funny. I think we will go to the Riesengebirge.

Reaction from Geneva

Papée, the Polish minister to Danzig, who had been a week in Paris, came in later. He thought Geneva had taught 'them' a lesson, and was particularly pleased when Lester told him something of his talk with Greiser – especially as the original proposal had been from Greiser.

> I said I was somewhat hopeful, but my sad experience of the past year made me cautious. I felt, however, that the stone wall I had been faced with during the past nine months, had been taken down. My policy was to wait to see actual results; not to pay too much attention to Forster's impertinent vituperation on the first occasion, but to deal with it only if the government's policy remained unchanged.

12 February 1936:

> Another bunch of newspaper cuttings awaited me. Across a page the *Daily Express* flaunted 'League's Irish Watchdog Returns to Danzig.' A special correspondent had been sent to report the riots which would, they hoped, greet me.

Failing this, he made a mystery out of my return – police didn't know; Government didn't know; no information at my office etc. The secret and mysterious arrival was, as usual, by getting my car to meet me at Dirschau at the frontier and thus save me a couple of hours in the train.

All quiet.

Family and social life went on. The children had a splendid time riding and the parents got all the gossip about every one of the horses in the stables, Fred and Prince, Titus and Lady, Lux and Hussar. One horse was having a foot massage and going to a farm for a rest and Ann didn't know in time to say goodbye to him; the question of which horses they would have for the Reitfest Horse Show would provide table talk for a day. Lester noted on 18 February that he had spent two mornings trying to fix up seven or eight dinners of twenty-two each: his difficulty was in trying to assemble parties of Danzigers who wouldn't walk out when they saw each other.

On 21 February his diary notes a natural phenomenon for a change:

> This afternoon in Zoppot – 14°C under zero – to see the frozen sea. Walked along the pier, solid ice for about 400 yards and closely packed ice-floes as far as one could see towards Hela or Danzig. Seawards they seem to stretch a mile. Boys and men were walking a quarter of a mile from the shore.

The family dog, Bully, gathered icicles on his jowls while carrying Lester's stick.

25 February 1936, diary entry:

> I lunched yesterday with President Greiser, prior to his departure on holiday. I mentioned to him some of the incidents involving violence during the last week or two, and he promised me he would see the Police President and the head of the SA [the Brown Shirts] before leaving Danzig and impress upon them that such things should not recur: that he had an understanding with the High

Commissioner and other interested parties and would insist upon the avoidance of any complication of the new policy.

According to various notes by Lester there seemed to be a general feeling that a period of comparative relaxation was expected. There were more comments from the press: 'Danzig Nazis give way; promise to keep Constitution,' said the *Daily Telegraph*. 'Another League Triumph,' wrote Vernon Bartlett, one of the most respected commentators, in the *News Chronicle* – a surprising verdict from one so experienced.

The Times of London headed a leading article, 'Success at Geneva,' and wrote that the two international problems that in other circumstances would likely have dragged on indefinitely 'have been set on the road to fair settlement'. (The second concerned Uruguay and the Soviet government.) And *The Times* attacked those British newspapers which were sloganising about, 'Dangerous Mr Eden,' who was allegedly, 'rousing the Hostility of the Germans'. The newspaper pointed out that the actions of the violators of the constitution went against a large body of opinion in Danzig itself. The *Daily Express* of London wrote that Danzig had climbed down and Herr Greiser had sent an order from Geneva that steps should be taken at once to amend the decrees that were held to violate the constitution. 'Nazis in Danzig will no longer be above the law and non-Nazi officials who have been dismissed will be given compensation.'

The level-headed, liberal *News Chronicle* was optimistic, too, in its leader columns. They praised Eden's bold part in facing the Nazis with the charges against them. 'And now the smouldering fires have been stamped clean out, and the Danzig question has ceased to exist as a threat to European peace' – that must rank as one of the major newspaper misjudgements of the decade.

In Danzig the *Vorposten*, the Nazi paper, said that the council was a great triumph for the Danzig National Socialists, in that all the demands of the opposition met with failure. The other Nazi paper, the *Neueste Nachrichten*, thought that the authority of the High Commissioner had issued from the meeting with important reinforcement.

Greiser's reply to Lester's report was hailed in the press as having made a climbdown. His respectful, almost apologetic approach was interpreted as a victory for the League. Much of it, perhaps the whole spirit of it, was more of the same Greiser-speak: 'We of the Free City of Danzig, regard ourselves as a child of the League of Nations.' There were on the council states which were great from the military and economic point of view, whereas Danzig was but a miniature state. But her great strength was her right. And, of course, the senate would collaborate in every possible way with the council, with the sole object of ensuring the maintenance of peace and right. Lester had heard it all before. Many times.

The Polish press said that Colonel Beck had gained a great success by exercising tact in the dispute between the senate of the Free City and the High Commissioner. This was the Geneva correspondent of the *Gazeta Polska*, who stated flatly:

> Poland has proved indisputably that within the zone of her influence and her possibilities, she is a great and favourable factor for order and international co-operation. Moreover during the 90th session of the Council it has been distinctly emphasised black on white that Poland has special rights in Danzig.

The Danzigers had bickered a great deal over the final report in Geneva. Lester says in his diary:

> Many things that Danzigers didn't like, but when they came to the final paragraph about Poland 'lending any aid that may be required to the High Commissioner,' it was the last straw. Out of the bag came the eternal cat: anything but that – although both of them [he meant Danzig and Poland] had been publicly boasting of their excellent relations and friendship.

It was hardly euphoria, but there was a feeling in League circles that the January meeting of the council had brought the National Socialists of Danzig to a more sober level. The press, the British press in particular, was, too, convinced that the

League had scored a victory, if only temporary, over the rulers of the Free City. Lester felt reasonably confidant that a period of relative calm might be expected, but he was not rejoicing. There were sound reasons for caution. Greiser had agreed in Geneva to a revision to certain decree laws.

Suppression of the press

On 21 February 1936 Greiser wrote to Lester with the text of the amended decrees and pointed to the setting up of a press court. The new rules on printed matter contained ten sections, and many sub-sections, with what might be a slight advance on the approach to press freedom of their German master, but which allowed full scope for the senate to take offence and initiate drastic action against any newspaper they liked to assault.

Thus, 'periodicals may be prohibited if their contents endanger public security or order'. Broad enough to condemn almost anything the National Socialist government might take offence at. Then, periodicals could be prohibited 'if they contain a call or incitement to a general strike or a strike in any undertaking of vital importance'. Similarly, they could be prohibited

> ... if in their columns, organs, institutions or principal officers of the state are insulted or maliciously held up in contempt. Officials who are deemed to be principal officials shall be determined by the Senate and announced in the Official Gazette. The duration of the prohibition, said the decree, may not exceed six months in the case of daily newspapers, and one year in all other cases. Moreover, publications printed abroad which served the purpose of political propaganda, and are not issued periodically, shall only be imported into the territory of the Free City of Danzig with the permission of the authority to be designated by the state.

What would be the verdict on a pamphlet issued, say, by the League of Nations Union of Britain?

There was a lull in prohibition of newspapers until May. Once the May session of the council of the League was over – and Greiser had been anxious not to have to appear – the tide of prohibitions started again. On 30 May *Die Neue Zeit*, organ of the house property owners, was banned for eight months, reduced to six. *Freies Volk*, the Social Democratic voice, was sentenced to six months' suppression the day before.

The *Volksstimme*, also social democratic, was prohibited on 7 July for five months, one week after the conclusion of the previous period of its suppression. On 8 July the *Deutschnationale Zeitung* was put down for five months, and on 18 July, the *Danziger Echo*, the Jewish organ, was given twenty months' suspension. On 5 August the *Volkszeitung*, organ of the Centre party, was suppressed for six months. Long before, on 7 January, the Communist *Roter Wähler* had been suppressed for one year.

Things were closing in.

The Rhineland occupied

On 6 March 1936 Hitler recalled the Reichstag and announced the reoccupation of the demilitarised zone of the Rhineland; his readiness to make a twenty-five-year non-aggression pact with France and Belgium to replace the Locarno pact; and 'offered reassurances, in somewhat general terms regarding Poland's access to the sea. And Germany would now be ready to return to the League.' Anthony Eden in the House of Commons denounced the German action, but said the future was more important than the present.

Lester noted Polish uneasiness. Many commentators reasoned that Hitler was, after all, moving troops into territory that was within the borders of the Reich. Had the French moved troops into the zone, Germany, it is believed now, would have withdrawn.

Would the French move, too late? The German consul in Danzig, von Radowitz, notes Lester, showed much nervousness and concern as to the outcome of the *coup de force* in the west.

Europe stirred uneasily. Lester thought of his family, should war break out:

> One aeroplane, or one machine-gunner might, in the present situation, precipitate the unthinkable disaster. A boat to Sweden or Denmark with my family on board would leave me here with a less anxious mind. But would one have time to pack them off?

Hitler made a speech in Munich. He wanted peace on the basis of equality: 'I go my way with the assurance of a somnambulist, the way which Providence has sent me.'

Meanwhile the League continued to lose face as Addis Ababa was occupied by the Italians and the emperor of Abyssinia, a member of the League, was forced to flee the country.

Greiser said that people who spoke of rumours of the Rhineland coup being repeated in Danzig were mad, because Germany required to keep on good terms with Poland. On this occasion Lester suggested to Greiser that it would be wise for National Socialists to direct their policy to healing the divisions between themselves and the other German parties, within Danzig, that is. Greiser liked the idea of a 'Deutsche Front' such as there had been in the Saar. Only patience and slow moving, said Lester, could bring that about. Co-operation, not absorption.

The May session of the council was the shortest on record. It lasted from 11 to 13 May and consisted of three short meetings. The only political point of interest was the decision that, in spite of Italy's formal annexation of Abyssinia, and her argument that as Abyssinia no longer existed, Italy should represent the territory at the council table, the council decided that the Ethiopian or Abyssinian delegate would be called to the table. This was decided at a private meeting on procedure; at the public session, a few minutes later, 'Baron Aloisi, the Italian, sat smilingly in his place.'

The question of Lester's reappointment was again on the agenda. Eden 'earnestly hoped I would accept reappointment for a period. He was aware that it was the unanimous view of his colleagues.' Then Avenol, the Secretary-General, spoke privately to Lester on the considerable uncertainty about the immediate future. There might, said Avenol, be a question of reducing some of the commitments of the League, now that Germany and Poland were 'on good terms', and the High Commissioner wasn't being called on to regulate disputes between Danzig and Poland. Avenol buttered this up by saying how important, then, in such circumstances, it would be that there should be in Danzig someone in whom they had confidence, as well as someone who knew the situation.

Lester said he would soldier on. He presumed that his own government would have no objection. 'Oh,' said Avenol, 'your government will be delighted.'

As to reduction in commitments, Lester thought this would be strongly opposed by Poland, if and when it came under discussion. With a changed military situation in Europe, Lester was of the opinion that Poland might regard the League in Danzig as, if not an actual protection, at least strengthening their moral and political position.

Things had, on the whole, been quiet in Danzig. But the administration remained Nazi in spirit and in many respects unconstitutional. The only way this trend could be radically changed would be by a committee of investigation. Lester had no resources. That had already been proposed in January, but postponed. There were many complaints still from the opposition: he had one or two kilos of such complaints on his desk, he said to Avenol.

Lester had little enough to reassure him. Papée had said to him that Poland, in relation to Danzig, would not make the same mistake France had in the case of the Rhineland, in not putting just one battalion across the Rhine. 'And he had reason to believe the Germans knew that.'

Last months in Danzig

Lester wrote in his diary that he thought Germany, just then, was not sorry to have the League and its High Commissioner *in situ* as a buffer to prevent the more extreme people from pushing matters too quickly. And never, he wrote on return to Danzig, had he seen Geneva in such disarray. No one could speculate on the future; no one could feel any certainty as to the European position even two months ahead. The Italian action, together with the flight of the 'King of Kings' had presented a situation in which the League appeared to have been defeated.

At a private meeting of the council of the League, Lester's reappointment for the following year brought many congratulations and good wishes. He also had advice from his colleague Frank Cremins, who

> ... urged me strongly to stay abroad i.e. in Danzig. No hope, he seemed to think, for me at home. Rather astonishing and discouraging; with my special experience, I had hoped to be welcomed back into our own service. Until two weeks ago I have never had one word of appreciation or encouragement from headquarters, personal or official, for my work on the Council, or for my work in Danzig. I wrote again to Joe Walshe [Secretary of the Department] asking for a direction from the Government as to accepting a renewed period here. Was semi-officially told 'that the President would not stand in my way of accepting.'
>
> The President himself is ill in Zürich and could not be consulted. He had, it is true, last July [when Lester was in Dublin] urged me to stay on 'as a feather in our cap'. Joe, for the first time for years softened his semi-official note by a purely personal one – congratulations on my success in Danzig. I am much afraid he doesn't want me.

Lester wasn't long back in Danzig before Greiser made an intemperate speech saying that the Polish–German pact would not last, and that then would come the realisation of their ambition. There was a protest from the Polish minister, and a complete denial followed. The newspaper which had carried the story, the *Volksstimme*, was suppressed for two months for 'false' reporting.

The Drang nach Osten

In *Mein Kampf* Hitler drove home the message that never again must Germany be in a position where she could be starved by blockade into submission. Land to the east was a necessity – land to be taken by war. He was by no means the first to press for invasion of territories east of the German borders. A leading propagandist on the theme, Paul de Lagarde, wrote in 1886:

> ... we need land at our doorstep. If Russia does not want to give it to us, she will force us to undertake an expropriation proceeding, i.e. a war, for which we have long stored up the reasons. The Germans are a peaceful people, but they have a right to live, and to live as Germans, and they are convinced of the fact that they have a mission for all the nations of the earth; if one hinders them from fulfilling their mission, then they have the right to use force. (Quoted by Carl Tight in *Gdansk*, Pluto Press, London)

Bismarck's *Kulturkampf* against the Catholic church throughout Germany had been accompanied on Prussian territory, where there was a Polish population, by a massive campaign against the Polish language. In 1887 Polish was banned from all elementary schools throughout the Prussian east. In 1887, too, Polish was banned even from a few private bilingual schools in Pomerania, and children heard speaking Polish were threatened with public flogging.

Among many German patriotic associations that sprang up along the eastern borders, the most powerful was the *Ostmarkenverein*, or Eastern Marches Society, which pressurised the government to extend laws forbidding the sale of land to Poles, tried to expel all non-Prussian Poles and, when a strike was called in a school near Poznan, where pupils refused to receive religious instruction or to say prayers in German, it was broken only when children were publicly flogged and their parents sent to jail.

Riots in Danzig

On 13 June what Lester described as 'our comparative peace' was shattered, when Nazis stormed a Deutschnational party meeting within a hundred yards of the High Commissioner's residence. Lester was miles away at the time in Zoppot. When he came back he was told of people clamouring at the doors, calling out that a massacre was going on. Ambulances came and fifty people were in hospital: the Deutschnational party supporters were in many cases elderly. Greiser came to see Lester, reporting that Forster had complained to him on the phone at 5.30 in the morning that fifteen of his men had been injured. Lester notes in his diary:

> After my formal talk, I told von Radowitz that the people in Berlin knew I was trying to prevent mischief but that, in certain circumstances, I would not hesitate to take the strongest action. If I were not supported, I would at once resign and explain why without too much diplomatic nicety.

The story went on. On 16 June the funeral of a Nazi was held with big demonstrations. All the state flags were at half-mast and offices closed. The head of the SA or Brownshirts came from Berlin. Lester went to see Greiser to warn him that, while the council was not sitting, he, Lester, had to take on every responsibility. Also that he might have to bring Danzig to the special sanctions sitting of the council on 26 June, ten days hence. Greiser said openly that he would regret that very much. Lester reminded him of the council's resolution in January that had asked Poland to support the High Commissioner, and told Greiser that he was going to see Papée that morning. Greiser hoped he would not make any formal *démarche* with Poland. As usual, Greiser told Lester in confidence afterwards that he was having difficulties with Forster.

Then Lester had a stream of protesters, including all the opposition leaders, with some of the weapons captured: a pistol, magazines, life preservers, a dummy hand-grenade. 'We all served in the war and won't be killed in cold blood,' some said. Lester made the normal point, in such abnormal circumstances, that their only strength was in legality.

At Greiser's request, Lester received a dozen young Nazi storm-troopers, all bandaged. 'Rather naive,' he noted. 'The police must act against all,' said Lester. Replied one: 'But not so hard.'

Then a young Nazi died in hospital. Lester reported more outrages, more interviews and 'the absence of confidence in the police forces very bad'. Ironically the young Nazi who died in the riot had a Polish father and a German mother but was brought up as a German. The medical certificate said that he had died from natural causes, but in the German press his death was referred to as 'cowardly assassination,' 'Red murder' and so on, and two SS men were killed in dubious circumstances in a village near the frontier.

For days there were more riots and outrages, in some cases, it was alleged, with the police looking on. Lester wrote a formal note to the senate as a warning. He also saw the German consul general officially to draw his attention to Forster's activity. Forster was believed to be behind all this. The consul general agreed. He said also that Forster did not, as he publicly claimed, represent the Führer.

Lester writes in his diary:

> Am keeping up steady pressure on all parties, and taking every preventive measure possible to keep the situation from developing into a crisis requiring international action, perhaps a request for force, which would complicate a situation in Europe already tense enough.

During the next few days Forster, Greiser, and the German consul general, von Radowitz, were absent for several days; in Berlin, Lester understood.

There were social occasions which proved an ordeal, too. Lester writes in March 1936:

Dined with Harbour President Nederbragt last night. A frightful dinner, as usual, in spite of two 'graces' by himself and Bishop Beerman.

We hadn't finished coffee before we were ushered into a room with chairs set ready. 'Mein Gott, a prayer meeting,' I said to Noë, a fellow guest. But it was a lecture by Nederbragt's daughter on 1000 years of Hungarian history; an imposing manuscript, 'mostly dates,' as Elsie said. At last it was finished and N. played some Hungarian airs on a tinny gramophone. Then another huge MS was produced – on the literature of Hungary.

I couldn't escape from the front chair. No drinks, no smokes. I tried to read the names of the books upside down. Another interval and a drink. I swallowed a brandy in a gulp, a 'life-saver,' and rose. I passed to the back of the room, congratulated Nederbragt, and to my horror learned there was another lecture to come. One and a half-hours of it had been enough. I said I must go. Elsie came up with another excuse. We insisted and left. Nederbragt threatens to be another public nuisance in Danzig. 'Him and his schoolgirl histories,' says Elsie.

When the three men, Forster, Greiser and von Radowitz came back from Berlin, it was clear, in spite of soothing words from Greiser, that Forster was still the man to be reckoned with.

Official German insult to High Commissioner

Then on 25 June came an official German assault on the position of the High Commissioner. The cruiser *Leipzig* visited Danzig and its commander was ordered from the highest authority not to call on the High Commissioner among his list of formal visits.

Accompanied by every possible personal indignity, the German government yesterday landed one in my midriff if not below the belt. I suppose it was not personal, but it naturally had its personal effect. The visit of the German

cruiser *Leipzig*, announced some weeks ago, took place
yesterday, and while I, all dressed up, awaited the arrival of
the officers for the usual official call, I received a message
from a subordinate official of the Senate that the officers
had informed the Senate that they had been instructed by
the highest naval authorities to pay no visit to the High
Commissioner. No explanation was offered. I immediately
cancelled the entertainment I had arranged for the officers,
and my acceptance of invitations in connection with their
visit. It appears that the officers went straight from the
Senate to the Polish Minister, arriving ten minutes before
they were expected. This, presumably, was in order to
prevent the Polish Minister knowing anything about the
affair, which they did not mention to him.

A German news source attributed the gesture to the incident
ten months previously when another German warship had come
to Danzig, and the former president of the senate, Rauschning,
had appeared at a post-dinner reception, causing Greiser and
others to walk out. The real reason, Lester wrote in his diary, he
was convinced, 'lay in strenuous efforts [he had taken] to
prevent Forster fulfilling his threat to take over the streets after
the recent incidents.'

Another factor was that nearly half of the population of
Danzig, mostly German, refused to be intimidated by the Nazi
government of the Free City, which rankled with the authorities
in Berlin. The same authorities, however, had to tread carefully
vis-à-vis Poland, for Berlin was anxious not to upset the balance.

The *Economist* said at the time that the continued existence
of the situation in Danzig, in which perhaps more than 50% of
the people were against National Socialism, was a very sore point
in Germany, and a continuous reflection on the occasional
popular plebiscites held there. As Lester noted in his diary:

> The Danzig question will in due course come to the
> forefront between Poland and Germany. I have always
> hoped it would come in the way of peaceful negotiations,
> and it has seemed to be a reasonable and intelligent policy

to prepare for that by keeping German nationalist feeling strong and well stirred up in Danzig, while maintaining, for the time being, a careful enough regard for the legal position, which otherwise might affect Polish relations with Berlin.

The present incident may also indicate other changes. After the consultations in Berlin, Greiser came back with authority to ban all meetings and processions, and with the orders which probably accompanied this to Forster, and the cessation of the daily marches of the Nazi troops, order has been restored. ... of course, the general European situation is again reflected here; the débâcle at Geneva and the apparent withdrawal of English policy within very small limits and the blow to British prestige in Germany following the victory of Italy.

Also with the return of the three from Berlin, the Propaganda Ministry had taken a hand, opening with a fierce attack on Lester, beginning with an article by Forster declaring that the High Commissioner interfered in internal affairs, and that, but for the League of Nations, all the opposition parties in Danzig would long ago have disappeared. The article demanded revision of the constitution in so far as the League's role was concerned.

On 30 June Eden, as president of the council, summoned Lester to come immediately to Geneva. Lester had not asked that the cruiser incident be discussed, but he had written a short account of it. Greiser had been informed that, as it was a matter between the League and Germany, not Danzig, he need not appear. The German press attacks on Lester continued, including from the *Diplomatische Korrespondenz*, the mouthpiece of the Wilhelmstrasse, the Foreign Ministry: Lester was, it said, 'personally and psychologically unsuitable and moved by animosity and partiality'. The British and Polish ambassadors in Berlin had been seen by von Neurath, the Foreign Minister, and assured that the incident would pass quietly. It seemed to the council that a short formal discussion would finish the matter. Then came the news that Greiser was on his way to Geneva. Here he was to become famous or infamous as never before in his life.

He had not been summoned to Geneva, but he came, via briefings in Germany, and delivered a speech on 1 July which the *Manchester Guardian* recorded as being in tone and language 'unprecedented in the history of the League'. It was, said the *Guardian* (which throughout described him as Captain Greiser) 'often more suited to a bar-room than to a meeting of the League Council'.

Greiser described the Danzig minority (the non-Nazi voters, who as the elections of the previous year had shown, numbered 42%) as criminals and cowards and said that he spoke for the honest part of the Danzig population. He again made the absurd statement that the majority were terrorised by the minority, and that Lester was responsible for this. The attacks on Lester, the *Guardian* correspondent noted, were quite unjustifiable, for he had been anxious to be just to the Danzig Nazis and his report was a model of impartiality. Greiser went on to say that Hitler and the late Marshal Pilsudski were the only statesmen in Europe, and the council should depose Lester and send another High Commissioner, or decide not to appoint any High Commissioner. The Free City, according to Greiser, had been set up to be a source of friction between Poland and Germany. The League's guarantee might be carried out under the personal responsibility of the president of the senate (himself), and thus peace and order would be restored to Danzig. The rights of the Polish minority in that case and the Polish state would not be touched. But he did not say anything about the rights of the German minority in Danzig.

After anodyne remarks by Eden and others, which did include support for Lester, Greiser, speaking again, was more insolent than before, and claimed to represent the whole German people. Greiser's headline eminence throughout Europe and farther afield was due more to an event after he had finished speaking: as he passed the press gallery, in response, it is said, to some laughter on the part of the journalists, he put out his tongue and put his fingers to his nose, 'cocking a snook'. Greiser, 'full of schnapps' according to Lester, swept aside the waiting correspondents outside the council chamber, and declared that the next time he came to Geneva it would be with a fleet of bombers.

Perhaps he was incited, too, by journalists who laughed when Greiser gave the Nazi salute at the end of his speech, but that 'did not justify the head of a government in behaving like a street urchin,' in the words of the *Manchester Guardian*. Greiser's speech was broadcast to crowds in the streets of Danzig. Attacks on Lester in the German press were violent. The *Völkischer Beobachter*, the official Nazi newspaper, wrote:

> Not a single proposal to make relations normal was listened to by Mr Lester. Every insidious attempt at sabotage by the opposition clique, on the other hand, found a ready hearing from him. Danzig has learned that the Commissioner is not the guarantor of peace, but the crystallisation point of the hostile Opposition.

The *Börsenzeitung*, close to the German War Ministry and the Foreign Ministry, declared that Lester was conspiring with the remainder of the opposition against the government of Danzig, and in Foreign Affairs had been a conscious fomenter of disorder. He had shown, on more than one occasion, that understanding between Danzig and Warsaw is not desired by him and is a thorn in his flesh.

The frustration expressed by Greiser, of course, stemmed from the stubborn fact that his majority, with all its powerful backing from Germany, could not erase the reality that one half of the Germans in Danzig refused to be Nazified. He said flatly that he expected the council to proceed with the revision of the constitution of the Free City and that he would not be recalled to Geneva to discuss the affairs of the sovereign state of Danzig. And, as the liberal *News Chronicle* put it in a leading article:

> It may seem curious on the face of it, that the truculence of a single ill-mannered clown should have caused more

sensation at Geneva on Saturday than the tragedy which
has overtaken the Abyssinian nation or the imminent
collapse of the whole structure of international law and
order in Europe.

True to form, the *Daily Mail* of Lord Rothermere headed its
leading article 'None of our Business'. It went on:

> This country is not concerned in any way with this remote
> town in the Eastern Baltic, and the British public is
> completely indifferent regarding its future. Nobody here
> would mind if the Nazis regained it for Germany.
> Unfortunately Britain has been dragged into the quarrel
> through her connection with the League.

Lester thought that Beck's contribution after the tirade of
Greiser was more than a bit offhand, and reported this to Beck's
second-in-command, Lubienski. 'I indicated that I had pulled
together some previous situations in Danzig, but this did not
look to be possible on this occasion, and it seemed to me that
my mission in Danzig had ended.' Lubienski, somewhat
alarmed, went to Beck. He returned saying that Beck would
speak again. Later, Lubienski was present when Lester, in the
presence of Walters, under-Secretary-General of the League and
Stevenson, Eden's second in the League affairs, said that the
Danzig situation had got beyond the possibility of action by a
High Commissioner with the limited powers at present given to
him. He was, he wrote, quite deliberately setting out 'to put it
up to Poland'. Beck was being a bit cavalier. Lubienski returned
from Beck (why, one might ask, was Beck not there at this
important phase?) to urge that 'any move on my part would
cripple any League action and play completely into the hands of
the people in Berlin, who had initiated the troubles, i.e. they had
briefed Greiser. And Lubienski begged me as a special favour not
to consider any action without further conversations with him.'
When Lester agreed, 'Lubienski said that he would not forget
this and seemed very much relieved.'

The council went into secret session immediately. Impressed

with the gravity and danger of the situation, Beck, at last roused, suggested to the council that Lester not return immediately to Danzig so that he, Beck, would have time to remind the Danzig senate that any incident affecting the High Commissioner would lead to intervention by Poland. In other words, Beck didn't care particularly what the Nazis did in the Free City as long as it didn't affect Poland adversely. But, said Beck, Poland would intervene energetically with Berlin in its capacity as a member of the League council to re-establish the prestige of the position of the High Commissioner, on condition that the council formally asked it to do so. Beck was an erratic person to deal with. He and Eden had a private conversation in the Carlton Hotel of Geneva at this time, as to how they could best impress on the senate of Danzig, and thus the Germans, that it would be dangerous to push too far their opposition to the authority of the High Commissioner. He told Eden that the best method of impressing the Germans with the importance Britain attached to the situation, without any doubt, was for Britain to send a warship to Danzig, under the pretext of a naval visit. Eden replied that he saw no possibility of suggesting such a measure to His Majesty's government.[3] Beck told Lester that ships were under steam at Gdynia in case of trouble. Poland feared, Lester said, that she might be left alone to face Germany, now especially, as the League was so weak. Beck declared that neither he nor his colleagues made anything out of politics 'and he added with some passion that he would co-operate with the devil to serve his country'.

The Polish promises of help had to be conditional. In Beck's papers it is claimed that the then senate of Danzig had behaved towards Poland better than any of its predecessors. He claimed also that in a secret session of the council in July 1936, he asked if Poland got into conflict with Germany in protecting the High Commissioner, would the powers on the council, particularly the Committee of Three (Britain, France, Sweden), effectively

3. This conversation is reported by one of Beck's close collaborators in the book by Colonel Joseph Beck, *Polish Politics 1926–1939*, published in French in Neuchâtel in 1951.

and immediately give support to Poland. He got his answer. Delbos of France 'a statesman of probity and honesty,' said that it did not appear to him to be possible; to which Beck replied that he did not think the government of Poland would imperil the safety of its country because the High Commissioner of the League of Nations had adopted such and such an attitude to the internal questions of the Free City. He, a member of the council, referred to Lester in the same context in these words: 'Or, M. Lester était sincèrement attaché a l'idéologie genèvoise.' ('For Mr Lester was sincerely attached to the Geneva ideology.') Was not Beck, then, also attached to the policy of the League? And his country?

So the Polish reassurances to the League that the High Commissioner would be well protected were hardly foolproof. Yet again, before Lester left for Danzig, Lubienski assured him that Polish preparations were complete and that they were ready if necessary. All Lester had to do was to give the word to Papée, the Polish representative in Danzig.

Lester spoke with Avenol, the League Secretary-General, a few days before he left for Danzig, and Avenol held that the League's position was becoming impossible in Danzig. The main mission was to act as a buffer between Danzig and Poland or even Germany and Poland, that the accords between these parties left the League to carry out a secondary mission regarding the constitution, and that this, in the present situation, tended to give the League an anti-National Socialist flavour, regarded in Germany as anti-German. That was Avenol's position, not Lester's. In the meantime, Poland sat back and declared her interest was only one-fourteenth in such matters, that is to say as one member of the council.

It seemed that the League members not only wanted, but needed, Lester to stay in Danzig, to be the Aunt Sally for Forster and Greiser and their followers; but, as indicated by Avenol, without any support or encouragement for the non-Nazi Germans, nearly half of all the Germans in Danzig, and the Poles and the Jews of the city.

continued on page 137

128

Great crane tower
on the River Mottlau,
Danzig.

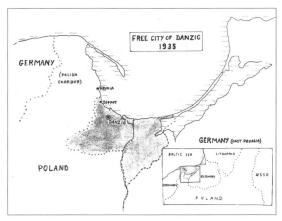

The Free City of
Danzig was the official
name but it was, in
fact, a small state –
including several
towns or small cities.
The area covered 750
square miles. For
comparison: Ireland's
smallest county,
Louth, is 317.82
square miles.

129

Old terrace houses in Danzig showing the stoop or platform before the entrance to the houses, reached by means of steps where the inhabitants sat out in the evenings.

The main street, Langgasse, Danzig, decorated with Nazi flags.

At Zoppot, the popular seaside resort,
Elsie Lester with her three daughters and,
on the right, Miss Minns, their governess,
July 1934.

Danzig tennis party, Easter 1936, from
left to right: Sean Lester, Countess
Finkinstein, Count Keyserlick, Count
Dante Serego.

Zeichnung: Waldl

—Wai geschrien, unser „Prügelknabe" schlägt zurück!—

Nazi propaganda liked to make its
enemies out to be caricatures of Jews.
This example is from towards the end
of Lester's term of office. The line at the
top reads 'Enough Lestering', the arm
points to the back door, while a clean-cut
Nazi looks on, waiting to be called in.
The caption reads: 'Woe, the victim
strikes back.'

Sean Lester fishing in the River Radaune,
near Danzig, 1936.

Sean Lester at the League of Nations in
conversation with Colonel Beck, back to
the camera.

Albert Forster, though not a Danziger, controlled the Nazi forces in Danzig. A personal protégé of Hitler's, he was untouchable. He was executed in Warsaw after the war.

From left to right: Sean Lester, Charles Bewley, Irish minister to Berlin, Albert Greiser, head of the Danzig senate.

Dr Hermann Rauschning, head of the Danzig senate or government, when Lester arrived, later succeeded by Greiser.

Julius Streicher, publisher of the infamous anti-Jewish sheet, *Der Stürmer*.

Japan withdrew from the League of
Nations in 1933 following its disputed
occupation of Manchuria. This cartoon
shows (clockwise) the Japanese delegate
addressing the council, defying the
League: Yen (China), Matos (Guatemala),
Colban (Norway), Fotich (Yugoslavia),
Madariga (Spain), von Bulow (Germany),
Grandi (Italy), Paul-Bancour (France),
Sir Eric Drummond (Secretary General),
Lord Londonderry (Great Britain),
Zaleski (Poland), Barreto (Cuba), Lester
(Ireland), Carry (Panama) (sketched by
Derson and Kelen, Geneva, 1932).

Lester could well have quit, drawing attention to the lack of powers in his hands. But everyone prayed him to stay on. Lester had no intention of delaying in Geneva more than a day or so after the matters in hand had been settled. Any delay might be interpreted as an abandonment of the Danzig post by the League. He had had an unpleasant experience the previous day when he had sat at the phone for three hours trying to get through to his family in the Free City. Wild rumours were circulating. 'The obstruction was deliberately put in my way at the Danzig Central [exchange],' and only when he got on to the Poles to communicate with the senate through their minister in Geneva, did he get through to find that things were quiet. 'A sleepy lady, somewhat irritated by such a late call,' Lester noted, 'gave me a welcome reassurance.'

On the Saturday when he left the secret meeting, he was surrounded by about twenty journalists who informed him that, according to radio reports, his house in Danzig was in flames and his family in flight. Two of the more responsible of the journalists said that was a rumour only on the news service of Radio Luxembourg, and therefore should be discounted. Indeed, he had got his wife out of bed to assure him that all was quiet.

Beck meanwhile had seen a somewhat deflated Greiser and had warned him that if Polish interests or the interests of the High Commissioner were interfered with, there would be intervention by Poland. Greiser disclaimed any intention on either count, but did send for the police guard around the house of the High Commissioner.

On 11 July, back, of course, in Danzig, Lester noted in his diary, 'The preventive work which I have been doing for two and half years is now rendered impossible by the attitude of the Senate.' 'I am awaiting,' he wrote to Avenol, 'with a deep sense of the big issues involved.' Lester's communications with Geneva were now limited, for security reasons. On 14 July he wrote a letter that he said would not reach Avenol for two weeks, presumably going via one of the diplomatic bags of their colleagues.

There was now only one small weekly paper of the opposition, the others having been suppressed for their reporting of the Geneva events. The complete National Socialist Danzig was being built up. The flood of journalists who had invaded the town for a putsch had largely withdrawn. Half a dozen policemen had been put around the High Commissioner's office since Greiser spoke at Geneva. There had never been one before then. None were stationed at the house entrance, only at his office: the opposition leaders thus stayed away.

In his diary of 12 September 1936, Lester describes a talk with Beck on 5 July, immediately after Greiser's outburst on Danzig policy, as 'perhaps the most dramatic conversation in my experience':

> The following morning I met a changed Beck who had spent a sleepless night. 'All my plans and policies are broken,' he said (alas for the solemn pact he had signed with Berlin). 'I am still a serving colonel,' he went on, 'and can always take my sabre.' That sent him down another step in my estimation. It is too easy a line of escape for a statesman. I said to him I did not think Germany was yet ready for war. I knew Poland sufficiently well to know that a Putsch in Danzig would mean war. That Putsch might, as he feared, take place, but only if Mr Hitler thought the Poles would accept a 'fait accompli'. He then told me that troops were moving up to the Danzig frontier and that the war-ships in Gdynia were under steam. 'If that is the situation,' I said, 'make sure that the Germans know it and the crisis will disappear.' As it turned out I was right. Austria and Czechoslovakia were to be dealt with first.

Greiser's helmet of honour

Greiser's return to Danzig after Geneva in July 1936 was the signal for an immediate move towards the full Nazification of the Free City. The Social Democratic *Volksstimme* was immediately suppressed for three months for publishing a manifesto expressing faith in the League and demanding new elections. Other opposition papers were seized on publication. The senate went into immediate emergency session, which was to lead to the suppression of all opposition parties. President Greiser received a special mark of approval from the local police. A photograph appeared in the Nazi press of the presentation of a helmet of honour to him in recognition of his manly attitude in Geneva and to emphasise the devotion of the police to him. It looked, in the photograph, just like any other German bucket-shaped helmet, but doubtless had an inscription to mark the occasion. As to Lester, the foreign press reported his calm demeanour. Wrote the *Daily Herald* special correspondent:

> [He] defied Nazi hooligans to do their worst when he arrived back here today from the stormy council meeting in Geneva. Outside the station his car was waiting. He dismissed it. With his wife by his side, he walked to his home through streets alive with plain-clothes and uniformed police. The authorities evidently anticipated trouble. Mr Lester did not care, and he was not molested. Round his house tonight, however, 40 armed police are mounting guard.

One man, at least, found some diversion in Greiser's antics at the League. Lester, back in Danzig wrote:

> At a dinner party shortly after, which included Count O'Rourke, the Bishop of Danzig, a cartoon was produced from the *Morning Post*, headed 'If the Greiser habit spreads.' It depicted a so-called school for Nazi diplomats, in which the participants were practising 'cocking snooks' and putting out their tongues, dropping banana skins for Eden etc. I have rarely enjoyed another man's amusement so much. The worthy Bishop sat gurgling and chuckling for about fifteen minutes over each new aspect of the cartoon. Eventually he insisted on taking it for the amusement of the Consistory, which was to meet the next day.

On 17 July Lester wrote in his diary, reminding himself that he had warned Beck and Papée not to try to make any bargains concerning himself: he had put up with indignities from people who were fighting the League, but he would not be pushed around or made a bargaining point by those officially on his own side. Back in residence, he was being systematically sidelined by the government of Danzig. He made a point in a letter to the senate about some new decrees and got no reply. He followed this up with a telephone enquiry and still got no reply. The Polish minister Papée was evasive, in spite of being reminded by Lester that assurances had been given by his government that they would stand by the High Commissioner and see to it that his position was not assailed.

Visitors to Lester's office were now being questioned by the political police. Even consuls were prevented from entering until they had established their identity.

> Some visitors were interrogated at length, including an American journalist who, having produced his passport and other documents, was asked what he was coming for. He said he wanted to see the High Commissioner. The policeman then inquired of the journalist had he already made an appointment, and he was allowed to pass when he said that he was going to my office to do so.

The detective suggested to one visitor that if he required information he would be better to go to the senate instead.

Gerald Griffin in *The Wild Geese* reports how Lester was appreciated back in England at this time:

> Cheers at Westminster for an Irish nationalist are not too common,[4] and an incident on 27 July 1936 was as much a tribute to the Mother of Parliaments as to Lester himself. Reviewing the international situation in the House of Commons, Mr Eden, Secretary of State for Foreign Affairs, said, à propos of Danzig: 'The League Council has frequently made it clear that in its view Mr Lester has

---

4. As well as not being too common, cheers for an Irish nationalist at Westminster may also not be particularly welcomed by the subject of the cheers or his compatriots. In this case they seem acceptable and correct.

carried out his most difficult duties in an admirable manner; he has earned and he deserves the complete confidence of the Council of the League.' There were loud cheers and Mr Eden went on: 'I am glad to hear those cheers, because I hope they will make it clear that all sections of opinion in this country sympathise with the difficulties of an Irishman carrying on an anxious task.'

Lester wrote to Avenol on 1 August that he had received not one visit from any of the opposition political parties since the police control was established. Senate members, he remarked on several occasions, were telling journalists and other enquirers that the High Commissioner would be gone by the autumn. In the middle of August, during the Olympic Games in Berlin, there was no anticipation of any immediate danger, and Lester took ten days' leave to tour the Scandinavian capitals. Before departing he had another conversation with Papée who again indicated, and more clearly than on other occasions, the determination of Poland to maintain her position in Danzig and if necessary to reorientate her policy in order to do so.

Shortly after that, the French chief-of-staff visited Warsaw and there was a return visit to France by General Rydz-Smigly, the virtual dictator of Poland and successor to the old marshal. This resulted in the renewal and strengthening of the Franco-Polish Alliance, which some responsible newspapers directly connected with Germany's Danzig policy.

Meanwhile the Danzig senate gave every indication of carrying out the Berlin policy of boycotting the High Commissioner and the League of Nations, so far as so-called internal affairs were concerned. 'Letters from me,' wrote Lester, 'on the Constitution have not been answered and decrees have been issued which I am certain are against the Constitution. The Council will next week begin a session in which it will be faced with another *fait accompli*: the destruction of the guarantee of the Constitution; and I do not see what the outcome can be.'

The Germans, he wrote in his diary, had tried to force his resignation by means of a 'nerve test':

I naturally have no longing to remain here, but I am equally determined that if I leave Danzig in these circumstances, it will be made clear in public that it is not because of any failure on my own part to carry out Council instructions with discretion and tact, but simply due to the change of policy in Germany, and the weakness of the League.

German newspapers now found Lester to be the most hated man in the Reich. It came down to some very personal remarks. He noted in his diary that the *Stürmer* had published photographs of Greiser and Lester together,

... my own photograph having been touched up a little, and this distinguished newspaper, which has for some time been under the direct control of the German Ministry for Propaganda, compared our personal appearances, naturally to my disadvantage. High Commissioners, if there are any in future, will have to be chosen on the basis of a Hollywood film star appearance. These, however, have really only been the lighter touches in a very anxious time.

But there were moves in Geneva. When Lester was there for a day in September, Avenol had mentioned in passing that he hoped shortly to be in a position to make an interesting proposal. He could say no more. A few days later it was announced that Azcárate had resigned from the post of deputy Secretary-General on being appointed Spanish ambassador in London. When Lester went down to Geneva again for the council and assembly of 25 September, Avenol asked him what would his feelings be if he were to propose him as the new deputy Secretary-General in place of Azcárate. Lester said he would feel very flattered, but he would like to think the matter over. 'I had never any thoughts of joining the Secretariat. At the same time, I did express my appreciation of what was a very big compliment.'

Avenol then told the Committee of Three, belatedly appointed to look into Danzig affairs, of his proposal. Eden came to Lester and asked him what he thought about it. Would he consider that he was being let down in any way? Lester told Eden he wouldn't look at it that way, it was a very high post and while he had been hoping to return to his own Irish service, he felt that he could hardly refuse such an offer. It would mean, he thought, a very good exit from Danzig. Eden said that neither he nor the committee wanted to stand in the way of his promotion, that the post was an extremely important one, and that in the normal course of events it might very well mean that he would later become Secretary-General.

'I replied,' Lester wrote, 'that the idea alarmed me, and if I really thought that would happen I would prefer to return to my own national service.'

It was inevitable that Lester's nomination would be regarded as a retreat from Danzig. The council did what they could to meet this. They put a restriction on the period when he would take up his new duties, by saying that it could not take place until his successor was nominated. Both the French and British, said Lester, were perhaps concerned with their own public opinion, and sensitive to any suggestion that Danzig was being abandoned. But if the Danzig senate refused even to acknowledge his presence – if he had no duties to perform – it would be farcical to continue with his term of office. The League was to make certain that his successor was more than acceptable to the Nazis in Germany and thus in Danzig.

In Danzig the news of Lester's new posting came as a very welcome surprise to the Nazis. It was treated on the basis of 'the recall of Lester' and the Nazi press rejoiced. A special festival being held that weekend, at which Greiser and Forster spoke, was made the occasion for celebrating 'the triumph over the League and Lester' and the opposition was told that they were now in for it at last. There was the nub.

But then came a bit of a shock for the Danzig Nazis. Lester had written a powerful report for the council, which had been passed on to the Committee of Three. He reminded them of the relevant article 103 in the Treaty of Versailles: 'A constitution for the Free City of Danzig should be drawn up by the duly appointed representatives of the Free City in agreement with the

High Commissioner to be appointed by the League of Nations. This Constitution shall be placed under the guarantee of the League of Nations.' He then went on to detail other duties of the High Commissioner but the basis was laid in that sentence about the foundation stone of the constitution.

Lester had included many criticisms and revelations of what had been going on in the Free City, even to the point of including the grovelling letter which Greiser had written to him as recently as 3 June, following Lester's re-appointment. 'I hope that your further term of office will be under a lucky star, and that your selfless mediation will, in the future also, work out for the good of the Free City of Danzig.'

Lester drew the conclusion from this that there had been a sudden change of policy in Berlin. The Committee of Three's report to the council led to a resolution giving a mandate to Poland to examine the situation with a view to the maintenance of the guarantee of the constitution and to report on the conditions necessary to enable the High Commissioner to carry out all his duties.

'At the same time there was a report in the newspapers,' writes Lester, 'that my successor would be a Pole. This all seemed to justify the suspicion, expressed by the *Vorposten* in its first leading article celebrating my so-called "downfall," that there must be a snag somewhere.'

Lester was always thinking of home:

> The one thing I was looking for was the return to the Irish service, and the shiver with which this suggestion has always been received in Dublin has been the most chilling. There was no Cabinet Minister in the Delegation in Geneva, – Cremins, Michael Rynne and Denis Devlin. I talked to them about the proposal and about my own hopes, and the encouragement I got to take the international job was unanimously enthusiastic. Rynne and Frank [Cremins] said that there was no job at home and no hope of any. Micky said that it was always possible of course that I would be given something like control of

passports. I wrote to Joe Walshe and left the decision in the hands of the Government, but said I would like to keep my contacts with my own Service. When I telephoned to Joe, he said he had talked to the President [de Valera] and both thought I should accept the post, which was such a very high one. On the other matter nothing could be said.

In October, Lester wrote in his diary of meeting Papée and intimating to him that he regarded his situation at the moment in Danzig as largely a formal one. He had reported the situation to Geneva and their remedy had been to ask Poland to take action. He told Papée that he 'considered the matter to be entirely in Poland's hands'. Papée said that he had seen Greiser and had warned him against some extreme steps. But Lester didn't think that Poland would try to maintain or would succeed in maintaining the constitution.

'Incidentally,' writes Lester, 'at one of the last Committee meetings, Eden had apparently asked Beck to ensure that life was made tolerable for me while I remained in Danzig, and Beck had given assurances ... both of them told me about this afterwards.'

Lester took the opportunity to have a lengthy holiday fishing in Ireland such as had not been possible for years.

Lester left, or was forced out of, Danzig, because he insisted on carrying out the orders of the League in conformity with the relevant article of the Treaty of Versailles. This, the League seemed to be saying, was no longer possible or desirable. A High Commissioner with whom the government of Danzig would not communicate was serving no purpose. There was no rush to appoint a successor, but when he came, his mission would not include that of being a guarantor of the constitution.

Après Lester le déluge

Poland, then, had the initiative and, to all intents and purposes, the control on behalf of the League. They were only getting in train when Lester made an entry in his diary on 22 December:

> The Social Democratic Party and all its kindred
> associations was suppressed a couple of months ago, the
> ostensible grounds being some revolvers alleged to have
> been found in the office of the defunct *Volksstimme*. The
> chief of the Catholic Party has been arrested and some
> other deputies are in Schutzhaft [protective custody]. Four
> Opposition Deputies had their parliamentary immunity
> withdrawn at a meeting of the Volkstag, and Mr Forster six
> weeks ago announced that he would have a special
> Christmas present for the Führer, which is variously
> interpreted, although the suggestion that it meant the
> return of Danzig to the Reich was, of course, quite
> groundless.

Lester had been, on and off, away for more than two months
on leave. He had told the Poles that he thought his absence
might actually be helpful, but that if a bad situation developed,
he would return quickly. One of the reasons for being away so
long was to make it very clear to Poland that she was now
shouldering the responsibility herself; as a member of the
council of the League, and by special mandate from the council.

Once the senate had decided, on orders from Berlin
presumably, to boycott him, there was nothing he could do for
Danzig or the League, and more particularly for the brave
minority. He was excluded from the run of events. He had a
promise from Poland in regard to himself, but no such promise
from that or any other quarter to guard and preserve the rights
of the non-Nazis, including the considerable number of
Germans who did not want to be Nazified. He and his family
were boycotted socially too – friends of the three girls became
unavailable.

The latest song from France, Lester had heard when in
Geneva, was 'Tout va très bien, Madame la Marquise.' While on
a long holiday away from home, Madame la Marquise
telephones to find out how things are going. Each of the
servants comes to the phone to say that everything is fine apart
from ..., and then each relates a different disaster that has

happened, culminating in a huge fire damaging the place, but 'à part cela, Madame la Marquise, tout va très bien, tout va très bien' (apart from all that, Madame la Marquise, everything is fine, everything is fine). Some wit in Geneva had a parody which included Avenol saying:

> Il était une petite bêtise,
> L'Ethiopie est conquise,
> A part cela, Madame la Marquise,
> Tout va très bien, tout va très bien.

> (There was something stupid:
> Ethiopia was conquered.
> But apart from that, Madame la Marquise,
> Everything is going fine, everything is fine.)

CHAPTER 7

Back to Geneva

On 18 February 1937 Lester noted in his diary:

> Take up new duties as Deputy Secretary-General of the
> League. Elsie recalled to my mind yesterday that it is less
> than eight years since I left Ireland – about the middle of
> April 1929. I had never before been in either Paris or
> Geneva!! In four and a half years I had attended scores of
> conferences, been a member of the Council for three years,
> presiding over it on one or two occasions, and over several
> of its committees – notably the Peru-Colombia and the
> Chaco affair – and I had been asked to go to Danzig as
> High Commissioner.
>
> I sometimes wonder what on earth I am doing here,
> being a man without ambition.

There was still much good international work to be done by
the League servants, notably in harmonising labour relations,
and there were successful departments dealing with drugs and
economic planning. Overall the League, however groping and
tentative, was a structure that the world still needed. Even
throughout the world war that was to come, countries still paid
to maintain a body that would carry on the first cohesive world
effort to organise peace and civilisation in international affairs.

In his earlier Geneva days Lester was given free rein while, as
John T Whitaker points out, 'other diplomats awaited
instructions from their Governments or studied League
procedure.' It was partly, says Lester, 'because of the
indifference of the Department.'

The appointment of the new High Commissioner took up a good deal of time in the early days of Lester's return – both Lester and Anthony Eden had argued against any appointment being made at all, but the Poles demanded that a High Commissioner be sent. Indeed Beck was much annoyed at the delay and even said that he would get support if he proposed leaving the League: 'Pure bluff,' wrote Lester. And of course Carl Burckhardt, who was subsequently appointed ('a remarkably good man in the circumstances, I think,' wrote Lester) took on a mission which was not the same as that confided to his predecessor, a fact openly proclaimed by the Danzig press.

There were lighter moments. Lester was in London in March 1937 to speak at a St Patrick's night dinner of the National University Club, and another day he fell in with some of his old journalistic colleagues at a reception given by the Free State commissioner in London, John Dulanty. Notable among them was Con O'Leary: 'Just fined by a Magistrate for smashing one of Hamar Greenwood's ABC shop windows.' (Greenwood had been Chief Secretary for Ireland 1920–2.) Said Con, 'I just couldn't help it, Sean.'

Other old colleagues from the *Freeman* days were there, but Con was the star turn. He kept pulling Desmond Ryan, former reporter and distinguished biographer, to every priest he saw and introducing him as 'a good little Catholic'. As Con was drinking whiskey, colleagues fled. Con introduced a man known as one of Scotland Yard's big five as, 'not a bad fellow, but a policeman and you can't trust policemen'.

It was a winding-down time for Lester, with many functions to be attended in his capacity as deputy Secretary-General.

He noted on 16 April that Avenol gave a lunch at which were Lord Astor and two bankers, Felix Warburg of New York and his brother, of Hamburg. Lester noted that he liked particularly the Hamburger. His family had been there for three hundred years and owned one of the two big financial (private) banks remaining.

Said the Hamburger: 'I have no vision of the future. I make

no plans. I do banking business each morning, giving my best advice, but if anyone asks me about the future I put them out of the door.'

Another Irish diplomat comes into Lester's diary of 23 April: Charles Bewley, Irish minister in Berlin, gave an interview to a newspaper on Irish–German friendship and said that Hitler had many admirers among the young people of Ireland. The Labour leader in Dublin, Norton, asked a question in the Dáil and Dev fenced: but it was clear that Bewley had gone a bit too far in his pro-Nazism, especially at the moment when the régime was in open conflict with the Catholic church and the papal encyclical had been suppressed in Germany. Writes Lester further:

> I don't forget how B. played up to me while I was High Commissioner in Danzig during the period immediately prior to the 'great offensive'. How I was then dropped like a hot cinder and I have not since had a line or a sign from him – even on my appointment. He is a skunk.

Immediately after that he adds:

> (Schoolboy).

At that time in Geneva there was quite a lot of talk of a possible *rapprochement* between Germany and Russia. Lester wrote:

> Ten or twenty years from now [Russia] will, I believe, be an immense and probably imperialist power. One good thing is that they have such huge territory and vast national resources that there should not be an economic necessity for expansion.

The League was represented at the British coronation ceremonies in May and there was a general series of discussions between the assembled statesmen.

Lester noted in his diary:

> Felt rather glum this morning, on looking out at Europe, at the League prospects. The initiative still rests with the

Rome-Berlin Axis. Hostile to the League. The Little
Entente is badly shaken, Poland under Beck hostile,
Austria nervous but seemingly in the current. Belgium
being strongly pushed to abandon Article 16 [the Article
which said League members should come to the aid of
anyone invaded], the Nordic States counting less and less
on collective help: Holland had declared that the 'passage
of troops' against an aggressor is a question only for the
state concerned.

His mind was always on Ireland. On 20 May he wrote:

Dev talks in the Dail of the possibility of the Irish Free
State leaving the League if it does not become 'universal',
in Europe at any rate. People here rather disappointed;
they expected better from Dev. But where the blazes will
Ireland be if she left the League? We withdrew from the
British Commonwealth of Nations – surely the necessary
corollary is that we hold with might and main to our only
place in the world! We will become more than ever an
'Island beyond an Island'. We would become domestic
politics for London – as seen from abroad. I do not take it
too seriously, because I do not believe our people are so
stupid. I doubt very much the interest Joe Walshe
[Secretary of the Department of External Affairs] has in
the League.

De Valera had been harried by the Fine Gael opposition in
every decent action he took in connection with international
affairs:

… irresponsible of men who would have done the same as
Dev if in his place. Sanctions against Italy; non-
intervention in Spain. They have tried to rally all our
abysmal ignorance of foreign affairs against him.

His last line is, 'Such party politics make me sick.'
At the League assembly on 26 May 1937 there was no
Abyssinian – only a letter from the Negus that he would not be

represented. A wit said that Abyssinia was now a corresponding member of the League. The Polish representative, Komarnicki, got up and said that his government now regarded the matter as settled. Writes Lester, 'It seemed a bit gratuitous and was first received in silence.' He put this remark in a certain perspective when he wrote:

> One recalled the time when Poland was also invaded, conquered, and partitioned, [he might have said wiped off the map] and in contrast with the action for many years subsequently of the Sultan of Turkey, who at each annual levée of the diplomatic representatives, asked aloud in the presence of Russian, Austrian and Prussian (the conquerors of Poland), 'Where is the Polish Ambassador?'

Against this backdrop Carl Burckhardt's reports from Danzig came as a bit of light relief. On one occasion he reported that Forster had mentioned Lester without violence. Writes Lester: 'But to tell the truth, I am a little bit suspicious of Burckhardt's tact on this point.'

On 8 June 1937 Lester writes:

> The Treasurer of the League, Jacklin, just back from London, where he had talked with Hertzog of South Africa and MacKenzie King of Canada. Both are pressing on Britain to dissociate the UK from any commitments or concern in Central or Eastern Europe and to eliminate Article 16, reducing the League to a purely consultative basis. ... As for England withdrawing more and more from Europe, excepting the West Coast and the Mediterranean, I only hope it would not really provoke war. I still could not see a major war in Europe which would not involve all, except, for a time, the smaller fringe.

Jacklin reported further on the English contempt for the Italians as a military or naval factor and disagreed with them. The new discipline had not yet been really tested, nor the difference which their air arm might make. Poor infantry material could be first class air material.

Social life on top of his ordinary duties became very hard. On 18 June Lester noted: 'This past two or three weeks, we have averaged about four parties a day. Appalling!'

The *Daily Telegraph* man in Berlin, CB Wareing, had just been to Danzig and wrote a few points to Lester. In his reply Lester said:

> I find myself looking back on recent years, with, of course, a pleasant sense of detachment and, thank goodness, without any kind of feeling except one of benevolent regret as far as the more unpleasant experiences were concerned. I feel it is all in a way a tragedy – a tragedy of European concern. At any rate all the visitors who came to me in the midst of my little troubles used to exclaim: 'What an interesting job you have!' Now I can fully agree with them, perhaps partly because some of the experiences were somewhat novel in the normal life of diplomacy.

Various turning points towards inevitable war have been marked out by historians. To Lester, the Hoare–Laval incident was the beginning of the end. This was a plan agreed between Sir Samuel Hoare, British Foreign Secretary, and Pierre Laval, French Foreign Minister, which was later approved by the British cabinet. It amounted to a sell-out of the Abyssinians to Italy, and was met with violent disapproval by the British public and many MPs. The Prime Minister, Baldwin, was forced to abandon the plan. He sacked Hoare and gave his job to Anthony Eden.

Sir Arthur Willard, a former Foreign Office man, lunching with Lester, said that Eden had lost his chance and authority in not resigning after the Hoare–Laval affair, and that Britain need not be looked upon as likely to favour any forward League policy – British policy was now one of alliances and balance of power, ignoring the dangers outside the line of immediate interests. In September 1937 Lester writes:

> What a world. Dangers in Spain, a crisis in the Mediterranean – wide open, but undisclosed, war raging

between China and Japan. Russia still undergoing 'a purification,' weakening her part in the balance of power. Too many problems and too many dangers.

An odd sign of the times: in a speech to the Assembly, Anthony Eden began by regretting that Great Britain was forced to rearm – that 450,000 tons of warships were on the stocks.

'Once,' writes Lester, 'we would have thought it an extraordinary opening of a League speech: to-day it was generally welcomed, he [Eden] said non-intervention had so far prevented the outbreak of a European war. Made some new offers in the economic field. A good speech.'

A very personal note:

> Have been having a hectic time. In my office from 9.30 till nearly 8.00 every day. And usually a delegation luncheon and dinner as well. But my holiday [he had spent August in Connemara] has stood to me, though I begin to be tired of the job. China and Spain and the reform of the Covenant are the big spots. British (and others) are careful about Japan, and timid does not seem too strong a word. ... Japanese bombardment of open towns was condemned in our Resolution. The British wanted their words referring to Japanese aircraft to be omitted. Old Jordan of New Zealand gave Cranborne the British Minister, a lambasting, a direct attack, and the Committee left the words in the Resolution.

Lester was on the council committee for technical collaboration with China, of which there was a supervisory commission. He noted that the Chinese epidemic question, 'which comes especially under me,' was moving slowly ahead. The council approved in a general way and referred the matter to the assembly. The only doubting voice was Poland's. And the only precedent for such action was on Poland's behalf in 1921, when epidemics began to sweep the country during the Bolshevik invasion: 'I should have blushed if I had been Komarnicki.'

Lord Astor, said Lester:

> ... had talked an hour with me on Europe and the
> necessity of eliminating the encirclement of Germany. I
> had said that if he wanted to abolish alliances – which were
> based on fear and suspicion of Germany – he would have
> to substitute something else. That could come, in my
> opinion, only by assurances under the real collective
> system. As he went out, I had said, don't forget that, the
> next time you write to *The Times*.

In a reply to another letter from Lord Astor, Lester says *inter
alia*:

> I am entirely with you in your plan that no doors should
> be bolted and that a great country like England, with its
> enormous wealth in territories can afford a healing policy
> towards Germany; indeed that such a policy in the end is
> the only alternative to the impossible policy of smashing
> Germany every generation. All through the Disarmament
> Conference that was what I had advocated and acted upon
> in my own small sphere as a delegate.
>
> I remember at one of our Commonwealth meetings
> urging in vain that the German demand for a certain
> proportion of tanks, anti-aircraft guns and heavy artillery
> should be conceded! Our experiences of that time, when
> we saw German proposals put forward by a more or less
> reasonable Government, rejected by France and Britain,
> while they, three or four months later would have been
> delighted to have made a settlement on such terms; but
> the price had gone up. I never forget in looking at the
> Germany of to-day, how much all these things have
> contributed from the outside to making the Nazi greed
> and the Nazi danger. There is no doubt a lesson to be
> learned from that period, but times have changed and the
> psychological factors have also changed; for the past two
> years Germany and Italy alternately have dominated
> international politics in Europe. They have had a series of

successes and have built up tremendous armaments. Germany fell back on the Sinn Féin idea of relying on herself alone. I doubt very much if a piecemeal settlement is possible or good. Perhaps it is because I am convinced that Europe is too small to envisage one or two great powers engaged in war, while the rest stood by to await the results. I don't think it is in the interest of either Britain or France, for example, to give Germany a free hand in the East and to comfort themselves that this diversion will leave their permanent interests intact. I heard the same argument in 1931 and 1932 when Japan was grabbing Manchuria; the second stage of that affair, which could I think easily have been foreseen, is in progress: and looking ahead a score of years or less, we shall both probably see further results of a magnitude infinitely greater.

In regard to the possibility of Britain giving up some of her possessions, Lester wrote:

> I would reserve every major concession until the general settlement approaches. I think that the first foundation for that general settlement, which I still hope for, will be when the Western Powers, with I hope the United States behind them, show that they will submit to no more threats and no more blackmail. I rejoiced in the Nyon Conference from no narrow motives, but because I believe that that was the way to helping Europe (including Germany and Italy).[5]

Astor, of course, was one of the so-called 'pro-German' group which included Lord Lothian, Major Astor of *The Times*, Lord Londonderry, Garvin of the *Observer* and others. So Lester probably thought it worthwhile to go on to other points. He

---

5. The Nyon Conference had been held in that place, near to Geneva, to avoid inviting Italy and Germany to come to the seat of the League. It held that British and French navies should control the Mediterranean, should counter-attack any submarine, surface warship or airship guilty of piratical attack on vessels other than Spain. Mussolini climbed down and offered to join in patrols: others accepted, knowing that the pirates all along had been Italian.

wrote that the relations between the 'haves' and 'have-nots' must be settled by concessions on the part of the 'haves' with regard to wealth and privilege, on the part of the 'have-nots' by submission to law or lawful procedure: 'I think that some degree of justice in international relationships is not only a dream; it can never be perfect, but it is the only hope for civilising international intercourse.' He went on to say that he thought the campaign for the return of colonies to Germany might change when it reached a certain intensity and when English imperialists were alarmed. Then the thought that was nearer to the Führer's heart might be presented – to give up, temporarily at any rate, the claim to a colonial empire in exchange for Central and Eastern Europe.

As a reminder of all this on 4 November 1937 the 'black-out' was tried in Geneva from 6pm until 7am, and partial exercises were made in several other cantons. Writes Lester: 'It was an extremely depressing experience – candles and blue lamps and covered windows and a pitch black night with low clouds.'

The Axis went on to further strength. On 8 November 1937, Lester notes that Italy had joined the Japanese/German anti-Communist alliance:

> This has created the greatest alarm in USA, England and France, which shows how little it is to be regarded as merely anti-Communist. *Le Temps* correspondent in Rome says it marks the end of Italian policy for an understanding with England, and Ciano [Italian Foreign Minister] on the same day said incidentally, that the three powers have two million tons of warships. With all this going on, the *Irish Independent* newspaper of the 15 November 1937, in a leading article on the dangerous international situation, attributed it '*inter-alia*' to 'the stupidly unchristian attitude of the Powers towards Italy'. How is that for an Irish Nationalist paper on a raw imperialist conquest [the conquest of Abyssinia]?

An odd note from back home. In referring to the new post of

President in the 1937 constitution, an English newspaper, according to Lester, had mentioned

> ... my friend Dick Hayes as a possible. He is a very fine type, Dick, with heaps of quiet character. But if it were offered, I should not be surprised if it took a great deal of coaxing to make him give up his Ringsend Dispensary for a public office.[6]

Shortly after that, on 24 November 1937, the *Sunday Dispatch* newspaper rang Lester up and asked his views on the proposal that he should be the first President of Ireland.

> 'What?' I exclaimed, 'where on earth did you hear that?'
> 'From a high source in Dublin.'
> 'Well I know nothing about it,' and I refused to make any comment.
>
> So it was published in the *Dispatch* and *Daily Mail* that I was talked of in Belfast and Dublin as a 'probable'. A non-political President is rather unlikely. Dev himself, or Sean T. O'Kelly with Alfie Byrne (!) opposition candidate.

Lord Halifax, British Foreign Secretary, ostensibly in Berlin to visit a hunting exhibition, took an unusual detour to Berchtesgaden (in the Bavarian Alps, where Hitler spent much time) and conferred with the Führer. 'I believe,' wrote Lester, 'that France and England are willing to make colonial concessions.'

In January 1938 the hundredth session of the council was in full swing. Lester wrote:

> France torpedoed sanctions in 1935–36 and Great Britain has since declared she accepts definite commitment only where vital interests are involved – France, Belgium and the Mediterranean. It is little wonder the small states have been asking themselves where they are, between the two blocks of Big Powers, and are anxious to avoid obligations

---

6. Dick Hayes was at one time film censor and author of several books on the Irish in France.

to act when Big Powers (and only then) are interested. The Italian hostility to the League and final departure and the German 'never' have aided in the demoralisation. But it is mainly the vacillation of England, the internal situation in France and, above all the fact that both of these great powers think of the League in terms of purely immediate national interests.

That was the fact, and that was the mood of Geneva at the opening of the year 1938, which was to bring about the Munich concession.

February 1938 brought news of some confusion, to say the least of it, within Germany: the fight between the army and the party resulting in the resignation of about eighteen generals. Very few doubted that the outcome was victory for the Nazi party. This coincided with or resulted in the appointment of von Ribbentrop as Foreign Minister, replacing the old von Neurath, one of the people who had helped Hitler to power. It had generally been believed in Europe that the army headquarters had been a sort of brake on the more violent elements in the National Socialist movement as far as foreign policy was concerned. But it seemed, wrote Lester, 'that this brake has now very largely been removed.' For within a very few days there was a sudden demand from Hitler for Schuschnigg, the Austrian Premier, to appear at Berchtesgaden. It appears that he was not even offered a seat during the interview but was treated like a domestic servant and given his orders. He was told that German military action could now be carried out with much less risk to Germany than the occupation of the Rhineland, and that England and France would not move to help. In the ante-room were waiting three generals, the commander-in-chief and the corps commander from the frontier. Hitler told Schuschnigg that he had learned from Halifax that England was in complete accord with Hitler on the Central European policy. Lester wrote: 'I have reason to believe that was a flat lie.' But what Hitler had learned from Halifax is now on the record: according to AJP Taylor, Lord Halifax said all that Hitler expected to hear.

He praised Nazi Germany as the bulwark of Europe against Bolshevism; he sympathised with the past German grievances and in particular he pointed to certain questions where possible alterations might come about with the passage of time. They were Danzig, Austria and Czechoslovakia. England, according to Halifax, of course was interested to see that any change should come about peacefully and that methods should be avoided which would cause far-reaching disturbance. Halifax's remarks, as interpreted by Hitler, were an invitation to promote German nationalist agitation in Danzig, Czechoslovakia and Austria; an assurance that this agitation would not be opposed from outside.

According to Taylor, Eden told von Ribbentrop something similar, and in France von Piper, on a visit to Paris, was amazed to note that the Prime Minister, Chautemps, and Bonnet, the Finance Minister, considered that a reorientation of French policy in Central Europe was open to discussion.

Austria was occupied on 14 March 1938.

Earlier Hitler had referred to Danzig, including the morsel:

> I may say that since the League of Nations has abandoned its continuous attempts at disturbance in Danzig, and since the advent of the new Commissioner, who is a man of some breadth of view, this most dangerous place for European peace has entirely lost its menace.

Lester wrote: 'I would feel somewhat unhappy in the circumstances, if I had earned praise from Hitler.'

The *Manchester Guardian*, in this reference to Danzig, said that it received only a partial welcome, as the new situation in which the Free City became a matter for Berlin and Warsaw was resented by most people in Poland. The majority of Poles, said the *Guardian*, would prefer the Danzig problem taken to Geneva. This feeling became stronger because in Poland as elsewhere the example of Hitler's method with Austria had caused increased apprehensions.

Spanish Civil War

The Spanish Civil War, which had broken out in July 1936, proved to be one of the main factors in the declining fortunes of the League. In their insistence that no complete break should be made with the Axis powers, Britain and France did their best to prevent the war in Spain from being dealt with by the assembly or council. Yet the Republican government was recognised by the bulk of League members as the legitimate government of the country. Thus it could insist on bringing international aspects of the war on to the floor of the assembly or council. The Republican government of Spain received aid from Russia and France: the rebels overwhelmingly from Germany, Italy and Portugal.

On the outbreak of the Civil War the French government forbade the sending of war material to either side, and by the end of August all European states had joined in a non-intervention agreement – entirely unconnected to the League. The non-intervention committee was set up in London.

The Spanish government felt itself wronged in that it was prevented from buying arms to quell a revolt in its own territory. And it well knew and denounced the fact that countries from whom they expected help were standing by the agreement, while the Axis powers were freely supplying General Franco. The agreement did not forbid the sending of men and volunteers and many poured in from the democratic countries. The German and Italian forces who came to Franco's aid were, in fact, sent there by their governments.

France and Britain proposed that the question of withdrawing foreign combatants from Spain should be immediately discussed between the three powers. Anthony Eden declared that his patience was almost exhausted. 'But the Duce,' wrote Frank Walters, historian of the League, 'had no misgivings about what the British government would do.'

Neville Chamberlain had succeeded Baldwin as Prime Minister, and he was an unshakeable adherent of the policy of co-operation with Italy. One of his first acts as Premier had been to write a personal letter to Mussolini expressing his admiration for the Duce's personality and his desire to collaborate with him in removing all misunderstandings between the two countries. On 20 February 1938, Eden and Cranborne resigned rather than sign a new pact with Italy in which the British government consented to the presence of Fascist forces in Spain until the Civil War was ended. But their resignation had no influence on British policy. Eden had waited too long. He had permitted public opinion to be misled as to the real situation in Spain, and indeed had himself contributed to keeping it in ignorance. In the last phases of the struggle, the Republican government invited the help of the League only in regard to certain specific objects.

There was never any serious possibility of the whole question being laid before the League: the field was left clear for the non-intervention committee in London, and in Spain, for the armed forces of the Axis.

On 22 February 1938 Lester wrote a letter to Eden:

> When I think of the circumstances in which you took up the Foreign Secretaryship after Simon and Hoare had been there long enough to be the causes of international disasters, and that you had been holding on during the most difficult period in Europe probably for the last century ... I sympathise with you in the difficult choice you have made and congratulate you on your courage.

When the London representative of the Secretary-General, HR Cummings, wrote asking for the overview from Geneva, Lester sent him an incisive analysis of the situation in Europe as seen from Geneva, and a virile defence of the League theory and practice, ending with the words 'though the League may be crippled, it cannot be killed'. Neither England nor France was prepared to fulfil the covenant, he wrote, 'but would like to hold the machinery intact to be used exclusively when their National interests required it, thus leaving commitment on the small Powers, without any corresponding insurance for themselves.'

Eden's resignation had the bad aspect of appearing to be yet another success for the Axis:

> '...who have held the Diplomatic initiative almost without challenge for the past three years
>
> A pro-League policy is an idealist factor, but I deplore certain aspects of British and French policy as being neither realist nor idealist; and in any case, the moral factor in certain emergencies is of tremendous military and political importance; and from a political point of view alone, foreign policy based on the League has a hundred per cent more possibility of winning and holding the Commonwealth co-operation, and to a certain measure also that of the USA, than a policy exclusively based on immediate national interests. Shortsightedness is almost criminal in foreign policy, especially for countries who have to face a combination of the 'have-nots', who do not like law and order because they have so much to gain by their absence. One hears again, here and there, the words 'perfidious Albion' but I cannot estimate yet whether the disillusionment in other countries will measure up to anything like that which followed the Hoare–Laval disclosures. The more balanced people, I imagine, have been expecting so much else since then. As for the League, one has to keep in mind that the attacks and campaigns, while ostensibly directed against this institution, and while concerned with breaking down any system which would make for a united front against aggression, are in reality concerned more vitally with the influence, power and possessions of France and England. If the British Empire could be divided amongst the have-nots, they would probably agree quite easily to any kind of a League. Our convictions and outlook here are not incompatible with hard-headed realism, on the contrary. For some time I myself have been convinced that the League had to mark time, principally because I did not expect its chief elements to hold a different view. When there is something to be

done within one's power, I believe in doing it with such judgement and tenacity and courage, as we may possess. The machinery here, as you know, is good; even from a German and Italian point of view. I don't think they are justified in imagining ideological or national prejudices as affecting the impartiality and integrity of the staff, but the machinery is not being used for major political purposes and it seems likely to remain so for, at any rate, some time. On the other hand, the idea which is enshrined in our Institution remains, I am convinced, humanity's only hope, and any other course for the world will bring another catastrophe. We may need a new spirit on the side of the 'haves' – I am sure we do – and, of course we need a new spirit clearly on the other side, but civilisation, especially in Europe, has reached the point where, even at the price of another catastrophe, man must find his way back to a system under which there will be law and, of course justice. One meets pessimists here and there – a considerable sprinkling these days – but in the Headquarters at any rate, I find, as I said, realism, courage and initiative (so far as that is open to an International Civil Service).

So Europe went on until the Munich crisis, with Czechoslovakia dismembered, without a reference to Geneva.

A few weeks after Munich, the head of the British Foreign Office, Sir Alexander Cadogan, was putting down on paper what was virtually a brief for Hitler to expand eastwards. He summed up his thoughts as follows:

1. The League system and collective security, are, if not dead, in a state of suspended animation.

2. Far from ordering the affairs of Europe, we, and the French, are on the defensive.

3. Let us make those defences good.

4. We must try to maintain our influence in Western Europe and the Mediterranean.

5. We must cut our losses in Central and Eastern Europe – let Germany, if she can, find there her *Lebensraum* and establish herself, if she can, as a powerful economic unit.

6. We must do everything possible to foster our trade with other parts of world and with the Empire.[7]

Less than a year later the British Prime Minister was to attempt to block that *Lebensraum* idea for Germany by the pact with Poland, and the League. 'Idealists' had little satisfaction in seeing the ruins of Chamberlain's 'realist policy'.

Lester had noted in his diary on 8 October 1938:

France and Britain have retired behind their Chinese Wall in Europe – the Maginot Line – and abandoned the rest of the continent to Germany. I do not think this is an exaggerated view of what has happened during the past month: even a few weeks ago France still had allies in Europe and an actual and potential strength: to-day she has none. De Valera, as President of the Assembly, on 30 September, had said that Europe had come to the brink of the abyss and had shrunk back appalled by what they saw.

Of the atmosphere just before the crisis Lester wrote:

The Sudetens' claims advanced week by week and we had in Europe a period of such tense emotion and fear under the threat of a world war as people have rarely experienced. Germany concentrated mechanised troops on the Czech frontier. The Czechs had one of the best armies in the world and was probably the best equipped. Nuremberg came and the speech of hysterical violence from Hitler. The French called half a million men to the colours. One night at the dinner for the British Commonwealth of Nations delegates – at which by the way de Valera attended for the first time and drank the toast to His Majesty – it was announced that Chamberlain

---

7. *The Diaries of Sir Alexander Cadogan 1938–1945*, edited by David Dilks, Cassel, 1971, p. 119

would, the following day, fly to Germany to see Hitler. Tremendous enthusiasm.

I sat by Andrews, the South African Delegate, and remarked that I supposed he would sell Czechoslovakia; I, no more than others, doubted the man's sincerity, but I doubted his judgement, his knowledge of Berchtesgaden and the latter agreed to the cession of all Sudetenland where there was more than fifty per cent of Germans etc. He returned home jubilant and obtaining the consent of the French, forced the acquiescence from Czechoslovakia. A meeting had been arranged for a week later and in the meantime the German press and radio increased their demands. The British Prime Minister flew back a week later to Germany; it was no great surprise to those who knew the Nazi method to find that during the week the price had gone up. Fresh demands were made upon Chamberlain and even he – as he later said – 'bitterly reproached the Chancellor'. The armies were mobilised in nearly every country in Europe. In Switzerland we had a blackout; the bridges to all frontiers were mined and the tank traps prepared, and the British fleet was mobilised.

Clinging to a hope of peace by negotiation, Chamberlain asked Mussolini to intervene only a few hours before the German general mobilisation was to take place. It was agreed that Mussolini, Hitler, Chamberlain and Daladier would meet in Munich. The first of October had been fixed for the German advance on Czechoslovakia.

On the night of 29 September the Four Powers came to an agreement. The Czechs withdrew to the line agreed upon; Chamberlain on his return to London waved a paper in the air and announced that he had, like Beaconsfield, come back from Germany 'carrying peace with honour'.

There is something indecent in this. 'Peace for our time,' he said, but that remains to be seen. The peoples of the world have accepted the peace with a great sigh of relief and Chamberlain's reception in London, as

Daladier's in Paris and Mussolini's in Rome, were those for a great hero; here and there a voice of warning was raised. Duff Cooper who was First Lord of the Admiralty resigned; no Minister resigned in Paris.

Winston Churchill, notes Lester, wrote to Paul-Boncour in a private letter, 'Nous avons eu le choix entre la guerre et le déshonneur: nous avons choisi le déshonneur mais, quand même, nous aurons la guerre.' ('We had the choice between war and dishonour. We chose dishonour, but we shall have war anyway.')

Lester wrote:

> What Chamberlain has done is a logical sequence of the policy pursued by Britain and France during the past two years; they paralysed the League of Nations; they gave no help to the weak attacked by the strong; they ran away every time a threat was uttered; now they have given Germany, for nothing but temporary peace, the fruits of a great campaign.

While the Czech crisis was going on, the League of Nations presented an extraordinary picture in Geneva. Arthur Sweetser, a League official, wrote to a friend in America:

> I deeply wish I could give you an adequate picture of this past amazing month in Geneva. We have never had anything in any degree comparable. The Assembly was the most extraordinary in the League's existence. It opened the day of the Nuremberg speech; continued throughout the negotiations, and concluded the day after the Munich Agreement. The scene was extraordinary. War was on the threshold; mobilisation orders were following one on the other, report and rumour flew wild; even the usually stoic Swiss had soldiers mounted on many bridges and plunged Geneva into an ominous black-out at the most critical moment. Several hundred delegates and experts from over fifty countries, plus a couple of hundred journalists from even more, paced anxiously back and forth in the Assembly

lobbies, trying to do their daily work but in reality affixed to the latest rumour, telephone or broadcast. It was almost impossible for them to keep their minds on their normal activities; indeed there was a tragic air of unreality about them which made it remarkable that they accomplished as much as they did. Unexpectedly enough, the Czechs didn't even present their case. They took the view that they were too hurt and wounded and their position too clear to justify explanation. For the first time since Locarno [1925], neither the British nor the French Foreign Minister was present.

As to purely family matters, with war possibly in the offing, Lester said:

Owing to my position, any hasty or panicky action was out of the question. But, under strong pressure, Elsie agreed that if war came, she would start with the children en route for Ireland. …We got the fur coats out of the summer cold storage – bought a new haversack to carry food – and half a dozen blocks of chocolate as iron rations. I changed money to give them adequate French and English currency. Then we waited. I was to stay at my post, of course, unless Geneva was invaded! I had told Elsie I would, while alone, have a 100% better chance of getting through than if I had others to think of, if flight became eventually necessary. She had agreed to go, on the understanding that once the children were safely in Ireland, she would come back; I said 'yes', knowing that such a return would be impossible.

The children must have been discussing the situation pretty thoroughly, because they presented a united front and declared that there would be a stay-in strike if any attempt were made to ship them off. Next day they entered the house, jubilant. Some English children had arrived from London, 'to escape the air raids! Daddy, how could you send us through London at such a time!' – with a triumphant air.

In November 1938 the Danzig question arose again. Lester simply repeated what he had said before, that the High Commissioner served no useful purpose now that Germany and Poland were settling matters over his head. He had, he reminded the Secretary-General in a note, pointed out that the ultimate future of Danzig was settled in the autumn of 1936, that is when the League bowed to Greiser's threats. 'Subsequent events have confirmed it,' he wrote. Nor did he regard the presence of the High Commissioner in Danzig as a serious element in maintaining the status quo, for he did not believe that the transfer to the Reich at this stage would now be a *casus belli.*

In the spring of 1939 Lester was in charge of what they called the 'Axe' Committee – reorganising and reducing the institution and its many activities. The budget had to be reduced on account of defections, although there were still fifty or more state members.

'It had been a hard task and unpleasant, too,' he said.

On 14 March 1939 Hitler occupied Prague. Wrote Lester:

> The arms of 40 divisions, Skoda and its 50,000 workmen, and 25 other armament factories pass into German hands. Ruthenia is occupied by Hungary. The Czechs are to have a régime less than a 'protectorate'.
>
> Lord Halifax says this action is not in accordance with the spirit of Munich. He is bold! But I don't agree with him. Chamberlain says we mustn't be deflected from objects of peace and appeasement. It sounds rather abject, and credulity is 'astronomisch'. Hitler's objective of at least continental domination cannot now be hidden behind unity of 'race' or 'self determination'. It is sickening to see a decent little country wiped off the map. And without a blow. Freedom shrieks again.

On 23 March Memel was joined to the Reich. Lester described it as:

> ... dirty and insignificant as an Irish provincial town, doesn't seem much of a prize. But it brings Germany

another step up the Baltic, and gives her control of the mouth of Poland's second river, the Niemen, as she controls the Vistula at Danzig. Lithuania loses her only port and economically falls into German hands. The port was neglected by the Germans before 1918, used only for wood export and the Lithuanians had done much to develop it. Romania signed a trade treaty with Germany, giving very substantial concessions. Hungary is in German hands 90%. Hungary claims 2,000,000 of a minority in Romania, a move could be initiated without the slightest difficulty and on most plausible grounds.

On 30 March 1939 Lester wrote, 'Almost unnoticed in the midst of other impending events, Madrid has quietly crumbled into Franco's hands after a thirty month siege.'

He continues:

Germany has opened an anti-Polish campaign causing fresh anxiety. Is it no more than an effort to prevent Beck's visit to London next week?

Britain proposed to double her territorial army. Not easy.

Leith-Ross [chief economic advisor to the British government (1932–45) and director general of the Ministry of Economic Warfare (1939–42)] with whom I dined a couple of nights ago, says one of the principal of the non-political difficulties about conscription, is absence of equipment. Still closer military relations between France and England are showing. A couple of days ago Avenol called Walters, Jacklin and myself to discuss our League position in case of emergency. Jacklin will send duplicates of accounts and important papers to a place in Western France – as banks in London and Paris are preparing. It will be chaotic at the best, but some preliminary work will be invaluable. Phelan pushed him, I think with his plans for I.L.O. evacuation. Polish-German relations continue to attract most interest and concern at the moment; after assisting Germany during recent years, attacking and weakening the League; sharing in the destruction of Czechoslovakia; she finds the diplomatic guns of Berlin beginning to swing towards her own frontiers. Her people's spirit and readiness to fight will delay or prevent any aggressive plans towards her.

Then on 1 April 1939:

Last night Chamberlain announced a Franco-British guarantee for Poland!!! To cover the weekend?? Or the period before more definite arrangements made? German demands have been made on Poland, but not yet in ultimatum form.

The circle of British policy is now complete.

CHAPTER 8

Exit the League from Danzig

Lester's successor as High Commissioner, Carl Burckhardt, had, as Lester put it, 'the talents of a novelist'. During his period of office he did everything with a flourish, and Lester enjoyed his flamboyance and acute brain. During Burckhardt's years in Danzig he reported regularly to Lester in Geneva: 'His sense of humour and drama makes him an excellent raconteur,' notes Lester. 'He had, as I expected, and as I did myself, developed a sneaking sympathy for poor Greiser.'

Burckhardt's stories from Danzig are recounted in his book *Meine Danziger Mission* ('My Danzig Mission'). He was disappointed that this book (1959) was not published in English. On the one occasion when I visited him at his home and discussed Danzig, Burckhardt asked why English publishers rejected it. 'Could it be the Masons?' he asked. It is, in fact, a lively book, but Lester, the former reporter, got him down in his diary with an immediacy that Burckhardt hardly matched in writing it up later.

Burckhardt was a professor at the University of Zürich and at the Graduate Institute of International Studies at Geneva, a historian of some reputation. In the words of Arnold Toynbee in the Survey of International Affairs 1936, 'he had given proofs that he had at any rate no special prejudice against National Socialism'. Hans Leonhardt, in *Nazi Conquest of Danzig* points out that he was more than that: he was *persona grata* in Nazi eyes, as evidenced by the fact that 'he had received solemnly in his home Dr Goebbels – bodyguard and all – when the latter played his well-known guest role in the general assembly of the League of Nations in 1933. On this occasion he had taken upon his shoulders to introduce the revolutionary envoys to the international circles in Geneva.' These were, according to a comment in *L'Europe Nouvelle*, 'peu disposés a s'ouvrir aux étranges barbares qui venait d'arriver dans la "capitale des nations".' ('... little disposed to open themselves up to the barbaric foreigners who had just arrived in the "capital of nations".)

Burckhardt had an ignominious exit from the Free City on the outbreak of war on 1 September 1939, in spite of earlier assurances by Weizsäcker, head of the German Foreign Office, that in such a case, all would be carried out according to correct diplomatic procedure. On 21 September 1939 Burckhardt's name had been mentioned at a meeting of the supervisory commission, and Hambro, the president, was scathing about an interview Burckhardt had given in Stockholm on his way home, in which he said that when he saw Hitler on 11 August he had gone to make a supreme effort 'to smooth out the road to a peaceful solution, but it was too late and I didn't succeed ... the Führer had already taken his decision ... a short while before and perhaps I would have had a chance, but I must say only "perhaps".' Hambro remarked, 'with brutal irony,' according to Lester, 'We didn't realise what a master-statesman we had amongst us, whose influence was so great that he might have persuaded Hitler when all else failed.'

On 22 September Burckhardt told 'his fascinating and exciting story' to Lester and Walters.

The battleship *Schleswig-Holstein,* which had been sent on a formal visit to Danzig towards the end of August, had contained, out of sight of everyone, a unit of assault troops. The usual duty calls and parties were arranged and in the course of the evening, when being entertained in the High Commissioner's house, the captain of the battleship remarked that sometimes an officer was compelled to do a thing which he would never dream of doing as an honest private individual.

Burckhardt had thought he was referring to his orders to attack without warning the small garrison of two hundred Polish troops on the Westerplatte at the mouth of the bay.

At eleven o'clock, Burckhardt told Lester and Walters, on the night of 31 August 1939, he was alone in the house (his wife and family had been sent home) and there came a violent ringing at the door. Three Gestapo men appeared. They instructed Burckhardt not to go to bed as the Gauleiter, Forster, would come to see him. Burckhardt replied that he would see the Gauleiter the following morning. The Gestapo cut the phone lines and occupied the ground floor while the High Commissioner went to his room. He was sleeping in the corner room at the back of the house, with big bow windows facing north towards the Baltic, and overlooking the garden. At 4.30am, he said, the glass of the windows fell into the room with the first explosions. The *Schleswig-Holstein* had suddenly opened fire on the Polish post office, and the railway station was also under attack.[8] The Swiss valet came into his room, exclaiming, 'nous sommes perdus, la guerre mondiale va nous tous engloutir.' (We are lost, the world war is going to engulf us all.) Lester here remarks: 'a vignette in the best Burckhardt style'.

The Gauleiter arrived at eight o'clock, armed to the teeth and with two uniformed *aides-de-camp*. Forster, standing in front of Burckhardt, announced:

> You represent the Treaty of Versailles. The Treaty of Versailles no longer exists. In two hours (looking at his watch), the Swastika will be hoisted above this house. You will be escorted to the frontier, or, if you wish to stay, you will stay as a private individual.

Burckhardt said he would go at once. Then, in slightly less official tone, Forster said: 'I hope this will not interfere with our private relations,' and in the best Johnsonian style, Burckhardt replied: 'Sir, I have never had any private relations with you and never wish to have.'

---

8. In fact, the war diary of the *Schleswig-Holstein*, according to a writer in *Die Zeit* of 1 September 1989, Karl-Heinz Janssen, gives 4.47 hours.

With a Gestapo man in every room, he got some clothes packed, and assembled his three compatriots: secretary, typist and valet and at ten o'clock went to the door.

Here came the last revenge of Danzig. The old butler of Lester's day, Borchard, had since retired, but retained some room at the top of the house. He had now reappeared and was fussing about, bullying the other servants as usual. When Burckhardt passed out, accompanied by his two little dogs, he saw, writes Lester, 'the old swine kick the dogs as they passed by'.

Burckhardt got into his own car in the presence of a Gestapo escort, with a small crowd gathered outside to enjoy the spectacle; he drove eastward, soon to leave the escort behind, and so on to Kaunas, the Lithuanian capital and, in a roundabout way, arrived back in Geneva. While he was in Stockholm, on the way back to Geneva, the German counsellor called on him, sent by Weizsäcker to apologise for the unceremonious way in which promises from Weizsäcker and others – that if he were forced to leave Danzig, he would be given decent notice and not treated ignominiously – were ignored. The counsellor also said that Weizsäcker's eldest son had been killed in the Polish fighting and he himself would be resigning as permanent head of the Wilhelmstrasse. He had only stayed there because he still hoped to check the wild men and keep peace.

Lester also found Burckhardt's account of his visit to Hitler on 11 August 1939 vastly interesting. Hitler had asked for Burckhardt and eventually sent his private plane to fetch him. After a quiet tea-table conversation, Hitler had two of his maniacal outbursts. If the Poles went a millimetre further, he said, he would erase them from the face of the earth and the face of history. His eyes were glaring and his face working and his voice rose to a shriek. The second outburst was over an article in the *Figaro* which made some personal reference to him. He told Burckhardt he could not let anybody touch his personal prestige, partly because he had come up from the masses, from the proletariat. Forster had been there throughout the meeting.

Now he was sent away and Hitler and Burckhardt were alone. Hitler said that they had found the Czech plans of war and that they had been the admiration of all his generals; and that they had bought the Polish war plans and they were childish and hopeless. He talked of Germany's need for food-growing space and said his scientists told him they could make German soil produce very heavily by intensive application of chemicals, but that this would lead to the soil becoming sterile. He therefore needed Poland's acres. This, said Burckhardt to Hitler, meant that his thoughts were still running on war, as such ideas were intended to defeat a world blockade. He pointed out to Hitler his tremendous responsibilities and the fate of millions depending on his decisions. Hitler replied, having turned his back on him, 'That decision no longer depends on me.'

Burckhardt had the impression that he was referring to the gang which surrounded him, including von Ribbentrop, Dietrich (one of the 1934 executioners) and others. There is another and simpler deduction to be made. Lester writes: 'I got the impression Burckhardt has a feeling of sympathy with Hitler. He regards him to some extent as he would regard an unbalanced woman, or perhaps, as Stoppani, a senior League official, has it, "the slave of his previous actions".'

Burckhardt said that in his previous interview Hitler, in addressing him, never looked straight at him. This time he did. Hitler said he would like to meet him again privately 'whatever happens'. Forster, as they drove away, remarked, 'You seem to have a tranquillising effect on him.'

The official text of the meeting with Hitler shows how the Chancellor came back more than once to the theme of land for wheat in the east. Perhaps most important was Hitler's suggestion to Burckhardt, that he, Hitler, would like to talk to an Englishman who spoke German, not a diplomat, but, in particular, General Ironside (promoted either by Hitler or Burckhardt to Marshal Ironside).

'Can you say that to the English?' Hitler asked.

The English were not moved.

CHAPTER 9

War

In March [1939], after the Nazi maw had swallowed the remains of Czechoslovakia, British policy changed, and an urgent and a last minute effort was made to construct a Peace Front. Poland was guaranteed, also Greece and Romania, Holland, Belgium and Switzerland, Turkey made an alliance. Tentative approaches were made to Soviet Russia. Very tentative, we thought.

Lester tells of meeting Walters, under-Secretary-General of the League, and William Strang, a senior man in the British Foreign Office over lunch one day. Lester said he thought the situation demanded urgency:

> 'What do you want us to do?' William said with a half smile.
>
> I replied: 'Make an arrangement with Russia at the earliest moment.'
>
> To which Strang replied: 'That's just what Walters has been saying.'
>
> Strang had once been Counsellor and Chargé in Moscow. So it was not unnatural, as Chief of the Central section in the F.O., that he should be sent to Moscow a few weeks later to help the Ambassador. He stayed about six weeks I think. The negotiations dragged on and ended only with the sudden announcement of a German-Russian Non-aggression Pact of a peculiar kind.

This *volte face* precipitated the crisis, already boiling up, and at daybreak on 1 September the Germans invaded Poland. On Sunday 3 September Britain and France declared war on Germany.

In August 1939 Lester had been on holiday in Ireland and returned on Monday 28, leaving his wife and family in Dublin, which 'leaves my mind free from a good deal of personal anxieties'.

He was quite unambivalent about his attitude to the war, as he wrote on 3 September:

> The Nazis must be beaten if there is to be any decency in such life and civilisation as may survive. In the war of twenty years ago, if we did not want England to be beaten [he would be talking here of the Sinn Féin element in Irish life], we were certainly not anxious for her unqualified victory. We were not pro-German, but pro-Irish and the land was in captivity. Now all our national interest lies with Britain and her allies. The freeing of most of Ireland – even if de Valera declares, as he does, that we will be neutral 'as long as possible', puts Britain in a better position than in 1914. No divisions to be kept in Ireland, a friendly government, a better moral position, especially with an eye on America, food supplies and a safe back door.

He saw de Valera's difficulties:

> To be honest, I should like to see the Government declare war, but it is difficult for Dev, especially with the Northern Question unsettled.
>
> After all, it is not so long ago since Britain represented in the eyes of our people, nearly all that Nazi domination is to them; and if they are at last standing up to the Hun it is, making full allowances for the British disgust of Nazi abominations, in their National interest. A failure at this time would have made Britain and France second class powers over-night. Their turn would have come, just as it came, in the end, for the too clever Beck, and in even worse conditions.

Lester now had to make household arrangements for himself. He wasn't too badly off, he said, 'Except for a low stock of Irish cigarettes and a weak cellar. It is now the time to live from day to day, and we are fortunate to have made so much provision.'

Like all of his colleagues and many other people, he was ruing the fact that the great powers had failed in leadership; failed, no doubt, in giving a better deal to Germany early on; failed to take low risks for the League and its conceptions; failed to realise what the Nazi really was: 'But it is not the time for all that.'

He foresaw a long war which might destroy the world's wealth again, involve the death of millions of boys and men and women and children:

> We are all at the moment in a kind of vacuum of thought. Tension has lasted for many years, easing off now and then, before being worked up to white hot intensity. The suspense has at times been intolerable. And when it passed, we knew it would recur in a few months in a worse form. I cannot even write. These two pages are worthy of nothing but the fire.

Early in September he reported that German propaganda swept Geneva with the theory that, for the British and French, this was not a real war, but a phoney war; that the French attack on the Siegfried Line was a pretence; that they and the British were dropping tracts but not bombing the bridges of the Rhine; that when Poland was crushed and Germany offered another *fait accompli*, and offered peace, they would accept it. Lester didn't agree: 'But it is part of the price paid for Munich, that it should receive so much credence. How much would the Poles not give to-day to have the sturdy Czech army at their flank!' (They had taken Czech territory in the carve-up after Munich.)

> And to record that unctuous wretch Komarnicki [Permanent Polish Delegate at Geneva], mouthing Nazi propaganda about the artificial State [Czechoslovakia] and Benes's errors in depending on France, and blatant exultation when their neighbour was torn to pieces, and

loud-mouthed certainty when one mildly inquired when Poland's turn would come. All this is in many people's minds and on some tongues. But Beck and his satellites were not the Polish people. And it all matters little to-day in the face of consequences.

While Lester was unsympathetic with the actions of the Polish government, he had a feeling for the country as a whole:

> Poland's history is so like our own. No Irishman can have other than sympathy and admiration for the Poles. But it must be confessed that post-war Poland developed, especially in recent years, a chauvinism far from attractive. I have already mentioned their disgusting attitude when Czechoslovakia was on the torture rack. They had not been cleverly treated by France, but their claim to play the role of a great power, their exercise of a raw type of lower politics, their stupid support of Germany when the latter was destroying the League and getting ready for the attempt to dominate Europe, the crude boasting of representatives like Komarnicki, lost them much sympathy and friendship. They went along so confidently.

He heard a broadcast by Dominions Secretary Anthony Eden on the night of 11 September. Eden said that after the war a new civilisation must be built with peace, justice and freedom as its foundations. Lester wrote: 'He did not mention the League of Nations, but, by whatever it is called, it will have the same aims.' Lester thought well of Eden:

> Two years before when Eden was chased from the Foreign Office the term 'idealist' was labelled on him as opprobrium. He has been proved, as I wrote to him at the time he would be, to have been the best realist of them all. I am glad he had the entrée into the War Cabinet.

He noted in his diary with satisfaction the *Manchester Guardian* leader for 2 September on Hitler which said:

> Even in his own shameless record of insincerity and

mendacity, there has been nothing to compare with the process by which, within the space of a few short months, Poland was transformed from being a friend to be flattered, into the enemy to be bullied and eaten up as were Austria and Czechoslovakia before her.

The last Polish flag was pulled down on 30 September on the peninsula of Hela, across the bay from Danzig.

Lester notes a privately printed pamphlet by Hermann Rauschning. As he says, no date or printer or publisher, but apparently written after the Russo-German Pact and before the war began. A powerful indictment, writes Lester, and quotes the ending:

> But we turn away from you as happens to every tyrant. We free ourselves from you in order not to share your guilt on the debasing of our children and the defeat of our people. We cut ourselves off from you and want to have nothing in common with that for which you hold to be German and the German future. All that was healthy in the Nation has cut itself off from your ideas. The other part may go down with you. A unique whisper is going through our people to-day. It is still a whisper, but it will become a shriek, and the shriek will become a reality: your time is past. Your time and that of your sworn helpers. For that, may God help us.

Things did not come about as Rauschning had foreseen. It was 1944 before any genuine protest arose in Germany. Lester's diary notes that Rauschning was then a refugee in Paris, 'and might well play a great part in a democratised, post-war Germany'. He did not do so.

Lester worried about the 'colourless – almost scared – look of the Irish press' under censorship. He suggested to Frank Cremins, Irish minister in Bern, to send home a detailed report of the Swiss press – the press of a small neutral country directly under the menace of German force, while Ireland was quite sheltered. 'No doubt,' he writes, 'the German Minister bullies, and our inexperience – not lack of courage or conviction – leads to a false understanding of what neutrality demands.'

The New York World's Fair was going on and League of Nations Day was celebrated on Saturday 21 October. There were various speeches on behalf of the League including one from Lester, by radio: 'The catastrophe [the war] marks a collective failure for mankind; a failure in which all of us have some share and on account of which we must all feel a deep humility.'

He pointed out that not all of the League's work would be brought to a complete halt by the war: its work for public health, for example, could go on; its worldwide service of epidemiological intelligence would be more and more necessary as national services became overburdened by the new emergencies. The League had built up a far-reaching system of study and co-operation on problems of nutrition: these were likely to take on more importance as food supplies diminished and poverty increased. The League's anti-drug work, which represented the most highly developed co-operation yet attained among the nations, would be increasingly essential. Similarly, with traffic in women and children, it faced the dislocations and poverty of war.

There was also some need of the League services in the field of economics and finance:

> Not by any means the least contribution that the League can make at this present moment is of a definitely moral and spiritual nature. It can, in fact, keep alive at least one centre of international collaboration and sanity, where men's efforts are co-operative and where whatever is possible in the way of international collaboration will still find welcome and assistance.
>
> And whether or not the League as such has a distinct role to play at the end of the war, the experience it has acquired during the past twenty years would be essential to those who would reconstruct the peace.

The League, he said:

... represents a groping of mankind for a better way of settling disputes than slaughter and the ruthless use of military force: unless it, or something like it, is given the necessary support, the world will never rise above a state of recurrent war and crises.

In November 1939, Lester writes:

A curious affair in Munich, where Hitler was celebrating the birthday of Nazism. He spoke for only half the usual time and then, with all his chiefs, left. Half an hour later there was a great explosion in the Burgerbräukeller, killing half a dozen and wounding sixty. Berlin says it was the British Secret Service. I was much more inclined to put it to the credit of the underground opposition; but it is being so promptly used to whip up anti-English sentiment, that I begin to doubt. Burckhardt to-day said to me it was the Gestapo, and would be used to prepare opinion for ruthless war – and the reprisals. Avenol thinks in a similar way.

At this time rumours and false information were deliberately fed out in Geneva.

Krauel, German Consul General in Geneva, who has just returned from Berlin, is talking in the following way to Permanent Delegates and others: Germany does not object to a League of Nations, but it must be reformed and become a true instrument of collaboration. She has no intention of attacking either Belgium or Holland, and from his talk, seemed to be fighting only England.

On 30 November 1939 a message came from the Swiss newsagency, quoting Reuters of London, announcing that according to press information from Helsinki, the Russians had invaded Finland. When the Finns appealed to the League, Lester wrote:

We came suddenly out of our political hibernation. Two weeks after the invasion began, the Soviets were ignominiously kicked out of the League and all members recommended to give such help to Finland as they could.

The council met on 14 December 1939 and exercised, for the first and only time in its history, the power granted it under Article 16 to exclude from the League a member which had violated the covenant. This was one of the most extraordinary periods in the history of the League. Neither Germany nor Italy had been officially expelled from the League, yet Russia was, as a result of that meeting. There were serious doubts as to the wisdom of the action, notably in the British Foreign Office. For it seemed that the Finns and the Russians between themselves might have come to a *modus vivendi*.

Negotiations had been going on between Russia and Finland for the ceding or leasing or exchanging of certain parts of territory which the Russians considered essential to their security. It was not out of the blue that the war came.

Lester notes that large public subscriptions were made in various countries, a million Swiss francs in Switzerland for example, also food and supplies and military material from others: 'Public opinion has pulled the Governments faster than they like in some cases – Holland and Sweden for example.'

The Irish government gave nothing, but encouraged the new Irish Red Cross Society to give a thousand pounds.

Writes Lester:

> Except for tiny remnants of fanatical – or bought – communists, world opinion is fiercely anti-Russian. It is even said to be divided in Germany, but what does public opinion in Germany amount to?

Most of Lester's work in November and December was with the 'Axe' committee. Between 1 January 1939 and 1 January 1940 over 50% of the staff had to be cut back – over three hundred people. 'A dreadful business,' he wrote.

Then he got sick early in December and attended the special assembly with a fever. After that he went to Ireland, 'Home and

Beauty', taking four days to get from Geneva to London. This was to be his last trip to Ireland until winter 1944.

When he got to Ireland the country was covered with fog. The family got into the car and headed for Ardagh Lodge, Clifden, their house. They crawled at about fifteen miles an hour with the windscreen open and, after a pause at Galway, stopped at Oughterard. The next day they made Clifden.

> A good week's rest at Ardagh, the weather so so. Christmas morning we walked over the bog to Lough Fada. A skin of ice covered it, but the sun shone and we sat for a couple of hours on a turf bank by the shore. Our return journey to Dublin was done in seven or eight hours and I settled down to three days of hard work in Dublin.

On the return journey through London he called to see Eden in the Dominions Office and spent one and a half hours with him at short notice. This resulted in a memorandum on the future of the League. He noted briefly that in his talk with Eden there was much discussion on Ireland and neutrality: 'No complaints,' he wrote.

On his return to Geneva he was sick for ten days.

German breakthrough

In the spring of 1940 the storm broke over Europe. After Finland, it was to be Denmark, Norway, Luxembourg, Holland, Belgium, France defeated and occupied. Switzerland was under constant threat. In the spring, Avenol the Secretary-General had decided that in certain circumstances, i.e. under orders from the Swiss government, or to save the Swiss government from too much embarrassment under German pressure, the League should move to a quiet town in France. The town chosen was Vichy, which in those days had no connotation other than that of being a spa town. Indeed he went so far as to send the archives to Vichy, only to have Lester bring them back a few days later. When Italy declared war on France and Britain on 10 July 1940, Geneva was almost cut off from the free world. The only route left was through the unoccupied zone of France, and then through Spain to Lisbon, a route which the Axis powers could at any moment bring completely under their control, and in fact did, in the case of a League deputation some time later, led by Lester, which was turned back at the Spanish border. But before that closed in, any League agencies that were to continue in free action must escape from Switzerland.

> Elsie Lester, back in Dublin, had decided to visit her husband and came across about the end of April. They had 'a pleasant reunion', rendered uneasy by pending movements of armies. Lester wrote that they kept advancing the date of her return. He had just got her return visas and she was to go home Sunday or Monday 12 or 13 May. … then on Friday 10th we said we would take the afternoon off and go fishing and picnicking in the Versoix. On reaching the office I learned that Holland and Belgium had been invaded that morning and telephoned Elsie to pack. The question was – was total war coming with bombing of towns? Would travel be possible or would she be separated from the children for perhaps months? I had warned them all that if she was trapped in Geneva, I would make her stay. News came of attacks on French aerodromes including Dijon. I held her back that night. Next day, in great uncertainty, we together decided she would risk an immediate start, she went off gaily and courageously on Saturday night. No news of her on Sunday. I was at the radio every hour. None on Monday until the evening. She was at Dieppe – Boulogne and Calais were, of course, closed. Then another twenty-four hours – London. What a relief. Sean Murphy [Irish ambassador] had helped her through Paris. I'll never forget the anguish of that waiting.

Elsie's train back across France was caught in the swift German advance. It was bombed and machine-gunned from the air. She and the other passengers had to crawl under the train, and the big tragedy, as she told it – making light of it all to the girls on her return – was that she had bought a new pale blue hat and it had got covered in black oil. A woman of great courage and high spirit.

In the meantime, wrote Lester:

> We were in the thick of a Swiss crisis and a Secretariat crisis. I had begged Avenol six weeks earlier to let me examine plans for a possible crisis, on evacuation. Between the two offices we still had 600 officials, many of them women; and their families. Avenol pooh-poohed it: suggested vaguely funk or nervousness, said all was ready, and when I said nothing was ready, he replied we would share the fate of the Swiss people. I welcomed that [wrote Lester ironically], and said it was easy, as it meant we did nothing and that I had no responsibility.

Over a month later, on Tuesday 14 June, Avenol called a meeting of high officials and again ordered prompt plans for evacuation. The tension in Switzerland had been almost agonising, and it increased. General mobilisation. On two nights the attack was expected. German transports were manoeuvring in Lake Constance, just across the border from Switzerland, and barriers had been removed from roads, and large German forces were concentrated. A third of the population of Basle left. The stock exchange was closed, there was a run on the banks. The new methods of attack, fifth column and parachutists, added to the fear. Hydroplanes could land in the harbour and taxi up to the Geneva bridges.

The biggest internal crisis of the League was to build up, with a serious threat that it be handed over to Hitler's New Order Europe.

CHAPTER 10

Wartime Intrigue at the Palais des Nations

There was now some confusion as to the future of the League of Nations. The question of the removal of its technical services to Princeton University in the United States began in earnest when Arthur Sweetser, long-time American member of the information section of the League, on extended leave, landed in the States at the end of May 1940 and began to work out a strategy. The United States was not in the League. Some educational and non-political organisation could be the route. Sweetser, early in June, consulted with representatives of Princeton University, the Institute for Advanced Study and the Rockefeller Institute for Medical Research. He pointed out that if permission were given, the League agencies would involve no expense: they would pay their way. The three institutions agreed, the plan was submitted to the Secretary of State, Hull, who said his government would raise no objections, but made it clear that the invitation was to be on the initiative of the above three institutions, and that the US government was not in any way associated.

The invitation was cabled to Avenol, the Secretary-General of the League.

Avenol himself was still in a state of some confusion, but basically seemed against any idea of transferring any part of the League across the Atlantic. Moreover he was going through one of his periods of expressed anti-Anglo-Saxon sentiment; the

United States being included in that designation. On 25 June 1940, writes Lester:

> J. Avenol called me and virtually charged me with conspiring with Sweetser to produce the Princeton affair. Very vigorous reaction on my part. Subsequent conversation calmed down to reasonable level. I again insisted on my view of the situation: I have for months urged the removal of technical sections, insisting that H.Q. must stay here to face physical dangers or discomforts of the expected invasion. The position was now changed. The physical danger had passed. Now it seemed to him that not only should the technical sections move, but also the Headquarters. There would be less and less possibility to live, independence would disappear; little enough work elsewhere, but none could be done here; ... the S.G. should move also; there were Latin cities abroad where a French S.G. would not be uncomfortable. J then told me that he had finally decided to remain S.G. (after very many threats to resign) and added that he did not forget that he had been appointed Secretary-General by fifty States 'including Germany and Italy'.

Lester ended his conversation with Avenol on what he called a 'somewhat sentimental appeal', relying on their years of work together, and that it was his wish that in whatever way he (Avenol) finished, it should be honourably and with a clean sheet.

Avenol gave Lester a message for the British staff that he would try to get them out of Geneva with every possible facility. On the same day Avenol sent out a note that an effort should be made to find out who wished to resign in the straitened circumstances of the League. The circular was not what had been agreed with the main directors. It ended with what was virtually an order to all members of the secretariat to sign a form of resignation; not only was it virtually an order, but it was made known that the conditions of resignation laid down by the assembly would probably not be applicable to anyone who did not take advantage of his request. There had been no consultation on most of these conditions and propositions and certainly no agreement, Lester noted.

Next morning, 26 June, Avenol saw Jacklin, the treasurer, apologised to him for harsh words recently exchanged and said he had determined to finish 'with a clean sheet', to which Lester adds an exclamation mark.

The see-saw went on. When Thanassis Aghnides, Greek under-Secretary-General, saw Avenol later, there was another violent outburst against Great Britain: she would now expiate her crimes; Hitler and Mussolini were great men; Hitler was not necessarily opposed to a League and admired 'our Saar work' etc. Aghnides said surely Avenol would not send away every British member of staff. 'Ah,' said Avenol, 'I won't have to send them away, they will have gone .... Run like rabbits.'

Loveday, an Englishman who was head of the Economic, Financial and Transit Department of the League, got a message from Avenol offering him a six-month mission in America alone, with full pay. Before receiving a reply, Avenol boasted a number of times that Loveday was going. Loveday wouldn't have anything of it. 'A gunk,' writes Lester, that being a good North of Ireland term, meaning, according to a local book on Ulster dialect, 'a shock or a mortifying and ludicrous disappointment'.

Avenol was now busy playing court favourites. He began a campaign of belittling Lester, and holding out to Aghnides 'vague but tempting suggestions'. Lester had for various reasons been counting his tenure of office from month to month and later week to week, but at this juncture, he daily expected an indication as to his future: 'I would not be used. Nevertheless, despite personal interests and inclination, did not sign the requested resignation.'

On 3 July Jacklin, the treasurer, when told that he could go when he wanted, replied that he would go when he wished – when his work was done. On this day, too, Lester got first word of the expected attempt to approach Germany. Avenol asked Aghnides if he could be in touch with Dr Krauel, the German consul. Aghnides refused – 'No result,' wrote Lester. Next was

Marius Viple, a Frenchman who was the head of information in the International Labour Office. Avenol saw him on 5 July in a meeting that lasted well over an hour. He pictured to Viple a new France, which was to be given a new soul to work in collaboration with Germany and Italy and keep the British out of Europe.

He asked Viple would he go and see Laval, to whom he was related. Viple said he would not for a moment consider any such proposal; he said that Avenol's anti-English attitude seemed strange coming from him; that nobody would listen to this in France, in any case, as he had long been known as 'la domestique des Anglais' (the maid of the English); that the Vichy government would not last, except with German military support; and that anybody who had anything to do with French affairs would be well advised to keep out of France for a considerable time. Finally, quite brusquely, that Avenol should not soil the honour both of France and himself in view of his position.

Apparently Avenol had been discussing for some time with various individuals, both in and outside of the secretariat, the possibility of forming a *directoire*. The idea seemed to be that this committee, consisting of a few outsiders and a few insiders, including Avenol of course, would be responsible with him for the conduct of affairs – virtually a hand-picked substitute for the council, assembly and supervisory committee. 'I know,' wrote Lester, 'that he approached Burckhardt, Swiss, and Bourquin a Belgian.'

When a directors' meeting was called on 6 July to consider staff reductions, the lists were discussed up and down. Yet the meeting on the whole was reasonable in tone. Everyone had expected fireworks but nothing much happened. On reflecting afterwards, however, writes Lester: 'I saw the list was almost exclusively European [Continental], or near European and sent him a note urging that the international character of staff be maintained.' This was on 8 July.

Avenol sent for Lester on getting his note about the international character of the staff, and argued that it was useless to look for any future outside Europe. He didn't mention the British, but said that Germany would militarily dominate Europe; he was not sure if Hitler wanted a League but fairly sure that Mussolini would, to form a certain balance.

> I said that the balance was rather an illusion and that in any case it was not the duty of the Secretariat to anticipate decisions of that character. A trust had been reposed in us, and if great changes were to come about, they should come about without our act of intervention in that direction.

Avenol spoke of the demoralisation among officials who would not have work to do and Lester replied that there was another moral issue at stake. Avenol said he was not sure if France would remain in the League, and what then would be the situation? He said further that he had no intention of preparing a budget for the next year. At this point Lester, in his diary, let off some steam on the subject of Joseph Avenol. Headed in capital letters 'ONLY EMOTIONAL RELEASE?' the note reads:

> He was plotting for the enemies of his country before an offer to lay down arms was accepted; he had plans to please them before the blood of his massacred countrymen was cold; he spoke with complacency of a new State, when the glory of the old was being mangled under the tanks of the invader; he conspired to betray the trust placed in him and to corrupt the honour of his associates in a debased self-interest. A pompous, self-opinionated creature when relieved of fears of his person and his belongings.

Avenol continued in July to enquire if anyone was in touch with Krauel, and Lester writes on 9 July:

> ... this week he is sending a mission to try to get in touch with Laval. The present plan is to use the League machinery for a new European League. Assumes early defeat of Britain and expulsion from European affairs.

United States gets a share of his splenetic hatred of Britain.
Retaining virtually no non-European staff. This policy may
be affected by the reception his agent gets at Vichy. Should
it not be favourable (he will probably propose as a
beginning, that the Secretariat should work for stricken
France), I believe he will again rapidly reduce the staff and
liquidate, probably remaining in office himself. One thing
he will not do, that is to remain loyal to the international
trust placed in his hands.

Avenol called a meeting on 15 July, to discuss

> ... the great difficulties the Swiss Government had in
> having the League here. He suggested that they might well
> be under pressure from the Germans on the subject and
> that we should help, first by going into the library (and
> thus looking more insignificant); secondly a number of
> officials, including the high direction, who had nothing to
> do directly with the practical technical work, should be
> sent on leave.

This of course would include Lester. Avenol himself proposed
to appoint one person to act for him, and to retire to the official
residence, La Pelouse. He would not resign, as that would, he
inferred, finish the secretariat. There was no body in existence at
the moment which could authorise his retiring, and he
mentioned as an example that the power-of-attorney given to
the treasurer would lapse, and the 'banks could refuse to hand
over our money'.

The Swiss de Haller said that there had been no *démarche* of
any kind from the Swiss government, but left it to be inferred
that the statement of the Secretary-General would be in
accordance with their wishes. At the meeting it became known
there were only sixty-five international officials and some thirty-
five Swiss out of the six hundred of twelve months before.

The government in Vichy seemed to be in more than one
mind also. In the end it appeared that it was not going to leave
the League, but that in view of its political implications, they

could not continue to have a French head of the secretariat. One suggestion made in Geneva was that the decision to hold on to the League might be, in a very minor way, a sign of less submission to Germany on the part of the Vichy government. If that suggestion were true, one had to remember that the League was a slender thread, still representing some link between Europe and the outside world, 'and its maintenance here,' wrote Lester,

> ... might begin to have a little promise of contacts other than that of a Continent united by conquest and bound into a subservient economic unit. ... Personally, I had almost given up thinking of possible political implications, being concerned more with what I called a reasonably clean finish. We shall see.

Avenol announced his latest move to Aghnides on 17 July: Aghnides was to be put in charge of the remnants of the secretariat transferred to the library. Wrote Lester:

> I and Skylstad [a Norwegian who was head of the League's minorities committee] were to be given paid holidays, unlimited. Aghnides was to have only certain powers delegated to him – not acting S.G. Avenol would hold other powers, while pretending to be in semi-retirement. Less power for the delegate than for the Under-Secretary-General. A mandate that could be revoked at a month's notice. No financial control.

Avenol had pleaded with Aghnides for an hour: 'Here I am, giving you my confidence and trust, and no one will help me.' He became rather desperate as Aghnides resisted and finally offered to let him keep Skylstad if he would take the job.

Aghnides said the proper method would be to leave the deputy Secretary-General, i.e. Lester, in his job. Avenol wouldn't hear of it. While he would say nothing against Lester personally, he did point out that following the proposed exclusion of Great Britain from Europe, Ireland too would be banned. Writes Lester, 'and I suppose I have a stubborn core; and I did appeal to his personal honour a month ago!'

Avenol also included the Americans in his exclusion from Europe, as part of 'the Anglo-Saxon world', and Great Britain must also be put out of the Mediterranean. It was his own idea, this new Europe – he had mooted it at an economic conference a few years ago, and it had been killed by the British and Americans. Now the Germans had taken it up. That was the reason why he insisted that the economic and financial services must not be allowed to go to America.

Aghnides begged Avenol to accept his own resignation, vainly. Like a bird in a trap – or nearly. 'I told Aghnides,' writes Lester:

> ... he must decide for himself. But I would help him if he reached a clear decision. He replied 'Avenol is a crook'!!!
>
> Avenol tried by trick [the circular] to get my resignation in his hands. Failed. Now holds out like a juicy carrot before a donkey's nose unlimited holiday with full pay and a chance to get to Ireland before it is too late. What a temptation! And how easy to judge others by oneself. I must, naturally, hang on. I am, I think, the core of the resistance.

The game went on. Lester sent a note to the Secretary-General 'to relieve pressure on Aghnides, by request,' he wrote:

> I have been reflecting on your suggestion that a number of officials should, in order to meet the expressed needs of the Swiss authorities, proceed on indefinite paid leave. One minor element may be my position as deputy Secretary-General. Your plan would, in my case, be extremely agreeable to me and it is a great temptation. But I feel I still must remain at my post of duty. I wish therefore to assure you that you may count on my full determination not to desert my post as long as I feel convinced there is a duty to be done.

Lester might well have added that this no doubt came as a

'gunk' to Avenol, who then announced to Jacklin that if the plan were not voluntarily accepted he would put it into operation by orders.

> So I assumed the crisis was approaching. Confirmation was brought back from Vichy that France would remain in the League, but they did not want a French Head of the Secretariat. ... will the bumptious bubble be burst (his morale is not really great); or (more likely) will he try – even from spite – to put his plan into force before he goes? I am assuming he would have a go despite all his hi-falutin' and legal arguments of four days ago; according to that theory of his, if he goes, no one will have the authority to give him his pension money!!! Still he continues to avoid consulting me. Information of impending crises sent to Eden.

Another turn in the plot came: a plan for getting rid of 'embarrassing creatures', as Lester designated himself and some companions. This was a suggestion which came indirectly, that the Secretary-General was weakening on the question of the Princeton offer, and proposed to send Lester, Loveday, and Skylstad on a prolonged mission to the United States to negotiate the matter. A new situation was now developing, however. As Lester wrote: 'We may expect in some ways a complete reversal of policy.'

On 25 July Avenol sent a long telegram to the members of the League, in view of the fact that the council and assembly were unable to hold a meeting. He briefly ran through his career since the year 1932, when the council and assembly unanimously elected him Secretary-General. He wrote of his devotion to duty; he wrote of failures and comparative successes of the League and of his part in them. He wrote of the painful duty of reducing step-by-step the secretariat to a 'level suitable to its financial resources' and, as it had been impossible for a majority of its members to meet, he pointed out that he had not had the benefit of the support of the supervisory commission which would have been the more valuable to him as difficulties increased.

The commission was to be summoned to meet in August.

Avenol said he had felt deeply the departure of loyal technical fellow workers and that he had tried to maintain, notably in the technical section, an experienced staff to keep alive the tradition of competence and devotion of the secretariat, but that 'since the assembly, the council and committees cannot meet at present, the constitutional powers of the Secretary-General are in fact in suspense.'

> Therefore while expressing my deep gratitude to all Members of the League of Nations who have been good enough to give me the support of their good will and confidence, I ask them to relieve me of the task which they have entrusted me. I propose to notify the date on which my resignation could take effect after the coming meeting of the Supervisory Commission.

He ends by saying that he is considering appropriate measures to ensure that the administration and the work of the secretariat shall continue. According to Lester, Avenol was said to be extremely indignant that Geneva was full of reports that he was

> ... preparing to sell the League; that he had sent Burckhardt to Berlin and Stoppani to Rome. I remarked that I have not heard the Burckhardt report, but how could Avenol be much surprised in view of his sudden change of opinion, so widely expressed, and have made many pro-German and pro-Italian declarations and such violently anti-British ones.

Charron of the secretariat told Lester very confidentially that the telegram of resignation sent by Avenol had been much improved by the elimination of bitter reproaches and personal invective on his, Charron's, suggestion. Lester notes dryly that the final report, which Avenol had retired to La Pelouse to write, 'leaving me in charge in the interim, promises to be an interesting document. One hopes it will also be a useful one.

Avenol, I heard, has given way on the question of my taking charge when he goes.'

Avenol sought to lay down claims to the continuation of his services as chairman of a special trustee committee for League finances. For this he would take a nominal 24,000 francs a year (in addition to his pension), have the right to live in La Pelouse with all the facilities of upkeep and, of course, have all his diplomatic immunities. Lester writes:

> I am definitely against this arrangement. If one could reasonably depend upon him, it would be pleasant enough to be able to give him all these comforts together with the authority he would hold over League finances, but I am afraid. ... Avenol continued to preach the doctrine of Europe under German control. To Vejarano [a Spaniard who was in charge of the International Intellectual Co-operation section of the League] he said on 24 July that the world was now divided into four divisions: Europe (under German control), Russia, Japan and America. For Europe one must not any longer think about frontiers; that countries (presumably France) must devote themselves to their language, tradition and culture; that 'a clean sweep must be made in the Secretariat'; new men were needed, that the League of Nations would be set up in Europe under German auspices; that Germany and Italy would dictate the peace at Geneva; he was going because he did not wish to be here to receive the orders from Germany and Italy.

There is a cryptic note in Lester's journal for 2 August 1940: 'J.A. at farewell luncheon in Bern. Poison laid here.'

But Avenol still had a few shots in his locker. It appears that a vital point in his future plans was the control of the capital funds of the League and the proposed finances committee was to meet that idea. But the funds were, to a vast percentage, in America and England. Avenol gave orders for them to be brought to Switzerland. Jacklin said that only over his dead body would this be done. Within half an hour, according to Lester:

... Jacklin had taken certain measures to limit the possibilities of mischief [e.g. redivision of the money into certain earmarked funds]; but there is still a substantial balance; Avenol demands a decision by tomorrow. He won't get an affirmative decision. I believe that, although the League power resides in his hands, he can still be beaten. Jacklin, once he is convinced, will be a good tiger hunter, or rather rattler-hunting companion.

The Bolivian Costa du Rels, president of the council, arrived in Geneva, sent with specific instructions from his government, and said that several other Latin-American governments had communicated with his government, too, reminding him of his duties as president of the council. On the way, he stayed at Vichy and met Baudouin, the French Foreign Minister, who was very clear that they did not want one of their nationals as Secretary-General of the League and that Avenol should go. Further, he should go soon and if he did not they would bring pressure on him to do so. Costa du Rels also brought the news that the French government thought that Lester was the man to succeed. He was going on to Bern, where he should put the same case to the British minister. In the midst of all this, Lester wrote in his diary:

> Elsie's support means all to me. I came across the following from R.L.S. [Robert Louis Stevenson]: 'If we find but one to whom we can speak out of our heart freely, with whom we can walk in love and simplicity without dissimulation, we have no ground of quarrel with the world or God.
>
> To my wife, S.L.'
>
> I have her always in my mind and heart. It's been so hard to be separated. She, too, will feel it just as hard, I know. I couldn't face all this, and the future, if I did not have her beside me in spirit. It's hard. And will be worse.
>
> And my other girls. I feel pangs when I look forward to the dead months to come.

Exit Avenol

Assuming that Avenol was going at the end of August, as he had said he would, the next business was a meeting of the supervisory commission, which was going to be difficult. It was hard to get all the members together in wartime conditions. There were many decisions to be taken about finance and general structures. Avenol threatened to complicate matters in deciding suddenly that he would come back to Geneva for the last three days of his term, from 28 to 31 August. Lester described this period as 'a touch of hell' and was constantly on his guard against 'the wiliness of an old dog fox'.

All states contacted by Avenol agreed to accept his resignation. As Lester wrote to Hambro: 'At any rate the internal crisis which he had maintained from day to day for two months is now, I think, approaching the end.'

When Avenol went to Vichy, he was received by Marshal Pétain. He twice endeavoured to see Laval, but Laval would not agree. Avenol was finally seen off by Costa du Rels on 31 August, a meeting which lasted an hour. He left the building, having said goodbye to only a few people and still having refused to see Lester, 'even on written request'.

Costa du Rels, who was Bolivian ambassador at Paris as well as president of the council, wanted to do the thing properly and arranged to pay a formal visit to Lester on the day he took up his duties as acting Secretary-General. He told Lester that Avenol would be present and that they should have a number of principal officials in the room. Said Lester: 'Although I was afraid Avenol might say something which would finally provoke me, I agreed.'

The function was arranged for 5pm on Monday 2 September 1940. Without any notification, and although it was arranged to suit him, Avenol did not turn up. 'His empty chair,' writes Lester, 'was a reproach to his manners, but no one seemed to be particularly hurt, except Jacklin, who regarded it as a "personal offence". The President of the Council was also naturally

continued on page 209

Summer 1937 in Carna, Connemara,
Sean with Dorothy Mary, his eldest
daughter.

Lunch at Annecy, 1938. From left to right:
Fred Boland (later Secretary of the
Department of External Affairs),
Sean Lester, unidentified and Eamon
de Valera.

Sean Lester in his Dublin home, Fairfield House, Highfield Road, Rathgar, December 1944, on his first return to Ireland since Christmas 1939.

Sean, Ann and Elsie Lester at Mühlen. Lester, as so often, with rod in hand, 1946.

Lester, relaxed, in September 1946, feeding his goldfish outside his official residence, La Pelouse, Geneva.

Sean Lester delivers his lecture to the Dublin International Society in the Mansion House, November 1948. Seated beside him are George Gavan Duffy and Sean McBride.

Ballanagh House, Avoca, County
Wicklow, where Sean and Elsie lived
from 1946 to 1953, after which they
moved to Recess, Connemara, where
the fishing was better.

Sean and Elsie Lester (right) with
their daughter Ann and her
husband Christophe Gorski at a
restaurant in Rome, 1958.

Ann and Patricia Lester skiing,
January 1936.

Aristide Briand, many
times French Prime
Minister in the twenties
and thirties,
photographed by Ernst
von Salamon.

Residence of the High
Commissioner to Danzig,
formerly a German army
headquarters.

Alger Hiss, one of the delegates at Yalta and secretary-general of the San Francisco conference, who was later indicted and jailed for espionage on behalf of the Soviet Union, but always protested his innocence.

CJ Hambro, president of the Norwegian parliament, who in 1929 became head of the supervisory commission of the League of Nations, which steered and sustained the League throughout the war. Frank Walters, the historian of the League, wrote of Hambro that he was 'most outspoken and persistent'. He was certainly a great support to Lester in his lonely vigil in Geneva during the war.

annoyed.' That was almost the end of Avenol, and from then on, Lester took over as acting Secretary-General

Incident at the Spanish border

For legal and financial reasons, it was urgent that the League have a meeting of its supervisory commission. 'Otherwise it might almost cease to exist,' Lester thought.

Lisbon was the chosen place. On 15 September Hambro, who was on a lecture tour in America, suddenly decided he could be in Lisbon on 28 September.

Spain and Portugal were neutral. Spain was quite obviously neutral on the side of the Axis. Portugal was nervous about having a committee of the League on its territory. After hesitations, diplomatic visas from the Portuguese came through for all, including two typists, one for French, one for English. Spain made difficulties. Lester, with a diplomatic passport, was denied a diplomatic visa. The party set off in a small bus on Saturday 21 September 1940, accompanied by Guerrero, president of the International Court of Justice.

They got through the Franco-Swiss border with difficulty and passed through a land of vineyards and vast parks of abandoned army vehicles. The frontier with Spain at Le Perthus gave no trouble on the French side. Guerrero, a Latin-American Spaniard, and Lester went forward first to the customs. The official turned up his book of instructions, and found an order prohibiting the passage of League officials or anybody connected with the League. (The party to Princeton and the ILO had got through at the last moment.) The new order against the League was dated 13 August. The official agreed to refer the matter to the local governor. The governor could not be found. Next day, Monday, the governor was found and his confirmation of the barring order arrived. Guerrero protested and urged reference to Madrid.

On Tuesday the reply came. The same. Meanwhile, Lester had urged that Guerrero should go on alone, carrying a few vital papers for the meeting. Guerrero agreed reluctantly and on

Tuesday morning applied for his own entry. He was then refused, although carrying a diplomatic visa.

They had waited until a joint request from Guerrero and Lester had been pushed to the ultimate point and final refusal came from Madrid through the governor. 'Kicked our heels like a batch of refugees,' wrote Lester. They were determined to exercise patience and push the protest to the limit.

Said Guerrero to the Spanish officials, 'You people have made a revolution to establish order in your country, and it seems to me you have worse disorder than you ever had.' The district commissioner and the frontier officers volubly protested, saying that order inside the country was magnificent. 'Ah,' says the president of the court, 'order begins at the frontier.'

Lester noted that one of the officials, recognising his nationality, remarked that Ireland was a friend of Spain and had 'sent volunteers to fight for us'. Lester thought to himself, 'O'Duffy's most deplorable Irish Brigade.'

If it were so that the two countries were friends, he said, that was no way to treat an Irishman wanting to pass through their country. How would it be if Ireland treated a Spanish diplomat similarly?

The officials became very apologetic and said that the order came the day after the ILO and League party had passed through about a month before, and was probably due to 'pressure' – meaning Italy or Germany or both. But if the League party did not get through, some important papers did. Lester writes:

> As we were walking back from the frontier when the final refusal to let anyone through was received, we noticed three diplomatic cars before the French Customs Office and recognised the Norwegian Legation en route for Lisbon after being kicked out of Vichy at the German request. With them was Berg, Counsellor of the Legation and formerly a League official. One of our immediate problems was to get a few quite inoffensive but vitally important documents through for the meeting. I asked

Berg if he would put something in his pocket for us and he agreed; so we walked back into the hotel and he was given our draft report. I congratulated myself on a bit of quick and useful thinking.

When Lester's party got back to Geneva, they heard there was jubilation at Avenol's residence (he was still in the Secretary-General's official house, La Pelouse) at Lester's being turned back at the border. With irony Lester writes, 'as indeed was only right and proper'.

En route to the border, two letters which Avenol had asked Jacklin to take to the meeting were shown to Lester. One was to Hambro, chairman of the commission. It was, as Lester wrote in his diary, cleverly restrained and dignified in tone, but complained that some useful reports he intended to prepare could not be carried out because Lester refused to allow him to have a special allowance of 60 francs per day and the services of two secretaries beyond the end of September.

The other letter was to Sir Cecil Kisch, who was travelling from London to the supervisory commission meeting. It was hand-written, as if Avenol did not want his secretary to read it. In it he expressed his heartfelt and profound admiration for the gallant fight the British were putting up; they were fighting not only for themselves, but for 'all of us in the world'.

It reflected Avenol's reaction to the continued British defence, but, as he disclosed to Jacklin, he hoped to be made the go-between for the French and British governments. 'He certainly is an incredible creature,' noted Lester. He wrote to Alexander Loveday, in charge of the League section at Princeton University at this time:

> Will you be astonished to hear that our amiable friend has suddenly become anglophile? I myself find it completely nauseating, but I am not surprised: the time-table he had established went wrong, for one thing; secondly, the background in his own country has been changing rapidly; thirdly he may still be thinking of a visit to God's own Republic; fourthly, he has the hope of receiving certain

211

favours from the meeting; fifthly, he thinks he has again reason to attack me because I refuse to continue from the end of this month, the payment of a special allowance apart from a three months gratuity, and suggested that he might be able to do with less than the two secretaries attached to him while I was doing his work and mine with one! However, all this is very comic and only provides the lighter side to a somewhat preoccupied man, but I am too busy to bother my head about the rascal.

The meeting of the supervisory commission was eventually held in spite of Hambro's last-minute failure to appear. Scrambled, with many phone calls, and finally a meeting of sufficient legality.

After the farce at the Spanish border, the authorities in Madrid came up with the classic non-explanation. The Ministry for Foreign Affairs claimed not to know about the order of the Department of the Interior forbidding League officials etc. to pass through.

Then they said they had sent a telegram informing the police of the League party's expected arrival, and emphasising the standing of the president of the International Court, Guerrero. Lester later heard that Guerrero had been informed that if he wanted at a later date to go through Spain, Foreign Affairs would send a secretary to the frontier to help. Costa du Rels, who had been able to get through on his own, came back with the same bland non-answers, having called at the Department of Foreign Affairs.

Lester already knew, of course, that he was *persona non grata* with Germany on account of Danzig. On 2 October he noted:

A telegram came through the other day from Lord Halifax expressing his sympathy with me on my unpleasant experience at the Spanish frontier. I was inclined to pass this without a thought, as an ordinary little diplomatic gesture, but on reflecting that it came from the middle of bombed London, I confess I was somewhat touched. They have their qualities, these people.

Back in Geneva Lester was to sit out four years until November 1944, when the Allied advance allowed him to get to London and then to Ireland for Christmas 1944. In 1942 his middle daughter Ann came out to join him for the duration, a great joy and comfort. But separation from his wife and other family, from 1940 to December 1944, was a penance such as, he would acknowledge, others all over the world were also to suffer, and in situations of more danger and hardship and deprivation. In all his misery, he never forgot his sense of service. This was service not only to the League of Nations but, as he saw it, to the civilised world at large. Fundamentally, he was an Irishman at the heart of Europe, as many had been before him. And while others had been in enforced exile from their own country, he was a volunteer.

Lester did not forget his Irish friends and they did not forget him. His diary entry for 28 October 1939 carries this letter from Eoin MacNeill, professor at the National University of Ireland and his old head in the Volunteer movement, who wrote:

> The manuscript copy of Adamnan's 'Vitae Columbae' written by Dorbene, Abbot of Iona, in or about the year 717, is the oldest known manuscript written by an Irishman that is now in existence. It is now in the Stadtbibliothek of Schaffhausen (Msc Generalia!) I wish to know if a photographic copy of the manuscript, preferably in the negative, can be obtained through the good offices of the Swiss governmental authorities.

Lester notes only: 'An interesting request from Eoin MacNeill,' but doesn't tell what happened.

Other friends with whom he kept in touch included his old colleague of the separatist press PS O'Hegarty, whom he had met at various times before the war; General MJ Costello, who had been army director of intelligence (later G2) when Lester was director of publicity in the Department of External Affairs; and Ron Mortished in the International Labour Organisation, whom he had known in Dublin. Professor Alfred O'Rahilly was a frequent visitor to Geneva for conferences, and the Blythe family had stayed with the Lesters in Danzig. At home in Dublin during the war, Elsie Lester was able to resume friendship with Desmond and Mabel FitzGerald and the McGilligans, the O'Hegartys, the MacNeills and Mulcahys and many other old friends.

No one who knew Lester would describe him as starry-eyed or sentimental. But Frank Cremins, who succeeded him as Irish permanent delegate to the League at Geneva and later was minister at Bern, was positively pessimistic about the League. At Christmas 1941 Lester spent two days with him in Bern.

One evening, Lester notes in his diary, 'the bold Frank informed me that the League was "all cod" and he had thought so since 1932.' To which Lester only adds 'Well, well.'

America?

In January 1942 Aghnides went over ground which all concerned with the League had pondered on for a long time. In a memo called 'Our prospects in certain eventualities', he noted that, now the US was in the war, it was possible that Germany might close up more borders in Europe; or that Switzerland could be invaded; or that Switzerland could be compelled by Germany to throw out the League; or even that the League might be closed down by Germany.

There was a case for the Secretary-General to go to America and perhaps later to London, leaving his deputy in charge. The Secretary-General's presence, it could be argued, was necessary in America in that he could be with his troops, so to speak, and from there the voice of the League of Nations would be clearly heard, not only in the free world. It would add to the public awareness of such work as the League was able to carry on, and give heart to the free world and also to the occupied countries.

There were other points on which Aghnides did not touch. Many of the occupied countries were still members of the League, nominally at least, though they did not pay their dues. For them the continued presence of the League on their continent may have meant something, as indeed Eden stated later to Lester.

Wartime put enormous strain on communications. Sometimes letters took months to cross the Atlantic, or even to come from Britain or Ireland to Switzerland. Aghnides worried that any worsening of the situation, meaning further moves by the Germans, could result in 'our inglorious death'.

Roger Makins, of the British Foreign Office, wrote on 2 January 1942 urging Lester to think of the amount of work that would be necessary before the end of the war and the beginning of the reconstruction period.

> We have to remember that, post-war, international discussions will be carried on by people who have either no knowledge of, or have half forgotten, what was done between 1918 and 1939. They will consider this work was a failure and will not realise in how many respects it was successful.

He was urging continuity of effort and continuance of all valuable technical work that was going on in Geneva.

Anthony Eden wrote to Lester on 28 May 1942, perhaps prompted by Aghnides, who had gone to London to join the Greek government in exile.

> I have of course been well aware that the situation of the Secretary-General in the centre of a German-controlled Europe is far from an enviable one, and I am all the more grateful to you for what you are doing. In this I feel that I can speak for all those Governments which are fighting to defend the ideals for which the League stands. The fact that you are still keeping the flag flying at Geneva has, quite apart from the technical work which the Secretariat can still usefully do, a moral and political significance which could perhaps only be accurately measured if you were ever obliged to haul it down. It is an outward sign of the hollowness and transience of the German 'New Order' and I therefore hope that you will find conditions not too

intolerable to enable you to carry on your rather thankless task for as long as you can. There are increasing signs that the tide is at last on the turn.

Meanwhile, meetings of the supervisory commission went on in Montreal in August 1942 and in London. Sir Cecil Kisch, a member of the supervisory commission of the League, wrote on 10 June sympathising. It was not an easy thing to keep the League in being during this period of crises:

> ... and what you are doing by remaining in Geneva and by directing the operations outside, is an essential factor in the matter and must make, in the end, a powerful contribution to the eventual revival of international co-operation, in whatever form this may come about.

On 20 May, Makins strongly urged Lester not to attempt to attend any supervisory commission meeting. It was not worth the trouble, he said, of coming out to be present, because he might not get back to Geneva. And that was of importance, of supreme importance, apparently.

> We are deeply concerned by the two problems of who is going to act for you while you are away, and whether you will be able to return. To take the second problem only, there is nothing that would suit the enemies of the League better than to see the collapse of the organisation at Geneva. It may therefore be taken as almost axiomatic, that whatever assurances you receive, you would in practice be prevented from returning to Switzerland. By the same token I am pretty sure that you would have absolutely no difficulty in getting out ... I will not say more about a matter which touches you very nearly, except that we should view with a good deal of concern, a situation in which you were debarred from getting back to Switzerland and the organisation began to disintegrate.

Britain and the Commonwealth countries contributed the bulk of the annual funding which kept the League going. Apart from the points well made by Makins and Eden, Britain had, perhaps, an especial, additional need to keep its commitment to the League fully up to date, on behalf of the governments in exile which it harboured in England. And it is not impossible that another element entered into their thinking. Already some of the League services had gone, to the United States as well as Canada, where the International Labour Office was seated in Montreal. For the Secretary-General to be in America could be taken as an indication of some loss of face by the British government. They had endured, and were enduring, war on their own homes; they had through the early difficult years kept the European flag flying, on their behalf and on behalf of the other governments. This was a European show, very much a British show, until America was bombed into the war. Would it not be reasonable to assume that the British government wanted to keep the show British and European as far as possible? America, with the (acting) Secretary-General of the League of Nations residing in the United States, would indeed be Big Brother. Naturally, not a suspicion of this thought appears in their voluminous correspondence with the League. Lester does not mention it. Viewed from to-day's perspective, it would be strange if at least an element of that thought did not ever enter the minds of the British Foreign Office. Not so long before, if Britain wanted a gun from the United States, they had not only to pay cash before they got it, but had to send a ship for it. There was no help left for them anywhere in Europe, their land forces were in disarray, much of their material having been lost at Dunkirk and they were awaiting the arrival of the victorious German army on English soil.

All the time there was the uncomfortable feeling of the League not being entirely welcome any more in Geneva. In 1940 the Swiss official who acted as liaison with Bern was withdrawn, and practically all contact discouraged. The 1940 contribution to the League had been paid in April. In the autumn the Swiss decided to cancel the item from their budget for future purposes. The League of Nations section in the political department was suppressed. When Lester became acting Secretary-General, he suggested he would like to pay his respects to the Swiss authorities, but if that would be embarrassing, he would pay his respects in writing. Six weeks later he got a verbal reply 'so contradictory as to leave me in no doubt that no further approach was required'.

For two years the Swiss government continued to avoid relations with the League.

> I did not expect them to take any risks for the League, but even in reflecting now [this in a letter of November 1943 to Jacklin, League Treasurer in London] as I was always consistently doing, on their difficulties, I must conclude that even modest expectations were not fulfilled. I don't like going so far as to write that Headquarters survived in spite of them, but I would find it difficult to come to any other conclusion.

League of Nations stamps were withdrawn from circulation in case it would offend one of the belligerents. In the winter of 1940–1 there was written refusal to supply oil for the League building, which was modified in later years. There was an official press order that nothing should be published about the League except official communiqués issued from the secretariat. This, notes Lester, was not strictly followed by the press. But until November 1943, the month in which he wrote to Jacklin, there had been in three and a half years only one friendly article in the Geneva newspapers. And yet, Swiss citizens held, at that time, half the jobs in the secretariat. 'But,' writes Lester:

> ... the decent newspapers were decently silent. The press as a whole is also now echoing a little the general overseas interest in the post-war possibilities of the League or its successor. It was rather pathetic to observe, for example, that a pageant in the streets of Geneva could show some symbol of the Red Cross work, but completely ignored that Geneva had been the seat for twenty years of what was, at any rate, the greatest experiment in human history for the maintenance of peace and international collaboration. No contribution for 1941, 42, 43 and 44. No one dares mention in public that Switzerland has

actually failed in many of her obligations as a member and as the host of the League.

As noted before, wartime communications were poor. Letters arrived not months later but, on occasion, two years after posting. Telegrams did not always speak with clarity or with the subtlety which were possible in the written and spoken word. So it was 1944 before Lester was plainly told that the League would not ever be re-established as it was. Hambro, head of the supervisory commission, sent him a telegram on 31 March 1944, which opened with the normal appreciation of Lester's loyalty, and expressed regret at the lack of personal contact, then went on to apologise that 'we' – meaning presumably the commission – had not succeeded in keeping him clearly informed of the international situation as it was changing outside Geneva.

> In spite of all our efforts we have to expect that the League of Nations will not ever be re-established as it was before. It is our task to protect and keep all that the League has built up in experience, in ideas, as well as in personnel in order to render service and help. We will have to find a way to set up a committee to discuss and plan for co-ordination, with the aim of setting up an organisation which will incorporate various activities in one body, which will contain them all. The Supervisory Commission is at your service for discussion on this subject.

Sir Alexander Cadogan, Under-Secretary of State at the British Foreign Office, clarified things for Lester in a telegram dated 16 June 1944:

> You may like to have some background to the attitude of His Majesty's Government towards the League of Nations. Fundamentally this remains unchanged for the present. But the time is clearly approaching for the substitution of some New World organisation for the existing League. Apart from the United States attitude, Russia will not forget her expulsion in 1939. She has since refused to co-

operate with any of the League organs. A world organisation must necessarily embrace the majority of victorious Powers without whose help it would be doomed to failure. The basis for future action is the Moscow Declaration of 1943 ...

And while the shape of the new world order was not evident, His Majesty's government felt that any further weakening of the existing League would be resisted. They would draw on the League's valuable experience in their preparation for the new world order: 'Many functions now carried out by the League organs will continue under whatever new order may be set up.' He quoted Churchill making the same point in the House of Commons, and outlined several made in the same debate by the Secretary of State for Foreign Affairs, one stressing the necessity for close co-operation, political and economic, between the major powers. He hoped that 'If our arms prosper in operations which have now started in the West' (the second front had been opened on 6 June), direct correspondence and consultation with Lester could be entered into. Cadogan sent 'warmest thanks and our best wishes'.

The valediction for the League after the long anxious years of holding out.

Writing to Jacklin, and many of his letters were more or less memos to himself at the same time, Lester had earlier reacted to transatlantic hints that the League was something of a political bogey, while all the new organisations arising were being given unbounded help.

I do not believe we are merely pumping a doomed ship. (If we are, I'd still go on pumping till we get an order to abandon it.) All the glory and great activity may be going elsewhere – which of us expects thanks in the end? But so far as I can see, the value of this little side show in the war cannot yet be determined. Decisions may be taken in the future that will give our work an air of past futility but that is not yet; and in certain political circumstances, the damaged ship may come in damned useful ... Whatever the end may be, I, for one, shall not regret the personal effort and sacrifice in the years which have seemed stolen out of my life.

CHAPTER 11

Interlude with James Joyce

Isolated from homeland and family, still settling down to his new role as acting Secretary-General of the League, Lester had a welcome reminder of Dublin when James Joyce arrived with his family in Geneva on Sunday 15 December 1940. Lester dates this entry in his diary Monday 16 December:

> I had some correspondence with and about James Joyce and his family. On Sunday morning got a telephone message from the Richemond Hotel, they had arrived there. I spent three hours with them in the afternoon before they caught their train for Lausanne.
>
> The famous Joyce is tall, slight, in the fifties, blue eyes and a good thatch of hair. No one would hesitate in looking at him to recognise his nationality and his accent is as Dublin as when he left it over thirty years ago. His eyesight is very bad and he told me it had been saved some years ago for him by the famous Vogt of Zürich, who had also operated on de Valera. His son, seemingly in the late twenties, came in first. A fine, well-built fellow, with a peculiar hybrid accent in English. He told me he is a singer and has sung in Paris and New York. He is married to an American girl and I had the secret hope that, energetic as he seemed, he was no mere hanger-on.
>
> Joyce and I soon got on intimate terms. He is completely unspoilt by his world success. Natural and pleasant in manner. I told him I had read very early his small book of poems *Chamber Music*; then *Dubliners* and

had reviewed the *Portrait of the Artist as a Young Man* (having first assured myself that he had no recollection, I said I had done it for the *Freeman's Journal*); and although I had not re-read the book for fifteen years, I still remembered very vividly the first chapter in which he described a Parnellite household in the crisis of the '90s; I am sure the review was very inadequate. I then told him that I had tried to read *Ulysses* but had to confess I never read it all. I remembered the impression of splashes of beauty, but the Dublin 'argot' at times beat me; I had often wondered how on earth foreigners got along with it. He told me it had been translated into French, German, Czech, Russian, Swedish and, I think, Italian. When I ventured my remark on the incomprehensibility of parts of it, Joyce said that he too had sometimes wondered what the Monsieur in Tokyo made of the Japanese translation. There was a touch of humour in his voice which showed me I had not been trampling too much and in too grave a way on his susceptibilities.

He asked me if I had read *Finnegans Wake*. I said I had read scraps of it when it was being published in 'transition'. He said it was even worse than *Ulysses* and had taken seventeen years to write it. I said: 'Is it a big book? I have not seen it yet'; and he replied: 'that reminds me of the story of the drunken Irishman walking from Drogheda to Dundalk and when questioned as to the length of the road, said it was not the length that worried him, it was the width!' He told me he has also published a book with the title something like *Thirteen Poems for a penny* (reminiscent of D. Kelleher's commercial display on the Strand). – He then began to rake up mutual acquaintances. He had shaken the dust of Dublin off his feet some years before I arrived there. I told him I was an Antrim man who spent his early life in Belfast. You need not tell me, he replied (my accent always sharpens again when I am with Irish). His father came from Cork, he said: his wife from Galway and he came from Dublin, so we were a representative group. He spoke of Oliver Gogarty about whom he enquired and about his hotel in the West. I had never met John Eglinton. He kept coming back to Herbert Hughes, the northern musician who spent so much time in London; I had met him not long before his death and liked him very much, but told him of my wife's long acquaintanceship with him. Hughes, he said, had published a peculiar book of at least a dozen of his poems having them set to music by twelve composers all of different nationalities. A nice little international tribute to Joyce. I mentioned Desmond FitzGerald's name with a very faint response. Dick Hayes, he knew only by name. As to Lennox Robinson, he inquired whether he was a particular friend of mine. I said I knew him fairly well and then he referred to a series of dramatic competitions given over the Dublin wireless; they ended after a couple of weeks, or rather the adjudication was changed; describing some of the adjudications by Robinson, he said that there was not the slightest doubt the man was completely tight; he had two adjectives which he employed without any other qualification for each of the competitors.

John Dulanty, the High Commissioner in London, he liked and respected very much and he talked of John Sullivan who was born in Cork, but left at the age of three for Paris, and who apparently became a fairly renowned singer in Europe. For Count O'Kelly, he spoke of his ability to write beautiful French, and when I mentioned Gerald's brochure on '*les petits vins*', disclosed that it was he who introduced Gerald to the Clos de St Patrice, probably, he thought, the oldest vineyard in France; the Château-Neuf du Pape was comparatively young and, in his view, seemed to be more or less a descendant of the St Patrice. I ventured a remark that it was not a wine worthy of the great name and he said, laughingly, that he would never drink it himself. There was another St Patrice on the Loire where the tradition was that St Patrick on his Rome pilgrimage had crossed the river on his mantle and on arriving at the other side had planted his blackthorn stick.

The parish priest in the village had told him that this had grown and flowered always in December and the shrub or tree was known as the *'fleur de St Patrice'*. Unfortunately, during the last war the Sacristan, or gardener, had a *'crise de nerfs'* following family losses and had hacked down the ancient bush.

Joyce told me that he had only spent ten days in Ireland during the last thirty years – some day I hope I shall get the story of his departure from him. He seemed to have gone first to Trieste, where he taught English. His children were born there and they did not speak any English until they were twenty, and in the family asides over the tea-table, I noticed it was always in Italian. I said to Joyce, 'Why do you not go home? I myself would like so much to do so.'

'I am attached to it daily and nightly like an umbilical cord': the family, who had gathered by this time, joined in protest, as it was true he kept Radio Eireann going on the wireless all the time. His son intervened and said 'One thing I am thankful to be in Switzerland for, is that I can now have a room of my own'; they had been living for six months in a tiny village, forty kilometres from Vichy. Joyce then began to discuss with him all sorts of details of the daily program; the son was outraged by the quality of opera broadcast. I said: 'I enjoyed the folklore songs most of all.' We laughed together over the last 'question-time', when the three girl-typists gave some screamingly funny replies. The only one I could remember was when one of them was asked the precise meaning of a 'bourgeois' and replied 'an Italian soldier'. Then Joyce remarked that one of the competitors, the one who got top-marks on the previous Sunday, when asked who had won such and such a literary prize two years ago, had replied, 'I am not sure, but I think it was Joyce;' there were short controversies with the competitor, but he was adjudicated correct. Joyce said that when the Dublin labourer gave this reply, which was correct, he stood up and bowed to the receiver.

They were going to settle in Zürich, where they had some good friends. I said I thought it was an unusual place for him to choose and asked, what about Suisse Romande? His wife then intervened and said that Zürich had always been associated with certain crises in their life: they had rushed from Austria at the beginning of the last war and had lived in Zürich very comfortably; they had spent their honeymoon there; it was there that Joyce's eyesight had been saved and now they were going back in another crisis. They like the stolid virtues of the people. Joyce, describing any Saturday night dinner in a restaurant when a score of men, fat and square-headed, would sit eating a great meal talking the patois of which he could not understand a word, while the wives stayed at home darning socks and cleaning silver until they were allowed out on the Sunday night. Joyce said he often wondered whether he had not been expelled from France because of his strongly expressed conviction that Switzerland's white wine (he only drinks white wine) was vastly superior to anything he drank in France.

They had left their place in Paris in May; it was filled with most precious books, first editions and presentations from all over the world, and with many good pictures. He had, he told me, some Jack Yeats' and asked about Paul Henry, whom we also admired.

Gossiping afterwards, he told me that he had been a rival to the young McCormack and in their early days in Dublin, his wife had some times tried to persuade him to follow the musical career and drop the writing. This was at a time when he was having a hard struggle and apparently it was 'a near thing'. Mrs Joyce – showing more signs of her cosmopolitan life, pleasant voice – joined in deploring McCormack's pathetic and tragic insistence on continuing to sing as he did when his voice had gone.

Joyce's practical blindness was most noticeable over the tea; he asked his wife to prepare a piece of toast for him and then decided with slight pathos to have biscuits, which were easy to find. Shaking hands with him, I noticed his wife who acted as his eyes, indicated to him to hold out his hand. When I asked him if he had read one or two recent books, mentioned Desmond Ryan's book of recollections, he showed me his difficulties; he has two glasses, one, a small magnifying glass which he has to use for reading, and when he writes he has another glass which must be affixed to his spectacles, and each time he had to read something while writing he has to make a change; obviously the poor fellow can read very little and slowly: one can understand the radio!

The second time I mentioned the question of his returning home, his wife said she had been trying to induce him to for the last two or three years. Joyce said nothing, but when I spoke of getting home in the present circumstances, he said the journey would have been quite possible for him, but he felt it would not be very dignified to go home in the present circumstances. Speaking about the daughter who has had a bad nervous breakdown and has been in a sanatorium for two or three years, he said she was a very gentle and sweet creature; he apparently had gone to visit her every week-end and that at first Sean Murphy [the Irish minister to Paris] obtained permission from the Germans to leave the occupied zone; O'Kelly, who had acted for Murphy said that when the application was made to the German Commandant in Paris, the latter granted it at once, having read and admired Joyce's work. The visa given by their Vichy government for the exit of his son, in view of very strict application of the rule preventing foreigners, and especially belligerents (the Joyces all had British passports) under the age of forty to leave the country, was difficult to understand and had astonished them. The application had been made for the four visas: Joyce, wife, son and eight year old grandson; they did not understand how it had been granted, but perhaps it was again the magic of Joyce's name.

Less than a month later Joyce was dead. Lester wrote to Mrs Joyce on 13 January:

Dear Mrs Joyce,

I have just received a telephone message from Zürich, telling me of your husband's death. It has been a great shock to me and I want to send at once a message of my deep sympathy. I had just signed the enclosed letter to him.

It was for me a delightful experience to have met him during your hurried passage through Geneva. I found him so charming and so unspoiled by his world fame and I was looking forward with very real pleasure to spending some good evenings with him. I am not going to say anything about the loss to literature in the poignancy of your own bereavement, but, believe me, I sympathise with all my heart and share in the sense of loss which all his friends must feel.

Yours very sincerely,
Sean Lester

P.S. I wish to attend the funeral and if I can possibly leave my post for the time, I shall be there; my responsibilities here are unhappily very heavy and may prevent my leaving.

Lester did not go to Zürich for the funeral. He suggested to Frank Cremins, chargé at Zürich, that he might like to go so that some official Irish person would be there. 'F. won't, says he can't leave. Too busy coding and decoding telegrams.'

Lester received a first reply to his letter, dated 18 January 1941:

Dear Mr Lester,

Thank you very much for your letter of January 14th. We were sad not to have you, a compatriot of Mr Joyce at the funeral. Lord Derwent spoke very well, also Professor Hanman. We had a tenor sing Monteverdi and Handel. It was a white and cold day and the sun was pale. I had the death mask made even more; a facsimile made of Mr. Joyce's head with his wonderful ear also on it. If the Irish State is interested in it perhaps they could write. At any rate I am going to have a copy made for Zürich and for myself.

I should very much like to meet you some time as you were always so kind to help Mr Joyce.

Yours very sincerely,
Dr Carola Giedion-Welcker

And another, from George Joyce in Zürich, dated 8 February:

Dear Mr Lester,

Many thanks for your kind letter to my mother, please excuse her for not answering it herself but she is yet much too upset to be able to attend to any correspondence. Many thanks also for the beautiful wreath you sent to my father's funeral.

I know my father was very pleased to have had the pleasure of meeting you during our short stay in Geneva. He was looking forward to meeting you soon again and having a real home evening in your company. Unfortunately fate decided otherwise.

As far as my sister's affairs are concerned I really don't know what I should do. Naturally I would like to carry out my father's wishes and have her brought here to Switzerland. I suppose the best way will be to get her an Irish Passport. On the other hand I imagine this is going to be a very costly affair. So I shall have to wait until I know exactly what our financial situation is going to be.

My mother begs me to thank you for all you have tried to do for my sister and wishes to be kindly remembered to you.

Sincerely yours,
George Joyce

Lester writes in his diary for 4 February 1941:

> *The Times* notice on Joyce quotes what it describes as 'the extremes of opinion' on his work. Sir Edmund Gosse wrote 'the worthlessness and impudence of his writings'; while the middle, puzzled state of mind is typified by A.E.'s remark, 'I don't know whether you are a fountain or a cistern.' (I think the nice mind has changed the word cesspool for cistern). 'In his student days' – says the *Times* – 'he was so self-opinionated and vain that he said to W.B. Yeats: 'We have met too late; you are too old to be influenced by me', to which the poet made answer, 'Never have I encountered so much pretension with so little to show for it.'
>
> They also record (a thing that I had forgotten) that Joyce went back to Dublin to start the Volta Cinema in 1912. I am pleased to see in conclusion of this notice: 'In person Joyce was gentle and kindly, living a laborious life in his Paris flat tended by his devoted, humorous wife.'
>
> Elsie tells me that the Irish newspapers have been very unsympathetic, referring to him as an author who was born in Ireland. One would expect the orthodox to wash their hands of one who challenged orthodoxy so impudently. She adds that a few 'poseurs' like Con Curran and Kenneth Reddin published some notes of their recollections; I agree they were probably intended as self-advertising.

CHAPTER 12

Ireland's Neutrality

O n 21 February 1944 the US ambassador in Dublin delivered what was known as the 'American note'. An official reply was issued by de Valera to the State Department on 7 March, and the exchange was published on 10 March. In Geneva Lester wrote:

> About a week ago it was announced that an American note had been delivered in Dublin requesting the immediate abolition of the German and Japanese representations there on the ground that they might possibly be a means of espionage and especially in view of the imminent big scale attack on Europe. My first reflection on hearing this was that whatever else was expected by the American Government they could not have expected an acceptance (if private negotiations had failed, an official demand had about as much chance of success as a snow ball in hell). It was not a question of a German Legation but of Irish independence. Some newspapers speaking of it said the Americans felt sufficiently strong not to accept a diplomatic setback by a refusal; but any Irishman knowing the Irish situation could have remarked 'it might be a pity but it was true that the Irish had not learned to accept ultimata.' There is nothing there of the spirit of Denmark.
>
> Shortly afterwards the British authorities tightened the control of passenger traffic between all Ireland and Britain, a control which had already been exercised throughout the war but with a good deal of consideration for the common

interest. That, I think, will probably be the end of the matter.

Churchill has just announced that the demand on Dublin was an American initiative but that of course Britain supported it; that the measures taken were desirable in case there could be any leakage from Britain to Ireland and thence to Germany. He then put his finger on the hardship inflicted by the measures, on the great number of Irish soldiers 'fighting courageously in our armed forces and in view of the many acts of personal heroism by which they have maintained the military honour of the Irish race.' He further justified the action by saying that if something went wrong with the first attack any suspicion of a lack of precautions in Ireland would create a lasting wound.

I must say I found all this quite reasonable and perhaps quite wise. If Eisenhower's first attack failed the Irish might be blamed! It is to be noted however that neither the British nor Americans have any trace of information suggesting that the Irish Government has failed to prevent German espionage. Cordell Hull later confirmed this. All the Irish correspondence by letter, or cable or wireless passes through Britain and the German Legation has no diplomatic courier. They had at one time a wireless sending set (as many Legations in Bern have) but this was put out of operation a considerable time ago; the machine was even taken into the custody of the Irish Government. No ship goes to or from Ireland without calling first at a British port of control. When I was in Ireland in December 1939, I asked what the position was about the danger of spies and was assured that the Irish and British secret services were working in the closest collaboration. I certainly believe that as far as Ireland is concerned no contre-espionage organisation could operate with half as much efficacity as an Irish organisation could. There may of course have been leakages, in USA, UK or Ireland but any that have been discovered have been from Britain itself.

I don't believe in neutrality as a general principle – I believe in collective security – but if Ireland had decided early in the war to enter, she would in the circumstances have been doing something utterly exceptional and amazingly generous and heroic. It makes me rather tired however if any outsider talks about a moral issue for a Government in Ireland not having taken that action. What was the position? We all know that the collective security system might have worked but it had broken down primarily because of the refusal of the Great Powers to take their responsibilities and fulfil their obligations in the years immediately preceding the war. It was no wonder that when war did come every European State and apart from the Dominions, every State in the world, hastened to declare its neutrality when the attack was made on Poland (they followed the example of the British, French, American Governments when the attack was made on Czechoslovakia though they did not assume in the same way the moral responsibility for the result). It was of course all wrong and it has proved extremely dangerous for every one concerned: Denmark with her irreproachable neutrality, Norway, Holland and Belgium, Yugoslavia and Greece, Russia and the USA were all in turn attacked and it was a direct declaration of war on them which was the cause leading them to abandon their neutrality. Three or four States have hitherto escaped in Europe, not through virtue of neutrality, but for various other reasons.

But the case of Ireland was still different to those others. Her independence had been won by much sacrifice and suffering after a struggle lasting longer than that of Poland. I was always gratified how quickly goodwill and common sense prevailed in Ireland to such a great extent. Some are inclined to forget that it is only twenty years ago, i.e. within the lifetime of most people alive in Ireland, that the Black and Tans were loosened to ravage the country. There is scarcely a criminal act of which the Germans have been guilty which did not take place in Ireland at that time, through not on the same scale. One remembers the shooting or hanging of hostages, the burning of towns and villages as reprisals, the hunting down of the guerilla bands of patriots, the mass imprisonments, (though not with all the horrors of the German internment camps). There were many cases (of which I personally saw some evidence) of torture and flogging. But the 'maquis' in Ireland and the leaders of the 'Résistance movement' were blandly described in the British Parliament by the British Prime Minister as 'a murder gang' to justify the measures of repression against an ancient nation struggling for its freedom.

I was interested to see the other day Stephen Gwynne writing in a British magazine about a book written by an ex-officer of the Royal Irish Constabulary who had 'served the King' in Ireland at that period. Like so many Irish families, a great many of his relatives are to-day fighting for Britain against the Germans. Gwynne who fought against the Germans in the last war, who was also opposed to the Sinn Féin policy and whose house was destroyed by the Irish side in the war of independence, says: 'Ireland's neutrality is painful to me as to any other man who served with the Irish Division in the last war. But reading Mr Gregory's book has made me see Mr de Valera did what was necessary. To have sided with Germany would have meant war; to have sided with England would have meant civil war, for Ireland was full not of historic memories, but of recollections of things done by English officers to Irish prisoners which were like what the Germans have been doing in this war. No one can enjoy reading of these things, but it is right that they should be read and remembered.'

In spite of what happened, the Irish Government adopted a most friendly and even helpful attitude in 1939. I have mentioned the collaboration between the police authorities. I remember also learning that very special facilities were given to, for example, the Naval Attaché in the British High Commissioner's Office as naval matters were thought at the time most interesting to Britain. Our entire foodstuffs went into beleaguered Britain and volunteers began to flow into her fighting services; when manpower began to be short, the Irish labour was allowed to migrate. It is said that to-day there are at least 150,000 men from the free Ireland in RAF, army and navy and a quarter of a million workers in the armaments factories: 150,000 volunteers from a country of 3,000,000!! The other day a British Minister compared the magnificent war effort of Great Britain with that of America in relation to their respective populations. If the people of the then neutral United States had been participating in the same direct way in the effort to save Britain and Europe the 150,000 volunteers would have meant about six and a half million (6,500,000) Americans fighting under the British flag and the 250,000 Irish workers would have represented ten and a half million Americans turning out armaments and materials under the rain of Germans bombs. Surely this has been a tremendous contribution and, in all the circumstances, a generous and a noble contribution. Would it have been possible from the United States twenty years after their War of Independence?

There was no Neutrality Law passed in Ireland forbidding the raising of loans by hard-pressed Britain, requiring Britain to liquidate her capital assets in the USA. In order to buy the shells and guns and planes needed in Europe. There was no 'cash-and-carry' law saying that not only must supplies be paid for on the spot in hard-cash, but that they must be called for, as no American ships were to be endangered or American neutrality threatened through the sinking of American boats carrying these supplies. The moral issue was the same in 1940 as in 1944 but the need was greater when Britain represented the last fortress of freedom on this side of the Atlantic. In her desperate need to meet the impending invasion Britain did get fifty small but valuable torpedo boats – and paid for them by a virtual transfer – a hundred years lease of vital strategic outposts in the American seas. For unarmed Britain in mortal and seemingly desperate peril, those fifty half obsolete warships would have been a great gift; but who can calculate the price that was paid for them? Lease-lend came into action sometime later. I don't know if enough of Britain's capital then remained to keep up the cash-and-carry policy any longer, but American neutrality, in spite of some far-seeing statesmen and in spite of substantial sympathy, was still the firm policy until Japan attacked American naval bases and Germany and Italy declared war on her. It was only a few days before Pearl Harbour that the American Congress passed the continuance of a military service act by one vote, which seemed like an indication of their will in nearly any circumstances to maintain their policy of a friendly neutrality.

As I have said, I do not believe in neutrality. I believe that the interests of all States are more or less intimately bound up, that peace is indivisible and that a threat of war in Europe or war in Europe is of vital concern even to the small Irish people on the fringe of the Continent. Still more is the fate of Britain. I believe that the interests of Britain and Ireland are to live in full friendship and close cooperation, economic and military, respecting the freedom for which many Irishmen have died in what seemed a vain struggle against a world Empire; respecting on the other side, as all neighbouring States should, the preponderant responsibility and role which the Great Powers must play or must be encouraged to play in the world. Anglo-Irish friendship is in the interest of Ireland and in the interest of Britain. The defence of Ireland is as vital an interest to Britain as the defence of her own coast because any foreign naval power established there would reduce Britain over-night to a third class Power and take her place as the guardian of half the Atlantic, controlling all the approaches to Europe.

It should be said however that in spite of signs of impatience and sometimes of irritation on the side of Britain, the conduct of the British Government towards Ireland has been so far as I can observe from a distance, as much beyond reproach as that of the Irish Government. De Valera has paid public tribute to them. I remember at the end of 1939 talking to the Duke of Devonshire, then Parliamentary Secretary to the Dominions Office of which Eden was in charge. I was asking him with considerable interest how the situation was seen from London; he told me how pleased they were to have a friendly Ireland even though neutral, cooperating in many ways. There seemed to be complete satisfaction, as a contrast to the conditions during the last war: they had no Irish problem on their hands and they were not having the moral handicap of keeping a small country in subjection against its will, while professedly fighting for the freedom of Belgium etc.

In 1914–18 the reaction in America was this time entirely different; powerful, well organised opposition by Irish people and people of Irish descent was creating a furore from New York to San Francisco. Ten to twelve British divisions were immobilized from the main war effort.

In 1940 came the fall of France and the control of the entire European coasts from Norway to Spain passed into German hands; British military armaments were apparently most dangerously inadequate even for the defence of the English coast. Ireland had a small and poorly equipped army, but raised a large local force and prepared to defend herself, as she surely would have done should the Germans try to attack. Again, at this critical period Irish neutrality was not a disservice to the British cause. Britain was of course deprived of the use of some southern ports which would have helped in the control of the Atlantic in case threat came from the Southern French coast. An aerodrome to help in the fight against the German attacks on shipping would also have been useful in the South.

These things however were not entirely without an offset. Britain, were she ever so willing, could not at that time supply armaments; Ireland's defence against a German attack, if it had ever reached the Irish shores, might have been weak through lack of heavy armament but it would have been persistent. The British Navy was there of course and it was a protection for Ireland; but it would be hard to find Irish people who believed that the protection was being given only in the interest of Ireland. When strength increased and when America in its turn came into the war the value of the Irish bases increased and the value of Irish neutrality decreased. The same of course was true regarding for example Portuguese neutrality; a port in Northern Portugal or even the Azores would have been even more valuable and Portugal was 'Britain's oldest ally'. At the same time moreover millions of Irish cattle were going into Britain, more precious than gold; whatever elements of our production that was superfluous to the half-starved needs of Ireland took the natural channel. From Portugal, about whom not a word was said at the time went the most vital of all war supplies, wolfram, to make German guns and shells and submarines. But the same was true of other European neutrals. Switzerland's great industry of precision goods was only going in one direction; Turkey was supplying vital minerals in large quantities; Sweden's iron ore had only one outlet. All these things going to Britain's enemies; but at the time there was quite a tenderness for these neutrals and impatience has only recently begun to be manifested; for very good reasons of course.

The present writer was told by General Costello of the Irish army, who had been director of intelligence when Lester was director of publicity in the Department of External Affairs, that the Americans who came to Dublin to look into the security situation at this time were soon convinced that everything necessary was being done. Costello said that the clinching factor to them was the great grasp of intelligence shown by Colonel Dan Bryan, then chief staff officer of G2, the Intelligence Department, and his 'moral authority'.

Further, Brigadier Dudley Clarke, in his post-war book *Seven Assignments* (Cape 1948), tells of a visit in 1940 as Calais was being evacuated, to an unnamed country – obviously Ireland. A cloak and dagger story with one incident which made the intelligence point again. After a circuitous journey to an unnamed city (Dublin) his guide brought with him a shadow to Clarke's hotel. It would be suspicious for Clarke to leave his suitcase locked, so the shadow went through the contents and removed the slightest evidence which might compromise the identity Clarke had temporarily assumed. 'I found I was experiencing real "security" at the hands of those who had learned to depend on it for their lives.' And when a bundle of temporarily removed items was returned to him, 'I was astonished to discover the thoroughness with which the job had been done ... no single detail, down to laundry marks, had been overlooked.'

CHAPTER 13

Towards the United Nations

It was November 1944 before Lester was able to cross France from Geneva and reach London. Here, after a short holiday with his family in Dublin, he was suitably and warmly fêted for his endeavours in Europe. The Royal Institute of International Affairs and the League of Nations Union gave a large party for him with some of the most illustrious names on the international scene in attendance: Lord Cecil, the giant of the League; Lord Perth, formerly Sir Eric Drummond, first Secretary-General of the League; ambassadors and political figures, many colleagues from Geneva days. And for a month, until Christmas, it was meetings and lunches and dinners and negotiations and interviews without break. After Christmas the same, with a visit to Paris, then Geneva, and back again to London.

In everyone's mind now, in early 1945, was the forthcoming conference in San Francisco, officially called the United Nations Conference on International Organisation, the main purpose of which was to implement and set in motion the hitherto embryonic United Nations. The secretary-general of the conference, Alger Hiss of the State Department, had a staff of over nine hundred people, according to an interview he gave to a newspaper reporter. The League, Lester was convinced, would be asked only in an observer role and, he wrote to Hambro, there would be no request to take part either in committee or primary discussions.

Twelve days before it opened, Lester, then in London, received an invitation from the US ambassador, John G. Winant (dated 12 April 1945), opening 'Dear Secretary General,' and informing him that the United States government 'as the host Government of the United Nations Conference on International Organisation', suggested that it would be helpful if the League of Nations were to be unofficially represented at San Francisco. The hope was expressed in this connection that the representatives of the League would hold themselves available in San Francisco for informal consultation relating to matters that might arise during the course of the conference, and which would be of particular concern to the League.

Due to wartime transportation difficulties and housing congestion, it was requested that the representation would not exceed two or three. There would be arrangements for the representatives to attend all public sessions of the conference, and the Department of State would be happy to assist in transport and hotel arrangements. Was it, in fact, an invitation to attend the conference at all? Lester wondered.

The supervisory commission of the League, even before it had an indication that the invitation would reach them, had decided that it would gladly authorise representatives to go if they could be of any assistance. But the League representatives should not be relegated to a position which might be quite appropriate for purely private associations or societies: the League of Nations was still a considerable organisation with some forty-odd members. It had not disappeared from the world scene. It had substantial assets and, it might be added, some staying power. A short press statement noted that the invitation had been received and 'in view of the effect which decisions to be taken at San Francisco may have on the future of the League of Nations and of the problems which may arise between the two organisations, the supervisory commission has authorised the Secretary-General to accept the invitation and to proceed to San Francisco accompanied by a few advisors.' The League assembly would meet later, it said, and examine the position.

On 12 April came the shattering news that Franklin Roosevelt had died. More than anyone else he had seemed to be the man who would lead the peoples into a new world: he had learned from the failure of the United States to follow up the victory of World War I to ensure a lasting peace, and had created a large staff in the State Department to make plans for the post-war international organisation – his predecessor Woodrow Wilson having failed to bring the American people into the League.

Lester wrote on 15 April to one of the senior men in the League at Geneva, Henri Vigier, saying that he took the view that it was not the form used in the invitation that was the important thing but the treatment they would receive, 'and I have no reason to anticipate that that would not be satisfactory'. He was optimistic. The invitation could well be described as more than a little offhand. And when Lester and his two companions, Manley Hudson of the International Court, and Alexander Loveday of the League staff in the United States, arrived at San Francisco, they found that no arrangements had been made for them to register, to obtain documents, to obtain admission to the buildings or the meetings of the conference. And they had been lodged in a third-class hotel.

Only three days after their arrival, on 23 April, were they able to register, and half an hour before the opening session one ticket arrived for the delegation of three. It was for a seat in the back row of the upper gallery – the gods, in theatrical terms, of the opulent Opera House, where plenary sessions were held. Loveday went instead of Lester, and came away dizzy after half an hour. Shortly after the opening session began, two further tickets arrived for the lower gallery or dress circle. Next day three tickets for the back row for the dress circle. Jacklin went. Lester went on the third day: '... but no seat had been retained and I was able to walk around the foyer; the dress circle was crowded by San Franciscans from the age of ten upwards.' There was vast confusion, too, as to hotel accommodation. Lester conceded that 'that sort of thing seems natural in view of the improvisation'. He was experienced and he was also too tolerant.

A fundamental point for the League delegation arose when

Molotov, heading the Russian delegation, objected to people belonging to neutral states being members of the delegations of intergovernmental organisations. This covered Lester; Phelan, head of the International Labour Office; and Olivan of the International Court – a Spaniard who had arrived. An official of the State Department named Mulligan then called on Loveday to suggest that the delegations might be reformed to meet the Russian objection. In that case, said the spokesman, Lester could remain and have complete freedom of movement in San Francisco – well, wonderful! (Phelan had not yet arrived.) Mulligan was himself a delegate, coming not on behalf of the Department of State, which had issued the invitation, but after having a talk with Alger Hiss.

Lester saw Cadogan of the British Foreign Office who said the Russians has been the cause of several difficulties: on the question of Poland and in demanding separate representation for the Ukraine and White Russia; and also in protesting at Stettinius, the Secretary of State for the United States, being president of the conference, though the Russians themselves had four presidential positions in the conference.

It was pointed out to Molotov that he had agreed to the terms of the invitations to the League and ILO without any restrictions or conditions whatever, and only then, in San Francisco, did he raise the question of the non-United Nations nationals. When this was pointed out to him, he had no reply; 'but simply looked sulky'.

In the meantime the president of the International Court, Guerrero, had arrived and he and Manley Hudson, an American, made up the court delegation. Wrote Lester, fifty years before the term was so widely used about the former Yugoslav territory, 'the Court had now been "cleansed" through the dropping of Olivan the Spaniard.'

The right of the League to choose its own delegation, and the international character of League officials 'for which we fought for many years and firmly established, made all this a serious matter'. Any neutrals at the conference, i.e. Lester and Phelan principally, were there not representing their governments but representing their international organisations.

When Lester referred the matter to Hambro he got the strong reaction he expected. An international official was international and he would not give way on that. But Alger Hiss was keeping up the pressure: he was preparing a revised list of delegates for 7 May, a cleansed list. Before returning home to Norway, Hambro pointed out that the international status of League officials would also be important for UN officials and told Lester that the recrudescence of the concept of the cleansed delegation came from Hiss after de Valera had called on the German minister in Dublin to convey his condolences on the death of Hitler (on 30 April). Hiss thought, or so he said to Hambro, that this might lead to trouble or incidents with regard to Lester, but Hambro agreed with Lester that if the principle of the international status of the international civil servant were not conceded, the delegation should leave San Francisco.

In spite of all this hustle and bustle ('almost unbelievable') Lester nevertheless thought that it would straighten itself out before the serious committee work began.

As secretary-general of the conference, Alger Hiss was basically responsible for some or many of the difficulties which the League officials went through, though perhaps acting strictly on US State Department orders. In 1989 he was to disclaim all intentions of snubbing the League people. He was replying to a letter from Sean Cronin, Washington correspondent of *The Irish Times*. Hiss reminded Cronin that San Francisco was a meeting of the victors, with a celebratory mood and someone, writes Hiss, may have thought Lester's neutrality might cause some embarrassment. Hiss himself manifestly did – and was seen so to do. But Lester's nationality, he protested, would not be a valid justification for a snub. Cronin had suggested to Hiss that there may have been a tendency to regard the embodiment of the League as an intrusive spectre at the feast. Hiss agreed with these words. In another letter to Cronin, Hiss said 'the Roosevelt Administration held the League in the highest regard, and rudeness by us to Lester would have been to dishonour the recently deceased President who was a major factor in the creation of the U.N.' Hiss was an implacable believer in what he said; and at all times.

Just occasionally Lester's temper broke out. He told one of the British delegation, Neville Butler, that personally he would not let himself be the cause of embarrassment. He felt that the spirit of the original invitation was hardly being fulfilled. And, 'I was getting rather tired of again being a cockshy; I had been accustomed in the last ten years to get more kicks than ha-pence, and perhaps could take some more, but I was not quite sure.'

General Smuts of South Africa was, for the League representatives, one of the more uplifting presences. He made a speech saying firmly that he was not going to allow people to blame the League for a failure which was a failure of the governments. He spoke too of America's responsibility by not joining the League originally. He had been asked, by whom Lester did not know, to have these passages excised. Smuts further said the League's organisational staff were the most efficient in the world. He spoke in terms of a general transfer.

Lester mused on a certain sense of unreality which pervaded the atmosphere at San Francisco during the first week of May, with world-shaking events taking place in Europe: Mussolini being killed and strung up by the legs in public, 'in the most beastly and inhuman fashion'; Hitler dead in Berlin; Berlin taken by the Russians; and the German armies all over Europe surrendering unconditionally.

On 8 May, Victory in Europe Day, Lester was wandering around the city with Jacklin. They came to Joe Kelly's restaurant where there were many Irish people, all wanting to buy them drinks. As to Lester: 'after three White Ladys and a Port or two, I drank water. It is to be noted that my fifty years record of never having one over the limit was fully maintained on Victory Night.'

There was a minor victory for the inter-governmental organisations (who felt they were being barely tolerated in San Francisco): it was decided that representatives of the organisations concerned – the League, the ILO, the Food and

Agricultural Organisation and UNNRA – could send observers to committee meetings.

Then on 13 and 16 May came the radio exchange between de Valera and Churchill. Lester wrote in his diary:

> Churchill made references to Ireland. There was an inescapable and proper tribute to the scores of thousands of Irishmen who had been fighting, but an attack on the neutrality position, especially with regard to the ports and references to de Valera, both somewhat frivolous and bitter. He certainly did not say all that could be said, and I felt that he might have been a little more statesmanlike with an eye on the future. There was an interesting reaction among the Irishmen in San Francisco who had been abusing and damning de Valera for the reported visit of condolences to the German Legation ... When Churchill, however, seemed to suggest that an attack on Ireland would have been justified, there was a widespread reaction ... Dev had replied to Churchill last night and some papers here carry a good summary. I must say I am astonished and very pleased at his general tone. It is infinitely more dignified than Churchill; when he reminded him that if England stood alone against aggression for a year or two, Ireland had fought alone against aggression for a much longer time; but he paid a great tribute – and this was clever and good statesmanship – to Churchill: 'In resisting the temptation [to apply force against Ireland] Mr Churchill advanced the cause of morality among nations and took one of the most important initial steps in the establishment of a basis for international peace. As far as England and Ireland are concerned, it may perhaps mark a fresh beginning.' In fact, de Valera, in my opinion, comes out extremely well in the matter, and I am relieved that he has given this guiding line, especially to people here who may in a short time be facing a violent controversy on America's participation in

the coming world peace [the setting up of the United Nations.]

One of the most arresting confrontations at San Francisco came not on the conference floor. It was recorded by Francis Williams, a member of the British delegation as controller of press and censorship in the Ministry of Information and a former newspaper editor. The subject was the Poles. There was a government of Free Poles in London and there was also a Polish underground; it had been agreed at Yalta in February that representatives of both should be given a safe passage to Moscow to open discussions on the future of Poland. This was a matter on which both America and Britain placed great importance. Williams writes:

> We had news that the members of the Polish Delegation had set off and that General Okulicki, their leader had had a preliminary meeting with the Soviet representative in the suburbs of Warsaw, after which the other leaders had joined him for the journey to Moscow. After that silence fell. Day after day in San Francisco the U.S. Secretary of State and Anthony Eden pressed Molotov for information.

None came until the evening of 4 May. It happened during a British delegation cocktail party. Williams continues:

> It happened that I was talking to Eden and Stettinius when Molotov, glass in hand, his interpreter as always at his shoulder, bodyguards close behind, pushed his way towards us. He bowed to Eden and congratulated him on the excellence of his party. Then with, so far as I could judge, no change in tone he turned slightly to include Stettinius in his remarks and said: 'By the way, those Poles you are interested in. We have arrested them.' Without giving time for a reply he moved away. ... the first shot in the Cold War had been fired.

On 25 May at the Palace Hotel in San Francisco a dinner was held, unofficially termed the Geneva dinner, because there were present not only Lester, Loveday and others from former League days but also ILO officials, World Court members and many who had attended as delegates. Lester spoke with his usual blend of understatement and idealism. There was a tendency, he said, and not only a tendency of the past, to think that the setting up of a machine would be regarded as in itself a solution for the vast complicated problems of co-operation and security. He spoke of delegates who went to meetings of an international body and defended their country's interest, often finding that in the long run they must find its best expression in the interest also of neighbours and the world community. It had to be faced that small sacrifices had to be made to avoid having to make greater sacrifices, to take risks, even in distant parts of the world. No machine of itself can be an adequate safeguard. Vigilance all the time, continuous work. And 'I need not say to this audience that no good League servant was ever denationalised or ever loved his own country the less for serving the world.'

On the assumption that all new-created human organisations start off with the inbuilt tendency to confusion and over- or under-planning, the conference at San Francisco may seem, from so many years later, to be not so different from any other as regards the pure mechanics, but there was a distinct air of superiority that the League of Nations had failed, rather than that the constituent nations had failed it (and America had welshed); there was an air of hubris that the two major powers, the United States of America and the USSR, were in at the foundation of the new body, and there was some resentment at the perceived arrogance of the Russians, though they had much to be arrogant about.

Alger Hiss was later to appear sensationally in American affairs. He had an impeccable background, at one time having been law clerk to the eminent Supreme Court Justice Oliver Wendell Holmes; he had worked with the Department of Agriculture and later in the State Department, and for a time had practised law privately; he had also attended the Yalta conference. In 1948 he was elected president of the Carnegie Endowment for International Peace. Then in 1948, the tide turned. Hiss was denounced by Whittaker Chambers, a senior editor of *Time* magazine, and a self-confessed former member of an underground Communist group, as an accomplice, before the House Committee on Un-American activities. Richard Nixon, later President of the United States, upheld Chambers's assertions that Hiss had copied and filmed State Department documents.

Hiss's typewriter, and microfilm that Chambers claimed to have hidden in a pumpkin – known thereafter as the Pumpkin Papers – were produced as evidence. Two Supreme Court judges, as well as Adlai Stevenson and John Foster Dulles, all eminent Americans, testified to Hiss's character.

His first trial in 1949 led to a hung jury. In a second trial in 1950, he was convicted of perjury and given a five-year jail sentence. He was released in 1954 and always maintained his innocence. He published a book, *Recollections of a Life*, in 1988 (Unwin Hyman). He died on 15 November 1996, four days after his ninety-second birthday.

Hiss was either the consummate spy of the century or one of the most wronged men of his day.

CHAPTER 14

End of the League and Return to Ireland

The charter of the United Nations was signed at San Francisco on 26 June 1945. A preparatory commission to get the new organisation rolling met in London in September, and the supervisory commission of the League came to London to meet it.

The League was still very much in existence, with forty-three member states, including some which were not members of the United Nations. The League owned the Palais des Nations and other properties in Geneva; it had a treasury of millions of dollars and a vast library and archival store. There were about a hundred officials.

Walters, in his history of the League of Nations, detected a strong tendency in the preparatory commission 'to allow all that concerned the League to sink as quickly as possible into oblivion. It was suggested that all that was necessary was to hold a meeting of the Assembly in London, at which the proposals of the Commission might be endorsed without discussion or delay.' But Ernest Bevin, the British Foreign Secretary, and Philip Noel-Baker, Under-Secretary at the Foreign Office, insisted that the assembly should meet at its own home in Geneva, 'where its rules and traditions could be respected and its last decisions taken in dignity and tranquillity,' wrote Walters.

Moreover, the meeting in Geneva 'was a debt owed to history, to the past achievements of the League, to the memory of the men who had gathered there in other days.'

And so it came about on 8 April 1946. Lord Cecil spoke of the hopes and aims of the League and of the true reasons for its defeat. Their efforts had not been lost and without the people who had founded it and shared in its work, the new world organisation could not have been established. He ended: 'The League is dead, long live the United Nations.'

The assembly voiced its gratitude to Lester and formally nominated him as the third and last Secretary-General as from 1 September 1940. The International Labour Organisation and the Permanent International Court were to survive the League. Then the assembly formally handed over its palace and material possessions to the UN and declared that as of the day 19 April 1946 the League of Nations should cease to exist.

The principal British delegate, Philip Noel-Baker, was among the more eloquent of those who paid tribute to Lester:

> Has any service had more exactly the leader required? Calm, patient, unambitious, resolute and brave, our Secretary-General had every quality that was needed. I like to think of him in 1940, when he assumed his charge, his staff scattered across the oceans, his budget cut by 75%, a few scores of helpers beside him in this once busy place, the enemies of the League, with the Continent already at their feet, the Nazis preparing to storm the last stronghold of liberty and peace, their armies across the lake, on the Salève, ten minutes up the road along the Jura. I like to think of Sean Lester at that moment, and when I do, the words of Seneca come into my mind: 'with nothing to hope for, he despaired of nothing.' The Assembly and the United Nations have justified his great courage and his hope.

At a dinner and reception given by the British and Commonwealth delegations on 16 April, Lester came straight from day-long labours and had not prepared a speech. When it was his turn, he spoke as others had done of the secretariat and he mentioned in particular Jacklin, the treasurer, who had kept the money coming in. The money and the support, he said was chiefly at that time from Britain, even in her worst moments in 1940. He wrote in his diary:

> I put up the flag by pointing out that it was ridiculous to suggest, as some recent article had done, that an Irish nationalist could not be a good internationalist or England's friend. Nationalism was so deep rooted as to be invisible, but none-the-less real. I believed, and would always believe, in the liberty of my country, but that did not prevent me from being a good friend of Britain and other members of the Commonwealth. Nor did it prevent me from being a good European and perhaps in a modest way a citizen of the world. When referring to friendship for England, I bent down, and *sotto voce* said to Noel-Baker, 'as long as she behaves herself.' It was a *sotto voce* of theatrical timbre, for there was a laugh.

It was a regular theme with Lester, that an independent Ireland would be not only a friend to England but a safeguard to her.

There seemed no end of luncheons and dinners. Lester writes:

> A group of Secretariat officials and some ex-officials invited me to luncheon. It was that group formed during the 1940 to '41 period, of officials who felt confidence in each other in the political field. About 30 of them were present. One of the most telling interventions was from the Danish Delegate, Finn T.B. Friis. He said that the League, carrying on throughout the war in the heart of Europe engulfed by the German Forces, had been described variously as a candle, a small light in the darkness. But he added a more positive note. He said that to get the Secretary General's annual reports throughout the war had been a great comfort to his people and a great encouragement. It may have been only a small flame in darkened Europe, but to them it looked like a great beacon.

Although the League had been declared dead, Lester's work was by no means finished. The task of liquidating the assets of the League was to be long and detailed.

Before the work began, he had been recognised as far back as December 1945 by the Woodrow Wilson Foundation in America which awarded him the Woodrow Wilson Award for distinguished service in maintaining throughout World War II the tradition of the organisation of the League of Nations, which President Wilson was instrumental in creating after World War I. The Foundation wished:

> ... to recognise your steadfastness and loyalty in holding to a difficult post during six long war years when normal support was very seriously lacking ... Above all, your vision and largeness of view in making available to the new agency of the United Nations the rich experience and valuable facilities of its predecessor.

Lester could not be present in America for the ceremony on 28 December 1945, but he wrote accepting the honour

> ... also on behalf of all my colleagues wherever they served, as a recognition of the steadfastness of those who, when the cause of free co-operation between free nations seemed almost a forlorn hope, would not yield their integrity nor allow force or the threat of force to mould their conduct.

He pointed out that in the Court of Honour of the League Buildings there stands a monument to President Wilson:

> The League of Nations itself has been his greatest monument and the world-wide services it has given during a quarter of a century, are the fruits of his thought and judgement. The catastrophe of war which could have been avoided by following Woodrow Wilson's sublimely common-sense vision, is his terrible and final justification. The people are now rebuilding that which they destroyed by timidity and neglect.

He predicted that the new organisation, the UN, would draw strength and inspiration from 'the same great American servitor of mankind'.

At the ceremony Arthur Sweetser, former president of the Foundation, recalled vividly the situation of Geneva when Lester took over as acting Secretary-General. Germany held a continent, and their armies lapped around Switzerland. To illustrate the point to his American audience, Sweetser described a colleague going trout fishing near Geneva, while on the opposite bank were German soldiers, in France, just across from him. Sweetser touched on a raw spot, as one who had served both the League and the United Nations, when he spoke of the American tendency to want to start new things, to cut away from everything in the past: 'We have tried to put on it [the League] responsibilities which I think do not belong to the League of Nations but to governments, including that of the United States for having made the first great break in the League.'

Sweetser brought the plaque belonging to the award to London. He had first proposed handing it over at a ceremony at a United Nations Association gathering in the Albert Hall: 'I put him off that,' said Lester. Then Sweetser proposed it be done at the final meeting of the League assembly. Lester likewise discouraged that, but finally gave in to a small dinner in the Café Royal, in the company of a few League people.

As soon as the meal was over, wrote Lester in his diary of 7 February 1946, 'I hurriedly grabbed the plaque and I light-heartedly set out to carry it to Park Place [his temporary flat] and, as soon as I had it on my shoulder, regretted that no taxi was in sight.'

It's a handsome, double-sided plaque, weighing three or four kilos, about 15 inches in diameter, made in bronze and on the back of it is engraved:

CITATION

TO SEAN LESTER

Acting Secretary-General of the League of Nations who upheld steadfastly throughout World War Two, the ideals, traditions and mechanism of international co-operation for peace.

Lester was invited to speak at the New York *Herald Tribune* Forum on 29 October 1946, and made a speech very much to the point: 'A start is again made with a new name, a new Covenant, a new centre, but the problems remain much the same.'

He said it had been suggested to him that he speak of the League in the war, but he had a few pertinent words to say to the USA. In 1939 the collective security system had broken down, weakened by its opponents, deserted or feebly defended by its supporters, 'while this great country itself again drew its cloak of neutrality around it, and thought it could escape from the sins of commission of others and its own great sin of omission.'

In 1940, he said, he had found himself the last trustee on behalf of forty-six nations while the territories of the European members had been over-run. 'I will not say we were hopeful in those days. I would rather say that, whether from pride or stubbornness, we could not down tools and go to our threatened homes. We went on with our work.'

Each year, he explained, a good number of members supplied the financial means:

> Even the exiled Governments such as Norway, Holland, Belgium, Greece, Poland, France, Czechoslovakia and others annually made symbolic contributions; one or two neutrals, including Portugal and Ireland, fulfilled their obligations in those years. While human calculations at that time could not be cheering, there remained, even in the worst moments, a deep conviction that some things could not vanish from the earth.

That chapter, he said, was almost closed. The magnificent buildings in Geneva had been handed over to the United Nations and, month by month, various responsibilities followed. 'It was a going concern that was transferred (as well as a solvent one)'. He said that his friend Trygve Lie, first Secretary-General of the United Nations, would 'find this heritage of some small value'. And he reminded his audience that the League had not failed, but that the nations had failed to use it: 'That is the lesson and the warning.' The new organisation, he said, would get from the new machinery 'results only in proportion to the faith, the effort and, if need be, the sacrifice we put into it.'

The detailed liquidation of the League was a slow, onerous, slogging and pettifogging business, which kept Lester wearily busy until the autumn of 1947. In June 1947 he wrote to de Valera, the Taoiseach: 'The period of my secondment from the National service is approaching an end, and I think the moment has come when I may address this letter to you.' He gave an outline of his work since he was appointed to Danzig, then to the secretariat of the League as deputy Secretary-General, both moves having been referred to de Valera and approved.

On 1 September 1947 Lester went to see the secretary of his old department, the Department of External Affairs, Frederick Boland.

> I went expecting a good deal of fencing. ... I did not want to make it too easy for the Department to make no proposals, but I had made up my mind to accept no post abroad, and I knew there was no obvious post in the Department, so when Freddie asked me what my plans were, I asked him what his plans were and he mentioned a few legations either open or in prospect. Boland also mentioned the possibility that Ireland would be entering the United Nations.

As the talk went round and round, Lester said to Boland: 'You and I both know that it is difficult to fit me into the

Department appropriately. I am something of an anomaly.' Boland agreed, and Lester went on to wonder

> ...whether I should not simply retire from the Service. I would prefer to go abroad only if I were convinced I was giving some special kind of service. It was over eighteen years since I had gone to Europe and I felt a strong inclination to settle at home. There might be occasions when I could serve on special missions or on public boards or committees. The latter idea seemed to strike him as of interest. I wrote a note to him the following morning saying that I found the openings he had mentioned did not attract me and that perhaps the best thing would be that I should not resume service. Incidentally, I mentioned to him that I had only discovered fourteen years too late that I had been seconded without any pension rights.

On 2 September 1947 Lester had an honorary doctorate in laws conferred on him by Trinity College, Dublin. The announcement of this evoked from a Belfast newspaper a remark on the whirligig of time which had brought Trinity College, for long noted as a strong-hold of the Unionist tradition in Ireland, to honour the friend of Arthur Griffith. The following year he had conferred on him an honorary doctorate in law by the National University of Ireland. In the introductory address Dr JJ Hogan, who was Professor of English (and later went on to become President of UCD), said:

> If it had been a matter of Danzig alone, no doubt Mr Lester would have had a very easy success. But we can all remember how tremendous forces from without bore unceasingly upon what should have been its local affairs; Danzig was marked out as the starting point of the Second World War. The eyes of the world were upon Mr Lester during those four years. We were proud that an Irishman should be in the place of responsibility and danger, and to know that he was acquitting himself well; that he stood firmly for what our great Edmund Burke described as 'a

manly, moral, well-regulated liberty', in looking through various publications of the time we catch glimpses of Mr Lester – quiet, reasonable, unflinching in circumstances that must have been almost beyond endurance.

CHAPTER 15

The Last Years

Lester was then approaching his fifty-ninth birthday. He was tired. There is no honours system in Ireland; suggestions that there should be one have been dismissed – many feel wisely. How could Lester's enormous experience of the politicians of the old and new worlds have been utilised to the benefit of the state? There is one way. Under the constitution, the government of the day can nominate eleven senators beyond those elected by panel voting to the Senate.

Lester's experience – which did perhaps make him an anomaly in his old department – could have been given recognition and he could have continued to render service to the state from the Senate. De Valera did not do it. Nor was he nominated by the coalition government which came into power in 1948 after a long rule by de Valera's Party.

When Lester wrote occasionally in his diary 'I am a man without ambition,' he did not mean that he was a man without a strong sense of service to his country. He had it in good measure.

He was happy in retirement with his gardening and fishing and his friends and his family. But Ireland, particularly in Dublin's relation to London and also to Belfast, could have benefited by his long experience outside the small world of the twenty-six-county state. He expressed no feeling ever of having been left out of things. He had done his duty by the state of which he was a loyal, even fervent citizen; in serving the League of Nations he had continued to hold high the reputation of

Ireland. It was the country which was deprived of a valuable contribution from a man of hard-won and successful experience.

There had been one recall to duty from outside. On 8 June 1948, the post office at Avoca, Co Wicklow, passed on to Lester a long telegram from Trygve Lie (Secretary-General of the UN), a follow-up to a call received that morning. Lie wrote, 'I am most anxious that you may see fit to accept my proposal to serve as representative of the Secretary-General and in that capacity as head of staff of the commission to deal with the India/Pakistan question.' The commission was to depart at once and would probably remain there three months. This was a matter of importance not only to India and Pakistan but to the whole world. And Lie was deeply appreciative of the invaluable contribution 'which you could make'.

Lester was about eight months back home. He replied that he was highly complimented by Lie's confidence in him on such an important mission, but, at present, difficult and urgent personal affairs made it quite impossible. Regrets and thanks. (His daughter Ann wrote mischievously on the sheet 'fishing season!')

After six years in Wicklow, the Lesters moved to Recess in Connemara, partly because the rivers of Wicklow had not enough good fishing, more perhaps because the family had for long a house in Connemara, and loved it. His retirement was as he had foreseen it, in a world of family and friends, of books and socialising in the Connemara countryside he loved. He had so often spoken of retirement within reasonable distance of a trout stream. Here, in Recess, he had the rights to miles of first-class fishing. He did not write memoirs, but he left a diary of his more public years, and he left an inheritance to his country which has not been adequately recognised. His knowledge of British politicians and diplomats was unique among Irishmen, to say nothing of his experiences on the wider international scene. He kept in touch with old friends of the early movement, Bulmer Hobson, PS O'Hegarty, Ernest Blythe, the McGilligans and others. Many called at his hospitable house.

Lester died of a stroke on 13 June 1959, some three months

short of his seventy-first birthday. His death came just weeks before the sea trout made their way up the river, as they did there on the first floods of July and swept along the lake shore, yards from his home. He is buried in Clifden, Co Galway, in the Church of Ireland graveyard.

After her husband's death, Elsie Lester was persuaded to build a house in Dublin for the winters, next to that of her eldest daughter. She would not be cut off from Connemara, where she and her husband had been so happy. Her spirited input into the marriage may be estimated from her decision, after selling the house by the lake in Recess, to have for herself a residence for spring, summer and autumn. She built a cottage overlooking Goirtín Bay, a few miles from her previous house, where the old family friend Bulmer Hobson lived in retirement. After a few years, she decided that her view was being obscured, so she built a second cottage about five hundred yards to the west, where the sea opened more to her. That was fine until she saw a neat, old-fashioned two-storey house on the Sky Road, high above Clifden that was for sale, some twenty miles away. She loved the western aspect, particularly with the evening sun over the sea. It was, she told the family, a suitable house for an old lady. It wrapped itself around her. She had good neighbours. From its eminence it had superlative views, and she lived there, with frequent visits from the family from about Easter until the autumn or winter began to close in on her. She made the journey to and from Dublin in a BMW car, suitably dashing for such a life-loving, busy woman. She had been a considerable support and organiser to her husband in all his intense career. As one writer on Danzig in the 1930s noticed, at times Lester himself remained cautious in comment, 'and left more outspoken remarks to his wife'. Not quite fair to either of them, but Elsie Lester was a fresh breeze in the often stuffy social and diplomatic life of the Free City. She was well read and, before meeting Lester, then involved in the Irish national movement, she already had a good library of Yeats, AE and other poets and historians and polemicists of the time. She exuded vigour and charm, and every house they lived in over their lives together was distinctive in its welcoming comfort and ease.

Elsie outlived her husband by fifteen years and is buried by his side.

Lester's report *The Work of the League During the War*, published in October 1945, opened with these words:

> The peoples of the world, searching for means to avoid the inhumanity and folly of war, constantly becoming more terrible and destructive, made a covenant and a league of peace. They did not keep the covenant; they broke the league; and a new war smashed across Europe and leaped the oceans. Aggression and ambition, on one side, timidity of Governments and short-sighted vision of the peoples themselves, on the other, led straight to the catastrophe.
>
> The League of Nations as an organisation no doubt had faults, but it is dangerous nonsense to say that war came because of those faults. The League did not fail; it was the nations which failed to use it. That is the lesson of the last ten years and it is a vital and terrible warning for the next ten years. The old League of Nations is going and the new League takes the centre of the world's stage. Whether, in many respects, it is better than the machine which is being discarded is not the most important thing. Success will depend on how it is used, on the justice, wisdom and courage of leaders and, above all, on the vision and determination of the common people. Such truisms cannot be too often repeated in view of the immensity of the task which again faces humanity. The new generation of builders and makers must not be misled into thinking that any defect in the ideals or organisation of the League of Nations was the cause of humanity's tragic failure. That failure was due rather to the statesmen and peoples of the League of Nations that contented themselves with lip-service, that could not face the lesser sacrifices to avoid the greater, and to those peoples and States which foolishly imagined they could be lookers-on. That will be the

verdict of history, simplified though it may appear in the welter and tangle of international relations.

Many of our Irish diplomats and politicians in the League of Nations and later the United Nations – and here I include also our army personnel – have demonstrated the same spirit and principles that Sean Lester showed in his time with the League of Nations.

Index

A

Abyssinia, 58, 86, 115, 126,
151–2, 153, 157
Adams, Major Vyvyan, 87
Admiral Scheer (battleship), 90,
91, 94
Aghnides, Thanassis, 190, 194,
195, 214, 215
Allen, Mickey, 8
Andrews, 166
Anglo-Irish Treaty, 1921, 15–160,
24
Anglo-Irish War, 15–16, 21
anti-Semitism, 39–45, 70–2, 84–5
Armagh Guardian, 6
Ashe, Thomas, 27
Astor, Lord, 149, 155–6
Astor, Major, 156
Austria, 89, 138, 151, 159, 160
Avenol, Joseph, 2, 20, 103, 147,
149–50
on Danzig, 128
Lester correspondence, 69, 90,
92, 137, 141
Lester's reports, 96, 99
move to Vichy, 185, 187
offers Lester deputyship, 142–3
post-war League, 188–99
reappointment of Lester, 116
resignation of, 197–200, 209
and supervisory commission,
210–11
war preparations, 170, 183
Azcarate, 142

B

Baldwin, Stanley, 43, 153, 161–2
Ballanagh House, Co. Wicklow,
205
Barrett, Donal, 26
Bartlett, Vernon, 111
Batiment des Commissions,
Geneva, 47

Baudouin, 199
Beaconsfield, 166
Beaupin, Monseigneur, 49, 50
Beck, Colonel, 105, *133,* 140, 149,
151
policy of, 60, 89, 112
relations with Germany, 127–8,
138, 170, 178, 180
seeks Polish Commissioner, 100
support for Lester, 99, 126, 127,
145
threat to Greiser, 137
Beerman, Bishop, 121
Belfast, 5–6
Belgium, 151, 158, 183, 185, 186,
233, 255
Benes, Edouard, 45, 179
Berg, 210–11
Bergmann, 68
Bernheim, Franz, 39, 41
Bevin, Ernest, 250
Bewley, Charles, *134,* 150
Bigger, Francis Joseph, 5–6
birth control, 49–50
Bismarck, Otto von, 118
Black and Tans, 15, 233–4
Blum, Leon, 39–40
Blythe, Anne, 16
Blythe, Ernest, 1, 2–3, 16, 23, *25,*
213–14, 260
Board of Deputies of British Jews,
42
Boland, Frederick, *202,* 256–7
Bolivia-Paraguay dispute, 34
Bonnet, M., 160
Borberg, 101
Borchard, 175
Borsenzeitung, 125
Bottcher, 97, 100, 101
Bourquin, 191
Boyd, David, *25*
Brauchitsch, Field Marshal von, 61

Briand, Aristide, 35–6, 48, *207*
Britain, 40, 44, 77, 127, 152, 233
  and Danzig, 97–9, 103, 106–7,
    109–11, 112–13, 126, 127,
    140–1, 143
  and Germany, 105–6, 158
  Hoare-Laval plan, 153, 163
  and Irish neutrality, 231–2,
    236–8, 246–7
  and League of Nations, 24, 33,
    43, 106–7, 159, 162–3,
    189–91, 193–5, 215–17,
    219–20, 250
  Lester in, 149
  Maginot Line, 165
  'peace ballot,' 43
  Polish guarantee, 171
  rearming, 154
  Spanish Civil War, 161–2
  World War II, 177–8, 183,
    235–6
Browne, Michael, Bishop of
  Galway, 69
Browne, Dr Noel, 49
Brownshirts, 110, 119
Bryan, Colonel Dan, 239
Burckhardt, Carl, 55, 149, 183,
  191, 197
  High Commissioner, 172–6
  reports, 152
Bureau of Military History, 14
Burke, Edmund, 257–8
Butler, Neville, 245
Byrne, Alfie, 158

C
Cadogan, Sir Alexander, 24, 33,
  164–5, 219–20, 243
Canada, 152, 217
Caritas, 68
Carnegie Endowment for
  International Peace, 248
Casement, Roger, 6, 13
Cecil, Lord Robert, 87, 240
Chamberlain, Neville, 161–2, 165,
  169

  Munich crisis, 165–7
  Polish guarantee, 171
Chambers, Whittaker, 249
Charron, 197
Chautemps, M., 160
China, 33, 35, 154
Churchill, Winston, 24, 44, 167,
  220, 231–2
  de Valera response to, 246–7
Ciano, Count Galeazzo, 157
Civil War, 16, 21
Clarke, Brigadier Dudley, 239
Clarke, Mrs Tom, 14
Clarke, Tom, 14
Clifden, Co. Galway, 185, 261
Collins, Michael, 29
Connacht Tribune, 8
Constitution of Ireland, 1937, 158
Cooper, Duff, 167
Coosan Camp, Athlone, 15, *26*
Cork Constitution, 9–10
Cosgrave, William T, 20, 22
Costa du Rels, 199, 200, 212
Costello, John, *30*
Costello, General MJ, 213, 238–9
County Down Spectator, 6
Coyne, Thomas, 40, 50
Cranborne, 154, 162
Craven, Mr, 87
Cremins, Frank, *30, 31*, 107, 117,
  144, 181, 214, 228
Cronin, Sean, 244–5
Cummings, HR, 162
Curran, Con, 230
Czechoslovakia, 40, 138, 176,
  233, 255
  Germans in, 45, 160
  occupied, 164–8, 169, 177
  and Poland, 171, 179–80

D
Daily Express, 8, 9, 79, 109–10,
  111
Daily Herald, 87, 139
Daily Mail, 106, 126, 158

Daily Telegraph, 47, 111, 153
Daladier, Edouard, 166
Danzig, 15, 22, 41, 43, 67, 129–30, 153, 160. *see also* High Commissioner
  anti-Semitism, 70–2, 84–5
  concentration camp, 69–70
  Constitution, 52, 72, 75, 104–5, 123, 128, 141, 143–4
  election, 1935, 76–92
    report on, 83–5
  government of, 58–61
  and League of Nations, 82–5
  League of Nations leaves, 172–6
  London mission, 85–90
  Nazism in, 79, 110–13
    full Nazification, 138–45, 146
  newspapers suppressed, 57–8, 63, 72, 79–81, 95, 113–14, 117, 138–9
  Putsch feared, 138
  riots, 1936, 119–20
  in 1930s, 61–73
Danziger Echo, 114
Danziger Volksstimme, 80, 83, 90, 114, 117, 138–9, 146
Danziger Vorposten, 75, 91, 111, 144
de Haller, 193
de Lagarde, Paul, 118
de Valera, Eamon, 23, 33, 46, 47, 58, 107, 117, 145, 165, *202,* 222
  and Bewley, 150
  condolences to Germans, 244, 246
  Constitution, 158
  and League of Nations, 151
    speech, 36–7
  and Lester, 70, 256, 259
  neutrality, 178, 231, 234, 237
  response to Churchill, 246–7
Delbos, M, 128
Denmark, 185, 233
Derwent, Lord, 228

Deutschnationale Zeitung, 114
Devlin, Denis, 144
Devonshire, Duke of, 237
Dietrich, 176
Diplomatische Korrespondenz, 123
Disarmament Conference, 33, 37, 38, 39, 155
Doig, Henry, 9, 12, 14
Douglas, James, *29*
Drummond, Sir Eric, 20, 240
Dublin Castle, 8, 9, 11, 12
Dublin Evening Mail, 8
Dublin International Society, 204
Dulanty, John, 149, 224
Dulles, John Foster, 249
Dungannon Clubs, 3–5, 11

E
Easter Rising, 1916, 11, 13–14
Eastern Marches Society, 118
Echo de Paris, 79
Economist, 122
Eden, Anthony, 36, 47, 77, 145, 160, 247
  criticisms of, 106–7
  and Danzig, 83–4, 99–100, 102–3, 105, 127, 149
  Danzig mission, 86, 87–90
  Foreign Secretary, 153
  and Greiser, 74–5, 124
  League council president, 123, 126
  League council rapporteur, 82, 111
  and Lester, 115–16, 140–1, 142–3, 185, 214–15, 215–16
  Lester on, 180
  rearming, 154
  Rhineland occupation, 114
  Spanish Civil War, 161, 162
Eglinton, John, 224
Eisenhower, General, 232
emigration, 4–5
Emmet, Robert, 23
Ethiopia, 115, 147

Evening News, 106–7
Ewer, Mr, 87
External Affairs, Department of,
    34, 39, 117, 238
  funding cut, 47
  and League of Nations, 151
  and Lester, 144–5, 148
  Lester retirement, 256–7
  Publicity Office, 17–18, 213

F
Ferguson, 105
Figaro, 175
Figgis, Darrell, *29*
Finance, Department of, 45–7
Fine Gael, 151
Finkinstein, Countess, *131*
Finland, 183–4, 185
First World War, 44
FitzGerald, Desmond, 17, 22, *27,*
    34, 214, 224
FitzGerald, Mabel, 214
Flandin, 102
Fleiner, Dr Fritz, 83
Food and Agricultural
    Organisation, 245–6
Foreign Office, 88, 89–90, 98,
    184, 215, 217, 243, 250
Forster, Albert, 61, 70, 95, 101,
    128, *134*
  anti-Semitism, 72
  and Burckhardt, 174, 176
  election, 1934, 85–6
  and Greiser, 55
  head of Danzig Nazis, 58, 59,
    64, 67, 106
  and Hitler, 107
  and Lester, 90, 108, 143, 152
  Lester on, 96
  manifesto, 72
  and Rauschning, 65, 79
  riots, 119–20, 121
France, 36, 39, 40, 77, 127, 226,
    233, 255
  and Britain, 107, 170
  and Danzig, 143

  and Germany, 44, 155, 156, 160
  Hoare-Laval plan, 153, 163
  and League of Nations, 102,
    106, 159, 162–3, 191–3
  and Nazism, 105–6
  and Poland, 54, 101, 141, 180
  Rhineland, 114–15, 116
  Saarland, 76
  Spanish Civil War, 161–2
  Vichy government, 193–4, 196,
    199, 200, 227
  World War II, 165, 178, 185,
    237
France, Elim, *29*
Franco, General, 161, 170
Freeman's Journal, 15–16, 149,
    223
  Lester in, 11–13, 19
  staff, *28*
Freies Volk, 114
Friis, Finn TB, 252

G
G2, 213, 239
Gaelic League, 2–3, 6, 22
Garvin, 156
Gavan Duffy, George, *204*
Gazeta Polska, 112
Gdansk. *see* Danzig
Geneva. *see* League of Nations
George V, King, 99, 101, 102
George VI, King, coronation of,
    150
German Legation, Dublin, 231,
    232
Germany, 169, 181, 236, 238. *see
    also* Hitler, Adolf
  anti-Jewish legislation, 39–43,
    44–5
  and Britain, 155–8
  expansionism, 138, 159, 185
  and League of Nations, 183,
    184, 197
  Lester welcomed, 56–7
  Munich crisis, 164–8

'new Europe,' 194–5, 198, 215–16
and Poland, 122–3
Polish pact, 1934, 54–5, 62
Rhineland occupation, 114–16
Saarland vote, 76
threatens Poland, 170–1
Versailles Treaty, 44, 78
Giedion-Welcker, Dr Carola, 229
Goebbels, Dr Joseph, 42, 44–5, 76–7, 78, 173
Gogarty, Oliver, 224
Goring, General, 76, 103, 109
Gorski, Christophe, *206*
Gosse, Sir Edmund, 230
Grass, Gunter, 61
Gravina, Count, 57
Greece, 233, 255
Greenwood, Hamar, 149
Greiser, Arthur, 56, 58, 67, 94–5, 106, 122, 128, *134*
'Deutsche Front,' 115
election, 1934, 79–80, 84, 85
and Forster, 55, 59
full Nazification, 138–45, 146
on High Commissioner, 82–3
hunt, 93
and League of Nations, 100, 169, 172
confrontation, 124–6
before council, 74–5
and Lester, 77–80, 90–2, 102–5, 108–12, 137, 138, 142–4
New Year address, 73–4
newspaper suppressions, 113–14
Polish threat, 117
processions ban, 123
riots, 119–20, 121
succeeds Rauschning, 66
Griffin, Gerald, 8, 140–1
Griffin, John, *26*
Griffith, Arthur, 3, 8, *27,* 257
Guerrero, 209–10, 212, 243
Gwynne, Stephen, 234

H

Halifax, Lord, 158, 159–60, 169, 212
Hambro, CJ, 173, 200, *208,* 209, 211, 212, 219
San Francisco conference, 240, 244
Hankey, Maurice, 87–8
Hanman, Professor, 228
Hayes, Dick, 158, 224
Hearne, John, 39
Henderson, Arthur, 35
Henry, Paul, 226
Herald Tribune, 79, 255
Heron, Archie, *25*
Herriot, 47
Hertzog, JBM, 152
Hess, Rudolf, 76, 78
High Commissioner, Danzig, 257–8
Burckhardt as, 149, 172–6
Lester as, 1–2, 41, 43, 51–75, 67–9, 116
British criticisms, 109–10
Council report, 143–4
final year, 93–147
Geneva reports, 73–4, 95–8, 101–5, 110–13
German obstruction, 121–5, 139–42, 146
house guarded, 137, 138, 139
hunting party, 93
Krauel meeting, 107–8
and League council, 82–5
London mission, 85–90
and Nazism, 58–63, 66–73
conflicts with Greiser, 77–80
diplomatic incidents, 90–2
reappointment, 115–17
resignation possible, 101–3
riots, 1936, 119–20
role of, 53, 56, 58, 82–3, 169
welcomed, 56–7
residence, *207*

Himmler, Heinrich, 62
Hiss, Alger, *208*, 240, 243, 244–5
  spy trial, 248–9
Hitler, Adolf, 2, 42, 58, 124
  'new Europe,' 245
  anti-Semitism, 71
  assassination attempt, 183
  Bewley on, 150
  and Burckhardt, 173, 175–6,
    187
  and Danzig, 54–5, 59, 89,
    108–9, 160
  de Valera condolences, 244, 246
  expansionism, 114, 118, 157,
    164–5, 169–71, 176
  and Forster, 107
  Halifax meeting, 158–60
  and League of Nations, 105–7,
    190, 192
  Munich crisis, 165–8
  Munich speech, 115
  Rauschning on, 61
  rise of, 44, 52
Hitler Youth, 68, 78
Hoare, Sir Samuel, 153, 162, 163
Hobson, Bulmer, 3, 6–7, 11, 12,
    15, *27*, 260, 261
  Easter Rising, 13
Hogan, Dr JJ, 4–5, 257–8
Holland, 151, 183, 185, 186, 233,
    255
Holmes, Oliver Wendell, 248
House Committee on Un-
    American Activities, 249
Hudson, Manley, 242, 243
Hughes, Herbert, 224
Hull, Cordell, 188, 232
Hungary, 169, 170

I
Imperial Conference, 1930, 23–4
India, 260
Institute for Advanced Study, USA,
    188
Institute of International Affairs,
    Geneva, 34

International Court of Justice, 209,
    242, 243, 250
International Labour Organisation,
    21–2, 32, 170, 209, 210,
    213, 243, 245–6, 248, 250
  in Canada, 217
Irish Bureau of Military History, 5
Irish Free State, 20, 49, 103, 107,
    117
  financial problems, 45–7
  and League of Nations, 22–4,
    33–4, 151, 194–5, 255
  neutrality, 231–9
  post of President, 158
  wartime censorship, 181
  and World War II, 184
Irish Independent, 157
Irish International Society, 21
Irish Red Cross Society, 184
Irish Republican Army (IRA), 15
Irish Republican Brotherhood
    (IRB), 5–6, 8, 11
Irish Volunteers, 14, 15, 22, 213
Irish Weekly Mail, 8, 9
Ironside, General, 176
Italian Legation, Dublin, 231
Italy, 40, 106, 107, 155–6, 236
  and Abyssinia, 58, 86, 115, 117,
    151–2
  Hoare-Laval plan, 153
  joins Axis, 157
  and League of Nations, 159,
    184, 197
  Spanish Civil War, 161–2
  World War II, 185

J
Jacklin, 152, 170, 190, 218, 220
  and Avenol, 200, 211
  British visit, 196
  League funds, 198–9
  role of, 251
  San Francisco conference, 242,
    245
Japan, 33, 34, 35, 107, 154, 156,
    198, 236

cartoon, *136*
and Germany, 157
withdraws from League, 37
Jenkins, Arthur, 56
Jews, treatment of
Danzig, 70–2, 84–5
Germany, 44–5
Upper Silesia, 39–43
Johnson, Tom, 56
Jordan, 154
Journal des Nations, 22, 92
Joyce, George, 229
Joyce, James, 61, 222–30
Joyce, Nora, 226–7, 228–9

K
Kelleher, D, 223
Keller, von, 40, 41
Kennedy, Hugh, 23, *29*
Keyserlick, Count, *131*
Kisch, Sir Cecil, 211, 216
Komarnicki, 152, 154, 179
Kosters, Dr Jan, 83
Krabbe, 97, 99
Krauel, Dr, 107–8, 183, 190, 192

L
Labour Court, 5
Langley, Liam, *26*
Laski, Neville, 42
Laval, Pierre, 77, 102, 153, 163,
191, 200
League of Nations, 1, 16, 47,
48–9, 49–50, 91, 108
1937-1939, 148
Abyssinia, 58, 86
'Axe' Committee, 169, 184
cartoon, *136*
Committee of Three, 142–4
and Danzig, 60, 79–85, 87,
89–90, 100, 110–13, 128,
145
Lester's reports, 69, 73–4,
95–8, 143–4
de Valera speech, 36–7
deputy Secretary-General, 142–3

funding, 46–7, 216–17
future of, 188–99
Greiser speech, 124–6
hundredth session, 1938, 158–9
Lester Irish representative, 19,
20–4
Lester's assessment of, 262–3
Munich crisis, 164–8
and Nazism, 72, 78
post-war changes, 189–92,
219–21
Rhineland occupation, 114–16
Russia expelled, 183–4
and San Francisco conference,
240–9
small nations in, 33, 34
social life, 47–8
Spanish border incident, 209–12
Spanish Civil War, 161–2
stamps, 218
supervisory commission, 208,
209–12, 216, 219–20, 241
and UN, 250–2
support for, 43–4
Swiss withdraw support, 214,
217–19
in Vichy, 185
weaknesses of, 105–7, 117,
150–2, 162, 255–6
winding-up, 250–6
World War II, 2, 179, 182–3
League of Nations Day, 182
League of Nations Union, 87, 113,
240
Leipzig, 121–2
Leith-Ross, 170
Leonhardt, Hans, 71, 81, 102–3,
172–3
London mission, 86–90
Lester, Ann, 110, *203, 206,* 213,
260
Lester, Dorothy, 15, *32, 201*
Lester, Elsie, *30, 32,* 46, 65, 94,
108, 121, *131,* 148, *203, 206,*
214, 230
marriage, 16

Munich crisis, 168
and Secretary-Generalship, 199
separation from, 213
train bombed, 185–6
widowhood, 261–2
Lester, Patricia, 5, *206*
Lester, Robert, 2
Lester, Sean. *see also* High
Commissioner, Danzig
Burckhardt's dismissal, 172–6
caricature, *132*
Coosan Camp, *26*
death of, 260–1
deputy Secretary-General,
142–3, 148–71
Avenol's plans, 188–99
on European situation, 155–6,
157, 158–9, 162–4
on League's role, 182–3
on Munich crisis, 165–8
takes over from Avenol,
197–8, 199
war preparations, 168, 170–1
war starts, 177–87
External Affairs, 17–18
family of, 64–5
health of, 184–5
honorary degree, 257–8
journalism, 6–7, 8–13
League of Nations diplomat, 19,
20–4, 33
birth control, 49–50
salary cut, 45–7
marriage, 15
on neutrality, 231–8
personality, 15
photographs, *25, 29, 30, 31, 32,
133, 204, 206*
political views, 2–6, 8–15
retirement, 256–7, 259–60
return to Ireland, *203*
Secretary General
isolation, 213–14
Joyce family, 222–30
post-war changes, 219–21

return to Ireland, 240
San Francisco Conference,
240–9
Spanish border incident,
209–12
US visit possible, 214–17
Secretary-General, 251–6
sporting activities, 35, 93–4,
131, 133, *134, 201*
L'Europe Nouvelle, 173
Lie, Trygve, 256, 260
Lithuania, 170, 175
Lockhart, Robert Bruce, 44
Londonderry, Lord, 156
Lothian, Lord, 156
Loveday, Alexander, 190, 196,
211–12, 242, 248
Lubienski, Count, 99, 126, 128
Luxembourg, 76, 185
Lytton, Lord, 47

M
McBride, Sean, 28, *204*
McCann, Pierse, *26*
McCormack, Count John, 226
McCullough, Denis, 3, 4, *29*
MacDermott, Sean, 13
MacDonald, Ramsay, 24, 47
McDunphy, Michael, 14
McGilligan, Ann, *30*
McGilligan, Patrick, 23, *30, 33,*
214, 260
Mackensen, Marshal von, 79
MacKenzie King, WL, 152
MacNeill, Eoin, 13, 14, 22, 28,
213, 214
MacNeill, James, *29*
MacNeill, Josephine, 28
McQuaid, Dr JC, Archbishop of
Dublin, 49
McSwiney, Terence, *26*
MacWhite, Michael, 20, 23, 46
Maginot Line, 165
Makins, Roger, 215, 216
Malkin, 98

Manchester Guardian, 42–3, 77, 87, 124–5, 160
  on Hitler, 180–1
Manchuria, 34, 136, 156
Marshall, Captain, 91
Masaryk, Jan, 45
Memel, 169–70
Methodist College, Belfast, 2
Minns, Miss, *131*
Molotov, VM, 243, 247
Morning Post, 139
Mortished, Ron, *29,* 213
Moscow Declaration, 1943, 220
Moske, Fr Emil, 74
Mother and Child Scheme, 49
Mulcahy, General Richard, 15, *26,* 214
Mulligan, 243
Mullins, William, *26*
Murnaghan, James, *29*
Murphy, Sean, *30,* 186, 227
Mussolini, Benito, 58, 105–6, 161–2, 167
  death of, 245
  and League of Nations, 190, 192
  Munich crisis, 166

N
National Socialist Party (Nazism)
  anti-Jewish legislation, 39–43
  control of Germany, 159–60
  Danzig
    increasing strength, 95–8, 100–1
  in Danzig, 1–2
    increasing strength, 122–3, 138–45
    press laws, 113–14
    riots, 119–20
  impunity of, 105–6
  rise of, 44–5, 60–1
  warning on, 89
nationalism, Irish, 3–7, 252
Nationalist Party, 11

Nederbraght, Harbour President, 121
Netherlands, 83
Neue Zeit, Die, 114
Neueste Nachrichten, 111
Neurath, Baron von, 47, 55, 59, 107–8, 123, 159
New York Times, 90
New York World's Fair, 182
New Zealand, 154
News Chronicle, 111, 125–6
Nicolson, Harold, 22
Nixon, Richard, 249
Noel-Baker, Philip, 48, 250, 251, 252
Nordic States, 151
Norton, William, 150
Norway, 40, 185, 210, 233, 255
Nyon Conference, 156

O
O'Broin, Leon, 13
Observer, 156
O'Byrne, John, *29*
O'Connell, JJ, 13
O'Duffy, Eimar, *25*
O'Duffy, Eoin, 210
O'Hegarty, PS, 213, 260
O'Hegartys, 214
O'Higgins, Kevin, *28*
O'Kelly, Count, 224, 227
O'Kelly, Sean T, 158
Okulicki, General, 247
O'Leary, Con, 149
Olivan, 243
O'Rahilly, Professor Alfred, 29, 213
O'Rourke, Count, Bishop of Danzig, 67–9, 139
O'Shannon, Cathal, 5
O'Sheil, Kevin, 29
Ostmarkenverein, 118
O'Sullivan, Donal, 23–4
O'Sullivan, John Marcus, *30*
O'Toole, OP, *29*

P

Pakistan, 260
Papée, 73, 93, 109, 116, 128, 140, 141, 145
Parker, RAC, 43
Patrick, St, 224–5
Paul-Boncour, 39, 47, 102, 167
Perth, Lord, 240
Peru-Colombia dispute, 34, 38–9, 148
Petain, Marshal, 200
Peterson family, *32*
Phelan, Edward, 21–2, *32,* 170, 243
Phelan, Fernande, *32*
Pilsudski, Marshal, 62, 77, 124
Piper, von, 160
Poland, 15, 40, 59, 151, 243
  British guarantee, 171
  and Danzig, 53, 62, 67, 95, 97–8, 100–1, 112, 116, 119, 144–6, 169
    promises, 126–8
  epidemics, 154
  Franco-Polish Alliance, 141
  Free Poles, 247
  and Germany, 65, 107, 114, 118, 122–4, 152, 160, 233
    pact, 1934, 54–5, 62, 117, 165
    threat, 127–8, 138, 175–6, 179–81
  Jews in, 39–43
  Kulturkampf, 118
  and League of Nations, 255
  and Lester, 72–3, 180
Portadown Express, 6
Portugal, 186, 209, 238, 255
Princeton University, 188–9, 196, 209, 211
Publicity Department, External Affairs, 17–19

R

Raczynski, Count Edward, 89, 98
Radio Luxembourg, 137

Radowitz, von, 114, 119, 120, 121
Rauschning, Anna, 64, 65, 66
Rauschning, Dr Hermann, 57–62, 68–9, 72, 73, 122, *135*
  election complaints, 79, 90, 91
  farm, 64–5
  newspaper bans, 63
  pamphlet, 181
  resignation, 65–6, 71
Recess, Connemara, 260, 261
Reddin, Kenneth, 230
Rhineland, occupation of, 114–16
Ribbentrop, Joachim von, 159, 160, 176
Riefenstahl, Leni, 71
Rising, 1798, 2
Ritchie, Mary, 2
Robinson, Lennox, 224
Rockefeller Institute for Medical Research, 188
Romania, 170
Roosevelt, Franklin, 71, 242, 244–5
Roter Wäweed hler, 114
Rothermere, Lord, 126
Royal Institute of International Affairs, 240
Russell, George (AE), 230, 261
Ruthenia, 169
Ryan, Desmond, 12–13, 149, 227
Ryan, Padraig, *25*
Rydz-Smigly, General, 141
Rynne, Michael, 144

S

Saarland, 76, 79, 87
Sahm, Ulrich, 54–5
Salamon, Ernst von, 207
Salomon, Dr Eric, 48
San Francisco Conference, 208, 240–9
Sarraut, 102
Scheliha, Rudolf von, 54
Schleswig-Holstein (battleship), 173, 174
Schramm, 70–1

Schuschnigg, premier, 159
Seneca, 251
Serego, Count Dante, *131*
Simon, Sir John, 63, 162
Sinn Féin, 3, 8, 11, 12, 156, 178, 234
Sino-Japanese conflict, 33, 35, 37
Skylstad, 194, 196
Smogorzewski, Casimir, 52–3
Smuts, General, 245
South Africa, 152, 166, 245
Soviet Union, 111, 118, 150, 154, 177, 198, 208, 233, 248
    and League of Nations, 183–4, 219–20
    and Poland, 247
    United Nations conference, 243
Spain, 40, 151, 186
    League border incident, 209–12
Spanish Civil War, 161, 170
Stack, Austin, *26*
Starkey, 101
Statute of Westminster, 24
Stephens, EM, *29*
Stettinius, 243, 247
Stevenson, Adlai, 249
Stevenson, RCS, 88–9, 126
    and Lester, 98–9
Stevenson, Robert Louis, 199
Stoppani, 176, 197
Strang, William, 177
Streicher, Julius, 44–5, 71, 77, *135*
Stresemann, 44
Stürmer, Der, 45, 71, 77, 85, 142
Stutthof concentration camp, 69–70
Sues, Maitre MW, 38, 41
Sullivan, John, 224
Sunday Chronicle, 87
Sunday Dispatch, 158
Sweden, 83, 127, 238
Sweetser, Arthur, 167–8, 188–9, 254
Switzerland, 83, 166, 167, 181, 193, 198, 226, 238, 254
    German threat, 185–6
    World War II, 184, 214, 217–19

T

Taylor, AJP, 159–60
Temperley, Major General AC, 33, 34
Tight, Carl, 118
Times, The, 87, 111, 156, 230
Tivy, Henry L, 8–12
Toynbee, Arnold, 172
Trinity College, Dublin, 5, 257–8
Turkey, 152, 238
Tyrrell, Elizabeth Ruth. *see* Lester, Elsie
Tyrrell, Alderman John, 16
Tyrrell, Air Vice Marshal Sir William, 16

U

United Nations, 2, 24, 49, 254, 255–6, 260, 263
    charter signed, 250
    conference to establish, 240–9
United Nations Association, 254
United States of America, 38–9, 157, 163, 193, 195, 233
    'American note,' 231–2
    Irish emigration, 4–5
    and League of Nations, 188–9, 196, 214–17, 219, 245, 248, 254, 255
    San Francisco Conference, 240–9
    World War I, 237
    World War II, 235–6
UNNRA, 246
Upper Silesia dispute, 39–43
Uruguay, 111

V

Vejarano, 198
Velghe, 49
Versailles, Treaty of, 1, 44, 53, 62, 78, 98, 174
    Danzig, 143–4
Vigier, Henri, 242

Viple, Marius, 191
Vogt, Dr, 222
Voigt, FA, 87
Völkischer Beobachter, 56–7, 125
Volksstimme, Danziger, 80, 83, 90, 114, 117, 138–9, 146
Volkszeitung, 63, 114
Volta Cinema, 230
Vorposten, Danziger, 75, 91, 111, 144
    hunting party, 93–4

W
Walshe, Joseph, 46–7, 117, 145, 151
Walters, Frank, 52, 96–7, 99, 126, 161, 173, 174, 208, 250
    Lester correspondence, 81–2
    and Lester report, 101
    World War II, 170, 177
Warburg, Felix, 149–50
Wareing, CB, 153
Weizsacker, 173, 175
Whitaker, John T, 148
Willard, Sir Arthur, 153
Williams, Francis, 247
Wilson, Hugh R, 39

Wilson, Woodrow, 16, 242, 253
Winant, John G, 241
Winke, Walther, 74
Winter Relief Work, 93
Wiskemann, Elizabeth, 87
Wnuk, senator von, 74
Woodrow Wilson Award, 253–5
World Court, 248
World War I, 1, 52, 65, 79, 237, 242, 253
World War II, 2, 51, 253
    German breakthrough, 185–7
    German surrender, 245
    Irish neutrality, 178
    Irish troops, 235
    outbreak, 173–6, 177–87
Württemberg, Baron Marks von, 83

Y
Yalta conference, 208, 248
Yeats, Jack, 226
Yeats, WB, 230, 261
Yugoslavia, 233

Z
Ziehm, Dr Ernst, 79, 90